Public
Management
in a
Democratic
Society

DISCARDED

University of Winnipeg, 515 Portage Ave., Winnipeg, MB. R3B 2E9 Canada

JF
1351
R462
1990

Public Management in a Democratic Society

Robert B. Reich

John F. Kennedy School of Government
Harvard University

PRENTICE HALL
Englewood Cliffs, New Jersey 07632

Library of Congress Cataloging-in-Publication Data

Reich, Robert B.
    Public management in a democratic society / Robert B. Reich.
        p.   cm.
    Includes bibliographical references.
    ISBN 0-13-738881-0
    1. Public administration--Case studies.   I. Title.
JF1351.R462 1990
350--dc20   89-38273
                                                           CIP

Editorial/production supervision: *Carolyn Serebreny*
Interior design: *Joan Stone*
Cover design: 20/20 Services Inc.
Manufacturing buyer: *Robert Anderson*

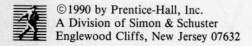©1990 by Prentice-Hall, Inc.
A Division of Simon & Schuster
Englewood Cliffs, New Jersey 07632

All rights reserved. No part of this book may be
reproduced, in any form or by any means,
without permission in writing from the publisher.

Printed in the United States of America

10 9 8 7 6 5 4 3 2 1

ISBN 0-13-738881-0

Prentice-Hall International (UK) Limited, *London*
Prentice-Hall of Australia Pty. Limited, *Sydney*
Prentice-Hall Canada Inc., *Toronto*
Prentice-Hall Hispanoamericana, S.A., *Mexico*
Prentice-Hall of India Private Limited, *New Delhi*
Prentice-Hall of Japan, Inc., *Tokyo*
Simon & Schuster Asia Pte. Ltd., *Singapore*
Editora Prentice-Hall do Brasil, Ltda., *Rio de Janeiro*

For Ellen

Contents

_____ *chapter 11* _____

Public Deliberation, 161

Further Reading, 176

Public Management in a Democratic Society

Introduction

For several years I have taught a course at Harvard's John F. Kennedy School of Government on the role of public managers in a democracy. Some of my students plan careers in, or at the borders of, government. Others already have served as public officials, sometimes for decades. Most want to be effective and responsive public servants in the future.

My students are painfully aware of the public's skepticism about government and frequent distrust of bureaucrats. There are too many stories of indifference, unresponsiveness, or worse. Most of them also understand how difficult it can be to get things done in the public sector, often because of the complex, diffuse, and ambiguous demands placed upon public-sector officials. In spite of this awareness, however, they are committed to public service and have resolved to make government work better.

Allow me to assume that you also are interested in improving the effectiveness and responsiveness of government, even if you have no present intention to serve in it. In this book, which grows out of my course, you and I will examine what it means to be both effective and responsive in government. As I do with my students, I want to draw upon your own experiences and understandings, regardless of whether you have worked in the public sector. You already know a great deal about working effectively and responsively within organizations—from school, from experience gleaned from jobs you have had, from watching others. Even a family is a kind of organization whose members also strive (at least on occasion) to be effective and responsive. But you probably have not thought about your experiences and intuitive knowledge in any systematic way. I hope that the following cases and discussions will help you develop a framework through which to think about these issues more carefully.

To be effective and responsive in government is a special challenge, because there is not just one public, as there is one boss, or one set of parents, or one teacher. The public comprises a vast number of people who want disparate—even, sometimes, inconsistent—things. And although most members of the public usually know what they want or need for themselves and their families, they are far less sure of the needs of the members of a community or state or nation, or even of the inhabitants of the same planet. To the extent that they have opinions about these matters, their opinions are subject to change, sometimes sudden change, depending upon how issues arise, how questions are posed, how choices are understood. The public rarely has access to all the relevant facts and often has little or no memory of what happened in the public sphere ten years ago or even last week.

The public gains some understanding of what it wants from its government—and public officials likewise gain insights into what the public wants—through special networks of intermediaries. Some of these intermediaries are organized groups committed to particular causes, such as welfare rights or the right to own a gun. Others are journalists, commentators, and editorial writers who not only inform the public about what government does but also help shape public opinion about what government should do. There are intermediaries within government, whose jobs are to translate, review, and pass judgement upon what other public servants are doing. Judges play intermediary roles by reviewing government activities on behalf of certain segments of the public and offering opinions about whether and to what extent public servants have functioned as they should. Sometimes legislators act as intermediaries, overseeing how laws are implemented and helping certain of their constituents get what they need.

This system is extraordinarily noisy, confusing, and time consuming, and it offers endless opportunities for blocking new initiatives and for sidetracking public servants from matters they would otherwise pursue. Thus, in being responsive to this vast vortex of intermediaries, public servants may feel (or be perceived to be) less effective than they should be at achieving useful and important things. Incidentally, this dilemma should offer no comfort to people who prefer that public servants do nothing in the first place. Even a minor government action done badly can have terrible consequences. Moreover, the system makes it as difficult for government to *undo* its mistakes as to do anything to begin with.

Years before I began teaching I was a bureaucrat trying to get things done while simultaneously responding to all sorts of pressures from higher-level officials, legislators, interest-group leaders, journalists, disgruntled taxpayers, judges, public-employee unions, and what seemed an infinite number of other such meddlers. I often thought how much simpler it would be if I could just take my phone off the hook and refuse to meet with anyone other than my immediate colleagues. No wonder the public is so often unhappy with government's performance, I thought; the public gives its servants no time to do anything but respond to public demands, complaints, and suspicions. It seemed like a vicious circle: The more responsive I was to outsiders, the less time I had to attend to my job; the less I did of my job, the louder and more insistent grew the demands.

I have a particularly vivid memory of one day at the Federal Trade Commission, where I labored as director of the policy planning staff. I had set aside the morning and most of the afternoon to review some provisions of a new regulation that staff members in the Division of Marketing and Advertising were proposing. The regulation would require cigarette manufacturers to include a special warning on packages and in advertisements involving any brand above a certain level of tar and nicotine: ''All cigarettes are dangerous, but this brand contains high tar and nicotine, which is especially injurious to your health.'' As I read the proposed rule, I began to wonder whether it might unnecessarily burden the manufacturers and at the same time have little public benefit. How did we know that consumers would use this information in guiding their decisions about which brand to select? I felt I needed more information.

I was just about to call the Director of the Advertising and Marketing Division when my phone rang. It was a staff member of the House Commerce Committee. He knew that I would be reviewing the cigarette regulation and wanted to talk about it. His boss, a congressman, would not look kindly upon Commission action, he said, and there were many other members of Congress who would feel the same. He reminded me that the appropriation hearing in which the Commission's future budget would be considered was fast approaching. Perhaps I could meet with the congressman? I agreed, already wishing that I hadn't come to the office that day.

A half hour later I received a call from the chief lobbyist of the American Tobacco Institute, with a similar message. He also wanted a meeting before I made any recommendation to the Commission on the cigarette rule. Meanwhile, the Director of the Advertising and Marketing Division had left a message with my secretary: The proposed rule was set to be debated by the full Commission in just two weeks; if we missed that date, it would be another six months before the commissioner's docket would again be open to consider the rule.

Then came another call, this one from the head of Ralph Nader's health group. She had heard rumors that the cigarette manufacturers were putting pressure on the Commission to scotch the regulation, or at least water it down. She liked the staff's proposal (she had obtained a copy somehow), and she was prepared to mobilize consumer groups at the first sign of backpedaling. She too wanted a meeting. I agreed, now resigned to getting nothing of substance done for the next few days.

Within ten minutes I was visited by the Commission's general counsel. Was I aware, he asked, of the recent decision of the Court of Appeals for the Seventh Circuit requiring that meetings between high-level agency officials and outside parties to discuss proposed regulations must be open to the public? He wasn't sure whether the court's ruling would apply to the Commission or, even if it did, what steps would need to be taken to make such meetings ''open.'' But I should be careful, just in case. If I were to have any such meeting, he recommended that a stenographer be on hand to make a transcript. Probably it would also be a good idea to note down all telephone conversations with interested parties, and summarize them for the record. I nodded in agreement, my mind growing numb.

Then a call from the FTC chairman—he wanted to see me at once. I hurried down the hall to his office. The chairman looked upset. This cigarette regulation is nothing but trouble, he said. He had received ten calls already this morning. The *Washington Post* was running a big story tomorrow. Seems that a former Commission employee, now working for one of the tobacco companies, had alleged that the Commission staffer currently in charge of the proposed rule within the Advertising and Marketing Division had a vendetta against the company. Apparently one of the staffer's parents, a heavy smoker, died of cancer and he was suing the company. I offered some advice about what the chairman might say to the press and agreed to look into the matter.

The remainder of the day continued in much the same way. The head of the American Cancer Association had heard that the regulation was being delayed and wanted to know why. The chief lobbyist of Common Cause wanted to know whether I had decided to make my meetings on the cigarette rule open to the public, and if so, could she attend? A reporter for the *Baltimore Sun* inquired about how I organized the staffing of new rules. Specifically, how did I control for potential conflicts of interest, such as personal vendettas? There had been a report. . . . And so on.

Needless to say, the commissioners did not have a chance to consider the proposed cigarette rule two weeks later; in fact, I spent most of the next two months trying to deal with all the commotion. Meanwhile, other proposed rules began to stack up on my desk.

Eventually, most of the brushfires were doused. Accommodations were made, compromises reached. The Commission finally issued a cigarette rule, bearing only the vaguest resemblance to the one that had been submitted to me months before. Tobacco companies would henceforth be required to list the tar and nicotine content of all brands on packages and in advertisements, without any specific warning attached to high tar and nicotine. Was it a good rule? I didn't know. My only feeling was a sense of enormous relief that it was no longer my responsibility.

This is an extreme example, but it serves to make the point. Managing the public's business within a democratic system is different from private-sector management, and different from public management in an undemocratic society. Democracy is noisy, intrusive, frustrating, time consuming, unpredictable, and chaotic. But it is also the best system of government yet devised for ensuring that government is accountable to its citizens.

So how should you, as a public servant, resolve the effectiveness-responsiveness dilemma?

One option is to strive primarily for *effectiveness,* by keeping the public and its intermediaries at bay. You first decide what needs to be done, and then you contrive a series of end-runs around the obstacles thrown in your path by legislators, judges, journalists, interest-group leaders, and others. You cajole, threaten, trick, or otherwise manipulate this vast system into letting you achieve your goal. You are thus a policy entrepreneur, whose success is a function of how clever you are at playing the game.

This approach seems at first blush to solve the dilemma. Had I been cleverer at manipulating the system, I could have designed and promulgated any cigarette rule I wanted. There is a certain attraction to the wily and shrewd public official like Robert Moses, the builder of New York City's infrastructure, who surmounts all obstacles with deviousness and determination and gets significant things done. But this manipulative approach poses at least two problems. First, if you successfully manipulate the system now, you may have more difficulty getting things done in the future, because your circumvention of the institutions of government and of the public's intermediaries gradually undermines government's credibility with the public. The public stops trusting the judgments of its intermediaries who are perceived to have been too easily persuaded or misled. The intermediaries are thus less capable of mustering public support next time, perhaps for policies or programs you want to implement. With fewer means of legitimizing what you want to do, you find that you have to work harder in the future to mobilize the resources you need. As the public grows more suspicious, red tape multiplies and more layers of review are demanded. The wheels of government slowly grind to a halt.

Robert Moses, for example, did achieve extraordinary things in and around New York City for more than thirty years: highways, bridges, tunnels, parks. He was the preeminent policy entrepreneur—manipulating, threatening, dissembling in order to get his way. And yet, one of his legacies was a distrustful public that tightly bound future public managers within straightjackets of bureaucratic formalities. Moses's end-runs around the informal system of public accountability elicited a far more formal and rigid system for governing in the future.

Of course, *you* may not be around to bear the full consequences of your deviousness, and even if you are around, you won't bear the *full* consequences because the public's distrust will be generalized across all of government, toward all public servants. You might conclude that this is a relatively small price to pay for the advantage of getting things done in the meantime. And maybe you'll be so successful at getting such marvelous things accomplished that the public won't mind that you circumvented or subverted the system of accountability along the way.

This justification raises a second and more profound problem, however. If you circumvent or subvert the system of accountability, you may not be able to discover what the public wants or needs in the first place. Effectiveness is a virtue only if you are effective at accomplishing something of public value. Your own judgments about what the public wants may be wrong.

The vast network of intermediaries—elected officials, judges, journalists, interest-group leaders, and the rest—is a source of knowledge about where the public interest lies. To disregard or to manipulate this network is thus to cut yourself off from important information. Robert Moses built lovely parks, but many New Yorkers couldn't get to them; they were located in the wrong places, were often inaccessible by public transit, and were designed in such a way that baby carriages couldn't negotiate the stairs leading to and from them.* I remember worrying that the cigarette regulation that emerged from the seemingly chaotic mix of political forces upon the Federal Trade Commission might not be a "good" rule. But how did I define "good" if not by reference to some measure of what the public wanted? And how should these wants be determined if not—at least to a significant extent—through politics?

Manipulation and subversion of politics reduce government's capacity to respond to what the public wants and needs, and simultaneously they reduce the capacity of the public to deliberate over its wants and needs. As a result, you and other policy entrepreneurs are left adrift, without democratic guidance. It is but a small step from this state of affairs to a government dominated by people like Oliver North, who have strong views about what should be done and possess the gumption and grandiosity to do it, regardless of what the public may desire. Worse yet, the public is left without an understanding of what it should or can achieve, and democratic institutions begin to wither.

The issue here is not one of personal ethics or of the moral responsibilities attending your job; it is a matter of how your job should be defined to begin with. A public servant is in the business of governing. Democracy is not a constraint on your effectiveness as a public servant; it is an aspect of the job itself. Part of your job as an effective public servant, therefore, is to sustain, even strengthen, democratic institutions.

A second option is to strive primarily for *responsiveness,* by doing whatever you are asked to do. Here, you have no preconceived agenda. You listen carefully and conscientiously to what elected representatives, judges, and the broad public (through journalists, interest-group leaders, and other intermediaries) tell you you should try to achieve. Where laws or directives are ambiguous, you seek clarification. You might ask a legislative oversight committee for guidance, or commence formal rulemaking procedures in which any potentially affected party may offer proposals and views, or you might seek guidance from the courts. In addition, you might commission surveys of public opinion, convene panels of "opinion leaders," and gather reams of data about how the public behaves. In all these respects you conceive of yourself as an honest broker—a neutral servant of the public—intent upon doing whatever it is that the public wants you to do.

This approach appears to overcome many of the disadvantages of policy entrepreneurship, but it presents problems all its own. First, even if you genuinely believe that you are acting in a neutral and passive way, there is no really neutral process for defining the public interest. Every

* See Eugene Lewis, *Public Entrepreneurship: The Organizational Lives of Hyman Rickover, J. Edgar Hoover, and Robert Moses* (Bloomington, Indiana: University of Indiana Press, 1979).

effort you initiate—an oversight hearing, rulemaking, a declaratory judgment from a court or adjudication, a public-opinion survey—carries with it a set of institutional biases favoring some substantive outcomes over others. The very design of the hearing or survey—how questions are posed, issues identified, choices arrayed—inevitably shapes the result. Public preferences are themselves affected by the social and political processes through which they are defined and articulated. A hearing, a rulemaking, or even an official survey is a public experience that gives rise to social learning about what is important and why.

There are related problems. I have already alluded to the public's lack of clear preference on most issues. Not even the public's intermediaries are likely to have considered any given issue in depth, and the few with an opinion are rarely in agreement; to the contrary, opinions are apt to be in some conflict (as they were when my staff proposed its cigarette regulation). Nor are intermediaries particularly interested in, or capable of, identifying enduring goals that transcend immediate issues and link issues to one another and to broader objectives. Their primary function is to reflect the immediate concerns of their constituencies or litigants, not to give continuity to whole streams of public choices. Nor, finally, are they concerned about implementation. The feasibility of the demands they forward, or the likelihood of inadvertent consequences flowing from them, are rarely within their ranges of vision. Thus, had I taken a totally passive role in the cigarette controversy, seeking only to respond to every political pressure emanating from every direction, no coherent policy would have emerged.

For these reasons, a passive approach to democracy is as flawed as a manipulative one. Responsiveness without concern for effectiveness leads to biased and incoherent results. Effectiveness without concern for responsiveness undermines democratic institutions and leads to policies unrelated to public needs. So what are you to do? As a public manager, how do you decide upon your goals and priorities?

Consider a third option. Here, rather than enter into a manipulative or a passive relationship with the public and its intermediaries, you develop a *deliberative* relationship. You bring to your job certain ideals and values and even some rather specific ideas about what you think should be done. But you nevertheless look to the public, and to its many intermediaries, as a source of guidance. Your relationship is deliberative in the sense that you are honest and direct about your values and tentative goals, but you also listen carefully to how the public responds to your agenda and are willing to make adjustments accordingly.

You are not a policy entrepreneur, because you make no attempt to manipulate either the formal system of accountability or the informal network of intermediaries. But neither are you a neutral and passive public servant, because you have things you wish to accomplish. You are instead a participant in an ongoing public deliberation about how problems are to be defined and understood, what the range of possible solutions might be, and who should have the responsibility for solving them.

The process is iterative and ongoing. You use a variety of devices to elucidate an issue, to show how it is connected to other issues and broader purposes, and to propose solutions. The communication flows in both directions: A first round of explication often will be followed by a second, after those likely to be affected by your proposals have had an opportunity to ponder them, understand their significance, and respond. A second round may be more detailed; it may involve a smaller group of better-informed intermediaries; the range of ambiguous or disputed issues may be narrower than at first; the spectrum of choices may be narrower and the data of higher quality, since there is now more agreement about what needs to be known.

Few issues will ever be resolved permanently. You will almost always be involved in further explication, showing how decisions made in the past affect present and future decisions, how single issues are linked, the consequences of clusters of decisions over time, and the broader goals being achieved. Rather than making ''decisions'' and then ''implementing'' them, your role is to manage an ongoing process of public deliberation and education—a *by-product* of which is a series of mutual adaptations, agreements, compromises, and, on occasion, stalemates.

You are an instigator: Your job is not simply to discover what people want for themselves and then to implement the best means of satisfying these wants. It is to provide the public with alternative visions of what is desirable and possible, to stimulate discussion about them, to provoke reexamination of premises and values, and thus to broaden the range of potential responses and deepen society's understanding of itself. To the extent that deliberation and reflection yield a broader repertoire of such possibilities, society is better equipped to cope with change and to learn from its past. The thoughtless adherence to outmoded formulations of problems, choices, and responsibilities can threaten a society's survival. Policy making should be more than and different from the discovery of what people want; it should entail the creation of contexts in which the public can critically evaluate and revise what it believes.

Such deliberation, far better than either manipulation or passivity, can also help define and sustain mandates over time. It can strengthen democratic institutions and the civic virtues on which such institutions ultimately must depend. Had the Federal Trade Commission embarked on an ongoing dialogue with the public (through the media, elected representatives, and interest groups) about the hazards of cigarette smoking and the various ways of reminding people of those hazards, it would have been far easier for the Commission to devise a set of regulations that would benefit the public without unduly burdening producers.

But deliberation is exceedingly difficult to do well. The public often tends to equate effectiveness with active decision making and successful implementation, concrete achievements that can be measured and on which reputations can be built. The nurturing of social learning about public problems and possibilities, on the other hand, is an elusive undertaking. A manager who tentatively advances several proposals and stirs controversy about them may appear indecisive or indifferent at best. Moreover, the public often wishes to avoid facing difficult issues and examining the values bound up in them; many people resent the tensions and ambiguities inherent in such deliberation. They prefer that you, as public manager, take the responsibility for making such decisions.

Public deliberation also can consume time and resources, with no guarantee that the resulting social learning will yield a clear consensus at the end. The process, in fact, may exacerbate divisions in the community and make it more difficult to achieve consensus in the future.

The experience of public deliberation is not likely to be enjoyable for either politicians or agency employees. Politicians will resent a process that is beyond their control, often involving issues they would rather not have to deal with (that is why those issues were handed over to you in the first place). Agency employees, for their part, are unlikely to understand the importance of fostering public discourse rather than getting on with the job of making policy. Their jobs and reputations depend on getting something done (or undone), and they will have little role in instigating or managing the debate.

Last, there are lingering doubts about the propriety of nonelected bureaucrats taking on this sort of responsibility. The line between ideological chest thumping and the instigation of public debate can be a narrow one. Still, the public manager may be in a better position than a legislator or senior elected official to foster debate over certain value-laden issues, since the manager deals with specific applications of general principles. It is through detailed and vivid applications that the public comes to understand the principles and the tradeoffs and stakes they imply.

Both manipulation and passivity are easier: You will be sorely tempted to take advantage of whatever opportunities present themselves for forwarding your own agenda. Alternatively, you will be tempted, at least on occasion, to take no stand at all—to abdicate responsibility for provoking debate because the issues are simply too "hot." But neither manipulation nor passivity appropriately characterizes your job. Your job as a public manager is to foster deliberation and thus to facilitate your own accountability.

The following cases and discussions are presented to enrich your understanding of public management in a democracy. Each case deals with a different facet of the challenge, such as what to do when there are sharp conflicts between branches of government or between different segments of the public, or when your political superior has a different agenda than yours, or when the Constitution requires different policies from those that the public seems to demand.

Most of these cases end just at the point where the public manager has to take action. I then ask you to imagine that you are the manager and must decide what to do. I lead you through a discussion, not unlike a class discussion we might have here at the Kennedy School, about the wisdom and appropriateness of various courses of action. I hope that by the end of the book you will have gained a deeper appreciation of the possibilities for managing in the public sector—in a way that is both effective and responsive and that simultaneously strengthens democratic institutions.

chapter 1

A Conflict
of Ideals

People are drawn to public service because they have ideals. One does not earn princely sums of money by engaging in public service. (There are, of course, exceptions to this rule, found among corrupt officials and those who trade upon their government contacts after leaving the public sector, but these people are not, strictly speaking, "public servants"; they are in the service of themselves.) Some may find the sheer exercise of power to be pleasurable, but power in the public sector is so widely dispersed and broadly shared—so contingent and temporary—that the sensation is at best illusory. ("He'll sit here," Harry Truman said of Dwight Eisenhower on the eve of Ike's inauguration, "And he'll say, 'Do this! Do that!' *And nothing will happen.* Poor Ike—it won't be a bit like the Army. He'll find it very frustrating.")* Public officials are venerated within some societies, surely another potential source of satisfaction, but this has not been the rule in the United States. In fact, today one enters upon public service *despite* its relatively low public standing.

Ideals can be powerful motivators. Visions of a good society or, more particularly, of good schools, clean environments, safe streets, food and shelter for the impoverished, healthy children and productive adults—all of these ideals and many others often summon talents and energies in excess of those summoned by any other incentive. Indeed, work in the service of such ideals can give purpose and meaning to one's life.

But not everyone agrees on what a good society comprises. On

*Richard Neustadt, *Presidential Power,* (New York: John Wiley and Sons, 1960), p. 9.

some issues, like abortion or prayer in public school, there is sharp disagreement. Even where most people agree on broad goals, deep-seated conflicts often exist over the best means of attaining them. Most people want peace, but some people believe that peace can be obtained only through a strong military defense; others believe that peace is better achieved through unilateral reductions in armaments. Most people are against racial discrimination and in favor of civil rights but have differing views about whether discrimination can best be overcome by busing children to schools in other neighborhoods or by giving minorities preferential consideration in college admissions and jobs.

Such conflicts should not trouble people who pursue their ideals independently—for example, by volunteering their time to specific causes, supporting not-for-profit institutions, or working on political campaigns. Commitment to their ideals is perfectly consistent with commitment to their jobs. But these conflicts may create difficulties for people who pursue their ideals through employment in the public sector. Under these circumstances, commitment to ideals may not always be consistent with commitment to job.

In a democracy, public servants are accountable to the public, which gives them all the authority they possess; the public *authorizes* their actions. This is true even for public servants who sit on regulatory commissions not directly answerable to politicians, or who hold civil service jobs deep in the bowels of large public bureaucracies, or who are appointed by political appointees who, in turn, are appointed by politicians who repeatedly have run unopposed for office. Regardless of how remote their positions from the average voter, public servants ultimately derive all their authority from the public, and continued exercise of that authority depends upon the public's continued willingness to confer it. Public trust is fragile—painstakingly created, easily destroyed. If the public loses faith in the ability or disposition of a public servant to act on behalf of the public's ideals, the trust is broken and authority is withdrawn.

What, then, is a public servant to do when ideals clash—when the public is sharply divided over ends or means or when the public servant's ideals are at odds with those of the public?

Consider David Goldman's dilemma.

California Legal Services, Inc.

In May 1966, the Office of Economic Opportunity awarded a $1.3 million grant to California Legal Services (CLS) to establish a statewide program offering free legal assistance to poor persons living in rural areas. In August of that year, David Goldman, a 30-year-old lawyer with a background in legal aid and public defender work, joined CLS as its deputy director. Over the next 2 years Goldman was to play a major role in making CLS a vigorous representative of poor people in rural California. Among the most publicized legal battles that CLS won in its early years were those that:

- Forced Governor Douglas Patton to restore $200 million that he had cut from the State's Medicaid program
- Brought about the complete overhaul of a municipal water system

- Made the U.S. Department of Labor halt the importation of *braceros* (Mexican field hands)
- Enabled citizens who were literate only in Spanish to vote in California elections
- Liberalized the state's welfare requirements.

One measure of CLS's impact during this period was the impressive collection of enemies that it accumulated. Stung by CLS's challenges, Governor Patton denounced the program on several occasions for "harassing" State agencies. Senator Kerrigan of California called on the floor of Congress for the dismissal of Goldman and William Holland, CLS's executive director. And at various times the program came under fire from such diverse groups as the Kern County Association of Cities, the Republican Central Committee of Kern County, the Stanislaus County Bar Association, several California Congressmen, the *Los Angeles Times,* the McFarland City Council, and the California Raisin Advisory Board.

This case describes the background of CLS's initial funding by OEO and of Dave Goldman's decision to join the fledgling organization. The first section summarizes the development of OEO's Legal Services Program as part of President Lyndon Johnson's War on Poverty. The second section reviews Dave Goldman's personal background and his philosophy of legal services. The third and fourth sections describe, respectively, the CLS funding proposal and the California Grape Strike.

This case was prepared by Stephen B. Hitchner, Instructor in Public Policy at the John F. Kennedy School of Government, Harvard University. Funds for its development were supplied by the Ford Foundation and the Alfred P. Sloan Foundation. The case is intended to serve as the basis for class discussion, rather than to illustrate either effective or ineffective policy-making and management. While the case is based primarily on field research, some technical and descriptive information has been disguised and is not necessarily factual. Copyright © 1975 by the President and Fellows of Harvard College.

THE LEGAL AID MOVEMENT AND OEO[1]

The first legal aid societies in the United States were established in the latter part of the nineteenth century. The number of such organizations grew slowly but steadily until the early 1960s, when some 240 legal aid offices were providing assistance to indigents in civil matters. Financial support for these services was obtained largely from private sources, primarily community chests (60%) and bar associations (15%). In 1962, the total amount of money provided nationwide for civil legal aid amounted to less than $4 million.

Besides being privately financed and privately controlled, most legal aid organizations in the early 1960s shared several other characteristics:

- Caseloads were extremely heavy. A study of seventy legal aid offices revealed, for example, that attorneys in thirty-three of the offices handled an average of 1,678 cases per year, and only in twenty-five offices did the attorneys average fewer than 1000 cases each.

- Few appeals were made in civil matters. In fact, not a single civil case handled by a legal aid lawyer was appealed to the U.S. Supreme Court prior to 1965. The Standards of the National Legal Aid and Defender Association, which most legal aid organizations followed, deemphasized the taking of appeals "to establish useful principles" except for those instances "when costs are available."

- Services were usually provided from a single office located near the courts in the business district of a city.

- Legal assistance to the poor was normally seen as charity, not as a right. One consequence of this view was the refusal of many legal aid offices to take bankruptcy and divorce cases, since these acts were deemed morally unsound.

Experimental Legal Aid Programs

Three experimental programs were begun in 1963 and 1964 that departed significantly from the traditional model of legal aid. These programs were to have a major influence on the development of OEO's Legal Services Program.

[1]The information in this section has been drawn largely from three sources: Earl Johnson, Jr., *Justice and Reform: The Formative Years of the OEO Legal Services Program* (New York: Russell Sage Foundation, 1974); A. Kenneth Pye, "The Role of Legal Services in the Anti-Poverty Program," *Law and Contemporary Problems,* Winter 1966; and "Neighborhood Law Offices: The New Wave in Legal Services for the Poor," *Harvard Law Review,* Vol. 80 (1966–67).

New Haven: As part of its pioneering "gray areas" program, the Ford Foundation undertook to finance the establishment of decentralized social service centers in low income sections of New Haven, Connecticut. These multi-service centers were to be operated by Community Progress, Inc., a nonprofit corporation set up under Ford's auspices. At the urging of Paul Ylivisaker, head of the Foundation's Law and Government section, law offices were opened in January 1963 in two of the neighborhood centers. The lawyers in these offices were to operate as members of a professional team, including social workers and other specialists, which would make a coordinated attack on the problems of poor families who came to the centers. This experiment was short-lived, however. CPI's law offices were closed after two months of operation because of bad publicity resulting from the defense of an alleged rapist by a CPI lawyer.

New York: In the summer of 1963, Mobilization for Youth (MFY), an anti-delinquency program sponsored by the President's Committee on Juvenile Delinquency, established a small legal unit in cooperation with Columbia University. Influenced by the thinking of its first director, Edward Sparer, MFY's legal unit soon came to focus its resources on achieving social change, principally through filing test cases in the fields of welfare, public housing, housing code enforcement, and unemployment insurance.

Washington, D.C.: In November 1964, the United Planning Organization (UPO), a nonprofit corporation directing a Ford Foundation gray areas program in northwest Washington, established the Neighborhood Legal Services Project (NLSP). With fourteen attorneys and three offices, NLSP was the largest of these three experimental legal aid programs. The efforts of its attorneys were to be directed toward cases that were related to UPO's non-legal programs, that were not being handled by other legal services, and/or that raised especially difficult legal issues with significant impact upon the poor. Special attention was given to consumer practices, housing problems, public assistance and veterans benefit programs, juvenile problems, and representation of adult criminal defendants in certain matters.

Legal Services in OEO

The Office of Economic Opportunity was created by the Economic Opportunity Act of 1964. Peace Corps Director Sargent Shriver, chairman of President Johnson's task force on poverty, was named to head the new office. Located in the Executive Office of the President, OEO was to be responsible for operating some antipoverty programs and for coordinating the rest. Of the programs OEO would operate, the Community Action Program (CAP) was the largest and most innovative. OEO was authorized to spend several hundred million dollars under CAP on community-based and community-planned antipoverty efforts modelled after the Ford Foundation's gray areas programs.

Legal assistance for poor persons was not mentioned in the Economic Opportunity Act, but OEO soon determined that legal services projects were among the kinds of community programs eligible for federal funds. Shortly after OEO was established, Sargent Shriver set up a task force to study the role that lawyers might play in the War on Poverty. In November 1964, Shriver made a widely publicized speech in which he announced OEO's plans for creating "supermarkets of social services" in poor neighborhoods. Legal assistance was to be one of the services that poor persons would receive at these "supermarkets." Shriver also called for the use of laypersons in jobs "which we have assumed could only be served by professionals, but which cannot wait for the professional to get to them." As examples he cited the use of laypersons as "homework aides, recreation aides, . . . health aides, . . . and legal advocates for the poor."

Plans for establishing an OEO Legal Services Program were firmed up during the first half of 1965. It was becoming increasingly clear that most communities would establish legal services projects only if actively encouraged by OEO. However, the OEO Legal Services Program could not become a reality until it had a director. Finding an acceptable person for this position proved more difficult than expected. Not until September 1965 was E. Clinton Bamberger, Jr., appointed by Sargent Shriver to head the new program. Bamberger, a 39-year-old trial lawyer specializing in the defense of insurance claims, was a partner in the largest law firm in Baltimore and recently-named chairman of the Maryland State Bar Committee on Legal Services. A liberal Democrat, he had been finance chairman for Senator Joseph Tydings' 1962 election campaign. He was active in community affairs and had served as chairman of the Baltimore Blue Cross.

At the time of his appointment, Bamberger tried to obtain a commitment from Shriver that the new Legal Services Program would be independent of the Community Action Program. Shriver insisted, however, on placing the Legal Services Program under the CAP administration to ensure the coordination of services that was a major goal of the War on Poverty. But Shriver agreed that Legal Services would be a national emphasis program, like Headstart and Upward Bound, giving it preferred status within CAP. Though Bamberger would normally report to CAP director Theodore Berry, he was promised direct access to Shriver whenever he wanted it.

As soon as Bamberger assumed his new position, he began looking for someone to serve as deputy director of the Legal Services Program. He found that person in Earl Johnson, Jr., who was at that time deputy director of UPO's Neighborhood Legal Services Project in Washington.

The Organized Bar[2]

The traditional privately-financed, privately-controlled legal aid movement, as represented by the National Legal Aid and Defender Association (NLADA), had long received the backing of nationally prominent members of the bar. The growth of the legal aid movement had been slowed, however, by the apathy or outright hostility of local bar associations. This attitude started to change around 1950 when many lawyers began to fear government encroachment on their profession. They shared the view of the NLADA president of that time, Orisen Marden, that legal aid societies were a valuable defense against socialization of the legal profession. This led to a significant increase in bar support for legal aid during the 1950s.

In the early 1960s, the organized bar, including the American Bar Association (ABA) and the NLADA, had no desire for government financing of legal aid. However, there was increasing recognition of the profession's responsibility for representing poor persons. Impetus was provided by the Supreme Court's 1963 decision in the case of *Gideon v. Wainwright,* establishing the right of an indigent person to free legal counsel in felony cases. Another factor was Attorney General Robert Kennedy's Law Day speech in 1964, which emphasized that the need of the poor for equal justice extended to civil matters as well:

> The poor man looks upon the law as an enemy, not as a friend. For him the law is always taking something away.
>
> It is time to recognize that lawyers have a very special role to play in dealing with this helplessness. And it is time we filled it. . . .
>
> Lawyers must bear the responsibility for per-

mitting the growth and continuance of two systems of law—one for the rich, one for the poor. Without a lawyer of what use is the administrative review procedure set up under various welfare programs? Without a lawyer of what use is the right to partial refund for the payments made on a repossessed car? What is the price tag of equal justice under law? Has simple justice a price which we as a profession must exact?

Helplessness does not stem from the absence of theoretical rights. It can stem from an inability to assert real rights. The tenants of slums, and public housing projects, the purchasers from disreputable finance companies, the minority group member who is discriminated against—all these may have legal rights which—if we are candid—remain in the limbo of the law.

In August 1964, Lewis Powell, a member of the most prominent law firm in Virginia and incoming president of the ABA, saw the availability of legal counsel to all persons, regardless of financial resources, as a priority issue for the bar. During the inaugural speech before the ABA's House of Delegates, he stated, "On the civil side, the bar has no less responsibility to see that legal services are available for those who cannot afford them." Addressing the problem of lower middle class persons who were not eligible for legal aid, he went on to say:

> Unfortunately, this type of person is more likely to encounter legal difficulty than persons in higher income brackets. Garnishment of wages, repossessions resulting from default on installment purchases, evictions for non-payment of rent, bankruptcies, the failures of husbands and fathers to provide support and maintenance—these are but a few examples of the type of legal involvement familiar to every lawyer, so commonplace to the citizen in the low income bracket. . . .
>
> It has been correctly said that respect for the law is at its lowest with underprivileged persons. There is a natural tendency for such persons to think of the courts as symbols of trouble and of lawyers as representatives of creditors and other sources of "harassment."

With Powell's blessing, the ABA staff initiated informal contacts with representatives of OEO in the fall of 1964 when it appeared likely that OEO would create a legal services program. Sargent Shriver's

---

[2]In addition to the previously mentioned sources, A. Kenneth Pye and Raymond F. Garraty, Jr., "The Involvement of the Bar in the War Against Poverty," *Notre Dame Lawyer,* 1966, provides further information on this topic.

"supermarkets" speech in November 1964 produced a flood of mail to ABA headquarters urging a strong stand against the incipient federal program, but Powell and his chief lieutenants continued to believe that cooperation with OEO was both possible and desirable. Writing his column for the January 1965 issue of the American Bar Association *Journal,* Powell maintained:

> Those who press for rapid extension of legal services are not likely to wait for the evolutionary development of legal aid and lawyer referral. There are indications that government itself, in seeking to eradicate "poverty," will enter this area. If so, it is to be hoped that there will be cooperation with the organized Bar and utilization of established agencies. Certainly, there should be no use of lay "aides" to render legal services, as this would neither be lawful nor in the public interest. Freedom and justice have flourished only where the practice of law is a profession and where citizens are represented by trained and independent lawyers.
>
> But adherence to sound principles, however essential, must not blind us to the reality that more effective means of distributing legal services must be devised. Legal aid and lawyer referral have proved their worth; far greater effort must be made to improve and extend them—especially the referral service. Beyond these, the organized Bar must explore broadly, and with an open mind, the possibility of other solutions.

In marked contrast to Powell's view, the NLADA Executive Committee had in December 1964 passed a resolution that opposed the creation of any new legal service agencies by OEO and sought to limit OEO funding to existing legal aid organizations.

Undeterred by any such signs of opposition within the legal profession, Powell introduced a resolution at the ABA's mid-winter meeting in February 1965 that endorsed the proposed OEO Legal Services Program. The resolution concluded with the declaration:

> FURTHER RESOLVED, that the Association, through its officers and appropriate committees, shall cooperate with the Office of Economic Opportunity and other appropriate groups in the development and implementation of programs for expanding availability of legal services to indigents and persons of low income, such program to utilize to the maximum extent deemed feasible the experience and facilities of the organized bar, such as legal aid, legal defender, and lawyer referral, and such legal services to be performed by lawyers in accordance with ethical standards of the legal profession. . . .

By diligent diplomacy, Powell worked to mobilize a broad spectrum of past and present ABA leaders behind his resolution. So effective was his campaign that the resolution passed unanimously when it came to a vote in the ABA's House of Delegates.

In succeeding months, the ABA (joined by the NLADA in some cases) cooperated actively with OEO in launching the Legal Services Program. The new program was given favorable publicity in ABA publications. Regional conferences were held by the ABA for bar leaders who desired information about OEO's plans, and technical assistance was provided to communities that wanted to apply for OEO funds. In June 1965, the ABA co-sponsored the National Conference on Law and Poverty in cooperation with OEO and the Department of Justice. Representatives of the ABA were appointed to the National Advisory Committee to the Legal Services Program when it was established in the fall of 1965. In the spring of 1966, the president of the ABA and the chairman of its Standing Committee on Legal Aid and Indigent Defenders urged Congress to increase financial support for the legal services.

National Advisory Committee

In the fall of 1965, the National Advisory Committee (NAC) to the OEO Legal Services Program was formed. It was charged with giving advice to the program's directors on policy matters. Among the members of the NAC were several representatives of the organized bar, including the president, president-elect, and past-president of the ABA, the chairmen of its Special Committee on the Availability of Legal Services and its Standing Committee on Legal Aid and Indigent Defendants, and the president of the NLADA. Also included on the NAC were several persons associated with the experimental legal assistance programs started in 1963 and 1964.

The NAC's discussion in the early months of its existence focused on the guidelines proposed for the Legal Services Program. Several potentially important guidelines quickly met with the approval of almost all members of the NAC. Included among these guidelines were the following:

- Legal Services grantees were to accept all categories of civil cases.
- Representation was to be provided in felony cases only on a temporary demonstration basis and even in misdemeanor cases only in jurisdictions where the state government failed to provide adequate services.
- Legal Services grantees were to be governed by separate boards of directors rather than by the boards of community action agencies.
- Offices were to be accessible, which in most cases meant decentralized neighborhood law offices, and attorneys were to be paid salaries comparable with lawyers in the community who possessed similar levels of experience.

Much more controversy was generated by consideration of policies toward representation of the poverty community on legal services boards, representation of poverty organizations, and advocacy of reform. The guidelines that finally emerged on these issues were as follows:

- Policy for the legal assistance program must be formulated with the participation of the "residents of the areas and members of the groups served." The poor must be represented on the board or policy-making committee of the program to provide legal services, just as they are represented on the policy-making body of the community action agency.
- Free legal service should be available to organizations composed primarily of residents of the areas and members of the groups served. However, the services should not be provided if the organization is able to retain an attorney for the type of representation it seeks. By pooling their resources, a group of individuals may be able to afford counsel in cases where an individual could not. At the same time, the combined resources of the members of an organization may be insufficient to retain an attorney to handle the particular legal problem in which the organization requires representation. A flexible standard should be applied. The factors to be considered include the size of the organization, the relative poverty of the members of the organization, and the cost of the legal assistance which the organization desires. . . .
- Advocacy of appropriate reforms in statutes, regulations, and administrative practices is a part of the traditional role of the lawyer and should be among the services afforded by the program. This may include judicial challenge to

particular practices and regulations, research into conflicting or discriminating applications of laws or administrative rules, and proposals for administrative and legislative changes.

The complete set of *Guidelines* was issued with the NAC's approval in the spring of 1966. At the same time it was issuing these *Guidelines,* the OEO Legal Services office was processing applications for grants. Over $20 million had been allocated for legal services in FY 1966, and the program's staff was eager to fund a significant number of projects before the end of the fiscal year.

DAVID GOLDMAN

David Goldman grew up in Brooklyn, attended Yale as an undergraduate, and received his LL.B. from Harvard Law School in 1960. He spent the next year at Northwestern University studying criminal law and then went to work for the public defender agency in Washington, D.C., where he quickly rose to the position of deputy director. In 1964 he was named Young Lawyer of the Year by the Washington Bar Association.

Introduction to Legal Services

Early in 1964, Goldman was approached by a member of Washington's United Planning Organization and asked to draft the proposal for UPO's Neighborhood Legal Services Project (discussed above). This task filled all his spare time for the next several months as he continued working with the public defender agency.

Shortly after he began to draft the NLSP proposal, Goldman met Edgar and Jean Cahn, two young lawyers who greatly influenced his thinking. Both Cahns had participated in the Ford Foundation's short-lived experiment with neighborhood law offices in New Haven, Connecticut. Since the middle of 1963, they had been part of a small circle of people in Washington who were attempting to generate support for a federally-financed legal services program.[3] The Cahns stimulated Goldman's interest in the role lawyers might play in helping to organize poor communities, and he assisted them in preparing their

[3]Edgar Cahn, who worked in the Justice Department, had drafted the 1964 Law Day speech for Attorney General Robert Kennedy. Subsequently he became a special assistant to Sargent Shriver at OEO. Jean Cahn worked at the State Department for Abram Chayes, the department's legal advisor, who was also a member of the small circle of legal service proponents. Later Jean Cahn worked at OEO as a special consultant on legal services.

seminal article, "The War on Poverty: A Civilian Perspective," which appeared in the *Yale Law Journal* in July 1964. This was the first published statement of the philosophy behind the experimental legal aid programs of the early 1960s. In their article, the Cahns maintained that the War on Poverty could succeed only if "the citizenry have been given the effective power to criticize, to dissent, and where need be, to compel responsiveness." To this end, they proposed the creation of university affiliated, neighborhood law firms "which could serve as a vehicle for the 'civilian perspective' by placing at the disposal of a community the services of professional advocates and by providing the opportunity, the orientation, and the training experience to stimulate leadership among the community's present inhabitants."

Goldman's proposal for the Neighborhood Legal Services Project was funded by the Ford Foundation in November 1964, and he was asked to join the Board of the new organization. A director was appointed, and at Goldman's suggestion, Earl Johnson, Jr., one of his close friends from graduate school, came over from the Criminal Division of the Department of Justice to serve as deputy director. In April 1965, Goldman left the public defender agency to join UPO as its administrative director. Several months later he was promoted to deputy executive director. In both positions, he shared the responsibility for general oversight of the legal services project, but he was not directly involved in its operations. He continued to serve on NLSP's board of directors, and in the fall of 1965 he was invited to join the National Advisory Council to the OEO Legal Services Program as one of its charter members.

Experience at UPO

At UPO Goldman was responsible for training community organizers, coordinating organizational efforts, and building political strategies around such issues as welfare, housing, and community planning. His work led him directly into such activities as organizing tenant groups and conducting rent strikes. Through this experience, Goldman became convinced that the full potential of legal services as an organizing tool was not being effectively used in UPO. The NLSP seemed to be misdirecting its energies. Goldman agreed fully with the criticism of the legal services program voiced by Kenneth Pye, chairman of NLSP's board:[4]

NLSP gradually became service oriented with-

out any decision by its board to proceed in that direction. . . . During its first year it failed to realize the objectives of an experimental program which would re-examine systematically the legal rules and procedures affecting the poor, which would investigate new areas and utilize new methods in the representation of the poor, which would coordinate effectively legal and social services for a joint approach to the problems of the poor. It did not develop into a program in which attorneys, relieved of heavy caseloads, could concentrate on a limited number of cases of significance to the community, could develop drafts of new rules, regulations and statutes, and could provide leadership in the formation and representation of neighborhood organizations. . . . The staff attorneys performed their tasks with an attitude of dedication and provided aggressive respresentation for individual clients. But many demonstrated an approach of cautious conservatism towards the subjects of group representation, participation in attempts to organize groups, and relationships with social workers and UPO organizers. . . . An atmosphere did not develop in which the neighborhoods could look to staff attorneys for leadership in community affairs. NLSP attorneys were outsiders who came to the neighborhoods to represent those needing legal services and who left when the task was done.

Goldman shared Pye's view that NLSP had become at best a first-rate legal aid society of the traditional type. He was convinced of the need for a new approach to legal service.

Approaches to Legal Service[5]

Goldman described the original concept behind legal services as the "service model." Here the idea is to increase the availability of legal services to poor persons so that they will be adequately represented within the political and economic system. Neighborhood legal offices will help individual clients with problems stemming from such things as landlord-tenant relations, wage garnishments, welfare, consumer credit, and family relations. This model assumes that the social order is fundamentally sound, with the legal services program serving solely as a means of ensuring that grievances of poor people are heard by the proper authorities. This has been the attitude traditionally adopted by the American Bar Association and other bar groups. The service model

[4]For a fuller discussion of Pye's views, see "The Role of Legal Services in the Antipoverty Program," *Law and Contemporary Problems,* Winter 1966, especially pp. 237–243.

[5]The discussion in this section draws heavily on "The New Public Interest Lawyers," *Yale Law Journal,* May 1970.

generally leads to extremely heavy caseloads, since legal services offices try to help every client who comes to them. Unfortunately, lawyers who are overwhelmed by heavy caseloads may fail to see areas where the model's basic assumption is faulty, that is, where the law itself must be reformed before it is possible for the poor to obtain equal justice.

This realization led many proponents of legal services to endorse the "law reform model," which emphasizes rule change and the representation of groups of poor people. Based on the example of *Brown v. Board of Education,* the objective of legal services under the law reform model is to establish broad legal principles and to change administrative rules in a way that relieves the plight of poor people. The basic instrument for this purpose is the test case, which is brought to attack unfair practices of government agencies or private companies and to establish new rights for the poor. Under the law reform model, service to individual clients is provided only as a means for winning the confidence of the poor community and for learning about the problems faced by poor persons.

In 1964 and 1965, most lawyers in the legal services community espoused some combination of service to individual clients and law reform, with increasing emphasis on the latter. David Goldman, however, believed that both these models of legal services were inadequate. He approached the problem from a different perspective.

> I had been a criminal defense lawyer and then had gone to UPO, where for a year and one-half we did street organizing. . . . I saw legal services as an arm of community organization, that is, the lawyer was to function as part of a political effort, at times as a lawyer, at times as an organizer, an educator, teacher, and PR man.

He was particularly sensitive to what he saw as the shortcomings of the law reform model of legal services:

> The worst thing a lawyer can do—from my perspective—is to take an issue that could be won by political organization and win it in the courts. And that is what legal services agencies did all over the country. They took the most flagrant injustices—the ones that had the potential to build the largest coalitions—and they took them into the courts, where, of course, they won. But there was nothing lasting beyond that. . . .

The basic theory of test case litigation is that a court case can be framed and directed toward the elimination of a particular wrong, like maldistribution of income, and can be a vehicle for the elimination of injustice. For test case lawyers, the problem is merely finding the particular rule or doctrine which embodies or causes the injustice and challenging it. This approach is a dead end for a number of reasons. First, it misconstrues the problem. The problem of unjust laws is almost invariably a problem of distribution of political and economic power; the rules merely reflect a series of choices made in response to these distributions. If a major goal of the unorganized poor is to redistribute power, it is debatable whether judicial process is a very effective means toward that end. This is particularly true of problems arising out of disparities of wealth and income. There is generally not much doctrinal judicial basis for adequately dealing with such problems, and lawyers find themselves developing cases whose outcomes are peripheral to the basic issues that these problems raise.

Secondly, "rule" change, without a political base to support it, just doesn't produce any substantial result because rules are not self-executing: they require an enforcement mechanism. California has the best laws governing working conditions of farm laborers in the United States. Under California law, workers are guaranteed toilets in the fields; clear, cool drinking water, covered with wire-mesh to keep flies away, regular rest periods, and a number of other "protections." But when you drive into the San Joaquin Valley, the drinking water is neither cool, nor clean, nor covered. If it's provided at all, the containers will be rusty and decrepit. It doesn't matter that there's a law on the books. There's absolutely no enforcement mechanism. Enforcement decisions are dominated by a political structure which has no interest in prosecuting, disciplining or regulating the state's agriculture interests. It's nonsense to devote all available lawyer resources to changing rules.

According to Goldman's analysis, the problem is:

> the creation of a mechanism that can create a substantial and lasting change in behavior, governmental and private. This is inevitably a political as well as a legal problem. We can try

to generate pressures on the parties involved by bringing public attention to the problem, or try to develop sanctions for noncompliance with existing laws, or attempt to develop institutional mechanisms to keep the problem visible. Sometimes a legal decision can produce conforming behavior. But, what happens when we go away—when the pressure abates? Legal victories can be so easily circumvented. If one avenue is blocked, five other alternatives remain open.

To his question "What happens when we go away?" Goldman's answer was that the legal service lawyers must leave behind them poor people who have become organized to keep the pressure on the governmental authorities. In other words, he believed that legal services should be based on the model of "lawyer-organizers" who provide legal services to the effort to organize poor communities. In cases where no organizational efforts are under way, this might mean that lawyers would themselves function as the organizers.

Goldman was explicit in describing how he thought lawyer-organizers should operate. Even though they might use test cases and other tools of the law reformers, their aims and methods would be very different:

If litigation is directed toward the different goal of organizing, the potentials and methods in pursuing a law suit significantly change. In such a context, law suits can consciously be brought for the public discussion they generate, and for the express purpose of influencing middle class and lower class perspectives on the problems they illuminate. They can be vehicles for setting in motion other political processes and for building coalitions and alliances. For example, a suit against a public agency may be far more important for the discovery of the agency's practices and records which it affords than for the legal rule or court order it generates. An effective political challenge to the agency may be impossible without the type of detailed documentation that only systematic discovery techniques can provide. It is on this base that coalitions and publicity can be built, and that groups can be organized to limit previously invisible authority.

This, of course, suggests a different orientation for the attorney interested in political change. He will spend a great deal more time in political organizing, in working on cases and

priorities that reflect the group demands of his clients and in developing cases in a way which reinforces their political integration and cohesion. Let me give you an example: Assume an attorney is seeking an injunction and he must make a decision as to the type of preliminary relief he will ask of the court. What criteria should govern that decision? An attorney focusing on political organizing might well delineate the narrowest rather than the broadest ground in seeking preliminary relief. For example, in a landlord-tenant dispute he might seek a restraining order preventing the landlord from using force or self-help. This is, of course, a clear legal right in California, and the likelihood of obtaining such an order would be high. Why would it be sought? Twenty tenants would go in with the attorney to court asking that they not be thrown out by the landlord before he goes to court and they'd walk out with a paper in their hands restricting the landlord's power. More than the protection, they'd have won a victory. They can go back to the forty other tenants who didn't go to court and say, "We won our first fight. Now we'll try a harder fight."

CALIFORNIA LEGAL SERVICES

Frustrated by his inability to redirect NLSP and tired of Washington, Goldman decided early in 1966 to look for a new position where he would be closer to the actual delivery of legal services and could better try out his ideas. He hoped to demonstrate the utility of the lawyer-organizer model to OEO and the legal services community:

I thought legal services was on the wrong track with its separation from community organization and its tendency to slip into law reform without recognizing the political dimensions of that approach, so I began looking for a place where the lawyer could function as an organizer.

Thinking that his approach would be particularly helpful to poor people in a rural area, Goldman investigated legal services programs in Florida and Arizona. Finally, Earl Johnson, who by this time had left NLSP to become Deputy Director of OEO's Office of Legal Services, told him about an ambitious program that was about to be started in California. The prime mover behind the California program was William Holland, a 26-year-old associate at a major

Los Angeles law firm. Holland had gone to Phillips Andover Academy, graduated Phi Beta Kappa from Harvard College, and earned his LL.B. at Harvard Law School, where he had won first place in the prestigious Ames moot court competition. He was being assisted in planning the new program by two students from the Yale Divinity School, Tom Jensen and Barry Clark, who had been organizing farm workers in the San Joaquin Valley.

CLS Funding Proposal

Johnson showed Goldman the funding proposal for California Legal Services, Inc., which Holland had prepared. It began with a quote from a Woody Guthrie song that the farm worker "comes with the dust and is gone with the wind." The proposal proceeded to describe the farm workers' situation in the following terms:

> Few will debate the desperate plight of these farm workers. Their average individual hourly farm wage is $1.35 as compared with the state-wide average factory wage of $3.05 an hour. Those who work at least 25 days a year in agricultural employment still are employed an average of only 134 days. It is not surprising, then, that the farm worker's average annual income from both agricultural and non-agricultural employment is approximately $1,378, which is less than half the $3,000 level at which poverty supposedly begins in this country. His median income is only $674.00. More than 84% of all farm workers in California—approximately 252,000 persons—earn less than $3,000 a year.
>
> When measuring the farm worker's impotence, it should be noted that he is exempt from the protections of the National Labor Relations Act, which guarantees other workers the right to bargain collectively; the Federal Fair Labor Standards Act, which sets the basic minimum wage and maximum hours for industries engaged in interstate commerce; and the Federal Unemployment Tax Act, which subsidizes 60% of the state unemployment insurance programs. On the state level, he is not covered by unemployment insurance, by a minimum wage, or by maximum hours provision. His wife and children will receive a minimum hourly wage of $1.30 if they undertake farm work but this rate does not apply to employers hiring less than five women and children, does not extend to 20% of the piece work which is performed for any employer, and is not accompanied by maximum hour or over-

time provisions. If the farm worker is a Mexican American, an Oriental, or a Negro, as most farm workers are, he is sometimes discriminated against. In the words of the Senate Subcommittee on Migratory Labor, the farm worker's plight is "shocking"; he is the "always excluded American," according to the Director of the Office of Economic Opportunity, and as he himself says, "We're always goin' some place but we never git no place."

After painting this depressing picture, the proposal continued: "So far as the rural poor are concerned, the familiar saying that we are a society of laws, not of men, is, at best, a half truth. Laws are passed, interpreted, and enforced by men; legal rights depend upon political, economic and legal representation. Yet this is what the rural poor, particularly the farm workers, have consistently lacked." Because of this lack of representation, the proposal maintained:

> it is not surprising that the laws which are intended to protect the rural poor frequently go unenforced. Section 923 of the California Labor Code guarantees to the individual worker full freedom of association and the right to organize and engage in concerted activities; but in practice, organizational picketing by farm workers, which is essential to any successful organizational campaign, is often enjoined. Under present California case law, trial courts possess broad discretion to enjoin picketing, even where the acts enjoined are non-violent, so long as the court determines as a matter of fact "that future picketing, even though conducted peaceably, would probably, if not necessarily be regarded as sinister in purpose."
>
> The State of California has extensive housing codes governing the operation and upkeep of labor camp housing, but the President's Committee on Migratory Labor has estimated that only a quarter to a third of the labor camps comply with these laws.
>
> Working conditions in the field are also regulated: employers are required to provide their workers with drinking water, toilets and hand washing facilities and periodic rest periods. Yet it has been observed that less than 20% of the employers in the state comply with these requirements.
>
> The State Labor and Education Codes contain extensive regulations governing the employment, working conditions, and hours of

minors, but inspectors from the Department of Labor find children working illegally on 60% of the farms they inspect.

Employers are required to furnish their workers an itemized written statement showing income earned and deductions made; but the nebulous and changing working relationship between farm workers and employers and the common practice of paying workers on a piece-rate basis means that accurate records are rarely kept or made available to employees. As a result the benefits of the Social Security Act and the Old Age Survivors and Disability Insurance Program are frequently not received by workers, even though they are legally entitled to such benefits.

Criminal prosecutions are permitted under the Labor Code, but they are rare. In 1957, for example, only one California farm employer was prosecuted for violating the State Labor Laws.

Many violations of the law go unreported because farm workers are fearful of retaliation, or because they are unaware of their rights: while many of the rural poor speak Spanish, the statutes contained in the State Labor Code and the regulations published by the State administrative agencies are written in English. When complaints are made to the Labor Commissioner and other state agencies, many are determined to be unfounded or unsubstantiated, because the complainants have no clear idea of their legal rights and what they must prove to enforce these rights. Complaints which are filed may not be successfully prosecuted because necessary witnesses, who migrate to other areas of the State, cannot be found. Sometimes, even the complainant disappears.

It is little wonder, then, that the California State Senate Fact Finding Committee on Labor and Welfare concluded in 1961, that "the manpower for compliance work is still far short of that necessary to accomplish a minimal adequate job. This fact is recognized by Federal and State administrators of the program, growers, and organized labor."

Holland argued that a legal services program could make a significant contribution to bettering the condition of the rural poor. His plan for California Legal Services, Inc., had several noteworthy features:

- Ten regional law offices would be established in rural parts of the state and be manned by 20

lawyers at salaries of $14,000 a year. The advantages claimed for a statewide program included greater ability to serve migrants, larger economies of scale, easier recruitment of well-qualified lawyers, and more independence from local community pressures.

- The problems of farm workers would be emphasized by CLS, although other poor persons living in rural areas would also be served.

- A small research staff would be created to study major problems particularly affecting the rural poor. The duties of this staff might include the drafting of legislation and the preparation of trial and appellate briefs.

- An educational program would be developed to train the program's attorneys and lay assistants. Various social and legal problems relating to rural poverty would be addressed.

OEO Action

Holland's proposal was submitted to OEO in March 1966. It was supported by a number of liberal, farm labor-oriented groups, including the Mexican American Political Association, the Community Service Organization, and the Emergency Committee to Aid Farm Workers. In April, however, the Board of Governors of the California State Bar Association passed a resolution in opposition to the proposal. The State Bar condemned the departure from "the concept of neighborhood legal services offices established and operated by residents of local communities" and CLS's intention to provide "its services to political and economic groups as well as individuals." The State Bar's resolution went on to charge:

The proposal is basically one of militant advocacy on a state-wide basis of the contentions of one side of an economic struggle now pending. Ostensibly designed to furnish only legal services to the poor, the proposal also encompasses the furnishing of political and economic aid.

Despite the State Bar's opposition, OEO's Office of Legal Services recommended that the CLS proposal be funded. Clinton Bamberger, Director of Legal Services, remarked at the time that "advocacy of the contentions of one side of an economic struggle now pending" was the best one-line definition of the War on Poverty he had heard. In May a grant to CLS of $1.3 million—the largest grant OEO had made to any legal services program—was approved by Sargent Shriver, Director of OEO. Before the grant was announced, Shriver called the President of the California State Bar, James Hemphill. When Hemphill complained that the CLS lawyers might be used by the poor in suits against the growers, Shriver replied: "Look, I'll make an agreement with you. If you will agree that no lawyers in California will represent the growers, I will agree that no legal services people will represent the pickers." That ended the argument.

Under the standard conditions applied to all OEO grants, CLS would be prohibited from engaging in partisan political activities. In addition, several special restrictions were placed on the grant, including:

- The program was prohibited from acting as legal counsel or supplying legal representation to any labor union or political organization.
- CLS could not undertake or sponsor activities to encourage the formation of the poor into collective bargaining units (but the program would be permitted to represent persons satisfying the program's eligibility requirements who requested assistance regarding their legal interests, including interests relating to labor relations).
- A majority of the Board of Directors for the program would be attorneys, and the Board would include two representatives of the State Bar.
- No staff attorneys could engage in the practice of law outside CLS while employed on a full-time, staff basis.

Also at Shriver's insistence, the CLS office proposed for Delano—headquarters of Cesar Chavez's union—would instead be located seven miles away in McFarland.

As with all OEO programs, standards were specified in the grant that determined who was eligible to receive services from CLS. The eligibility standards limited CLS to representing persons who earned less than $2200 per year plus $500 per dependent. Also like other OEO grants, the grant to CLS could be vetoed within 30 days by the governor of the state in question. A gubernatorial veto was subject to override only by the Director of OEO.

Visit to California

David Goldman was intrigued by what he learned from Earl Johnson about CLS. He contacted Bill Holland to express his interest in the new program,

then flew out to California a few weeks later to meet Holland, Tom Jensen, and the handful of persons they had recruited to their cause. In their company he began a four-day trip through the Central Valley, visiting farm labor camps, talking with Cesar Chavez in Delano, and meeting workers in the fields. Goldman, Holland, and Jensen talked extensively about what the future might hold for CLS. All three men agreed that CLS should be used as an instrument of social change, though their ideas about how to do this differed. Bill Holland seemed to be thinking mainly along the lines of the law reform model, but unlike others following this model, he was primarily interested in the coalition-building potential of the legal challenges. Tom Jensen, with his background in organizing farm workers, thought that the legal services should somehow be tied to grass roots organizational efforts. However, not being a lawyer, Jensen lacked concrete knowledge of the ways in which lawyers could contribute to community organizing. In the end, Goldman found that both men were highly receptive to his ideas, and he to theirs. Together they began to evolve the concept of a legal services organization that saw the work of lawyers in political terms. By the end of the trip, Goldman had decided that CLS presented the opportunity he was looking for and that he could establish a good personal relationship with Holland and Jensen. He agreed to return in August to serve as CLS's deputy director. Special permission was obtained from OEO to pay Goldman an annual salary of $19,000 ($3,000 more than Holland was receiving as Executive Director) on the grounds that this salary was still below his current salary at UPO.

THE GRAPE STRIKE[6]

At the time David Goldman met Cesar Chavez in Delano, Chavez's union, the National Farm Workers Association (NFWA), was engaged in a major strike against the Di Giorgio Fruit Corporation, one of the largest agribusiness corporations in California. The NFWA had already achieved several victories on behalf of its members and was the object of nationwide attention. A national boycott of Schenley wines and liquors had been launched by the NFWA in December 1965. Four months later, Schenley, the second

[6]The information contained in this section is drawn largely from two sources: Jerald Barry Brown, *The United Farm Workers Grape Strike and Boycott, 1965–70: An Evaluation of the Culture of Poverty Theory,* Cornell University Latin American Studies Program Dissertation Series, 1972; and John Gregory Dunne, *Delano: The Story of the California Grape Strike,* 1967.

largest grower in the Delano area, agreed to recognize the NFWA as the sole bargaining agent for all of its farm workers in the counties surrounding Delano.

Delano

Delano, a city of about 14,000 people, is typical of the agricultural communities that line the great Central Valley of California. The Valley is the heart of California agribusiness, the state's largest industry. California produces between 35% and 40% of the fruit and vegetables sold in the U.S.; most of this produce comes from the Central Valley.

Grapes are the major crop raised around Delano. With the exception of the Di Giorgio and Schenley agribusiness corporations, most of the Delano growers are local, resident ranchers of Yugoslav or Italian descent. They are self-made men, hardworking and independent, who personally supervise the operation of their ranches. John Dunne, a journalist who visited Delano in the summer of 1966, characterized the growers as "clannish and stubborn," saying that they "still speak in the accents of their fathers and not in the featureless inflections of modern, affluent California, and they cannot believe for one moment that they might be in the wrong."

National Farm Workers Association

Cesar Chavez, whose parents were migrant farm workers, learned to be an organizer from Fred Ross of the Community Service Organization (CSO), an outgrowth of Saul Alinsky's Industrial Areas Foundation. In 1952 Chavez accepted a job organizing CSO chapters throughout California. Rising rapidly in the organization, he was appointed director of the National CSO in 1960. However, he became disenchanted with the organization as it prospered and seemed to lose touch with the people it was designed to serve. Chavez explains:

As the organization grew, we found ourselves meeting in fancier and fancier motels and holding expensive conventions. Doctors, lawyers and politicians began joining. They would get elected to some office in the organization and then, for all practical purposes, leave. Intent on using the CSO for their own prestige purposes, these "leaders," many of them, lacked the urgency we had to have. When I became general director I began to press for a program to organize farm workers into a union, an idea most of the leadership opposed. So I started a revolt within the CSO. I refused to sit at the head table

at meetings, refused to wear a suit and tie, and finally I even refused to shave and cut my hair. It used to embarrass some of the professionals. At every meeting I got up and gave my standard speech: we shouldn't meet in fancy motels, we were getting away from the people, farm workers had to be organized. But nothing happened. In March of '62 I resigned and came to Delano to begin organizing the Valley on my own.

How the union was started is now a legendary story that Chavez has been called on to repeat many times:

By hand I drew a map of all the towns between Arvin and Stockton—86 of them, including farming camps—and decided to hit them all to get a small nucleus of people working in each. For six months I traveled around, planting an idea. We had a simple questionnaire, a little card with space for name, address and how much the worker thought he ought to be paid. My wife, Helen, mimeographed them, and we took our kids for two or three day jaunts to these towns, distributing the cards door-to-door and to camps and groceries.

Some 80,000 cards were sent back from eight Valley counties. I got a lot of contacts that way, but I was shocked at the wages the people were asking. The growers were paying $1 and $1.15, and maybe 95 per cent of the people thought they should be getting only $1.25. Sometimes people scribbled messages on the cards: "I hope to God we win" or "Do you think we can win?" or "I'd like to know more." So I separated the cards with the pencilled notes, got in my car and went to those people.

We didn't have any money at all in those days, none for gas and hardly any for food. So I went to people and started asking for food. It turned out to be about the best thing I could have done, although at first it's hard on your pride. Some of our best members came in that way. If people give you their food, they'll give you their hearts. Several months and many meetings later we had a working organization, and this time the leaders were the people.

The union grew slowly through 1963 and 1964. Chavez established a Farm Workers Credit Union, a small Farm Workers Cooperative (to purchase automotive supplies for NFWA members), a Farm Workers Press (which published a bi-weekly newsletter), and a service center that helped members with welfare and legal problems. He and NFWA vice president Maria Sanchez lobbied California state legislators for the extension of disability and unemployment benefits to farm workers. By August 1964, the NFWA had 1,000 member families spread over seven counties. NFWA's membership voted in November 1964 to give Chavez a salary of $40 per week; he thus became the first farm labor organizer in history to be supported by the workers themselves.[7]

Encouraged by its growing strength, NFWA engaged in two small, local strikes around Delano in the summer of 1965. The major issues in both strikes were wages and union recognition. NFWA also organized a rent strike and protest march when the Tulare County Housing Authority announced plans to raise rents at two of its labor camps; investigations by state and county authorities ensued and the rent hikes were rescinded.

The Grape Strike Begins

Chavez believed that it would be another five or ten years before NFWA would be prepared for a major strike, but events in September 1965 forced his hand. A large group of Filipino workers arrived in Delano for the grape harvest and discovered that the Delano growers were offering lower wages than they had been paid in the Coachella Valley. The Filipinos were members of the Agricultural Workers Organizing Committee (AWOC), an AFL-CIO-backed effort to organize farm workers that had been started in 1959. When the growers proved unresponsive to demands for a raise, approximately 1,000 AWOC members went on strike. Chavez has explained how the Filipinos' action affected his union:

> We had just finished the Martin strike when the Agricultural Workers Organizing Committee (AFL-CIO) started a strike against the grape growers, Di Giorgio, Schenley liquors and the small growers, asking $1.50 an hour and 25 cents a box. There was a lot of pressure from our members to join the strike, but we had some misgivings. We didn't feel ready for a big strike like this one, one that was sure to last a

[7]Chavez places great stress on his union being self-supporting: "One of the first things I decided was that outside money wasn't going to organize people, at least not in the beginning. I even turned down a grant from a private group—$50,000 to go directly to organize farm workers—for just this reason. Even when there are no strings attached, you are still compromised because you feel you have to produce immediate results. This is bad, because it takes a long time to build a movement, and your organization suffers if it gets too far ahead of the people it belongs to."

long time. Having no money—just $87 in the strike fund—meant we'd have to depend on God knows who.

Eight days after the strike started—it takes time to get 1,200 people together from all over the Valley—we held a meeting in Delano and voted to go out. I asked the membership to release us from the pledge not to accept outside money, because we'd need it now, a lot of it.

The NFWA received the help it needed from many groups, including other unions, religious organizations, and civil rights groups. Chavez counted in particular on the support of the church:

> I've been making friends with the clergy for sixteen years, especially the Migrant Ministry. And as for the Catholic clergy, how could they stay out of this one? All the Mexicans are Catholic. The church is the one group that isn't expecting anything from us. All the others, the unions, the civil rights groups, they all want something in return for their support. Not the church.

The strike continued throughout the fall harvest season. Much of the flavor of what was taking place is captured by the recollections of a NFWA member about an incident that took place in October:

> When the Filipinos went on strike, we had $87 in the treasury and we knew we wouldn't be ready for a big strike for maybe five or ten years, but we could never keep our heads up if we crossed their picket lines. So we called the membership together to have a vote. In the early days of the strike, the growers used a lot of violence, especially the Dispoto brothers. They would come to the picket line and just keep bumping into the strikers and knocking them down. One of the growers had a spray rig drive over to the picket line and 16 people got sprayed with insecticide. But the police never arrested them.

> As the strike became more effective, the police really got mad. One day, Sergeant Dodd of the Kern County sheriff's office told the picket captain that a new directive had come through and there would be no more shouting along the roadside in Kern County since everyone knows there is a strike and there is no need to disturb the peace by shouting at them. One

of the strikers started to read Jack London's definition of a scab over a bullhorn and Sgt. Dodd told him, "You read that and I am going to arrest you. I have read that definition and consider it threatening and vile and I see no reason in getting these people [the strikebreakers] stirred up, do you?" When that happened, Reverend David Havens, who was on the picket line, with us, took the paper and began reading it. He was arrested.

That night we called an emergency meeting. The Tulare County sheriff's office also seemed ready to ban shouting and we decided to make a test case. Everyone in the room volunteered to be arrested. Rev. Chris Hartmire, who is the director of the Migrant Ministry, asked nine ministers to join with the strikers. Forty-four volunteers, including 9 ministers and 12 women strikers, went out to the fields, found a scab crew and lined up along the roadside and began shouting "*huelga*" ["strike" in Spanish]. The police arrested every one of them right in front of the newspapermen and television cameras.

That day, Cesar was up at Berkeley talking to a student rally. When news of the arrest came, Cesar asked the students to give up their lunch money to go for bail for the strikers. He collected over $6000 and several hundred students promised to come join our picket lines. We started holding prayer meetings around the jail. The kids were there crying for their mommies, and we made it clear to everyone that Delano was just like Selma, Alabama. From then on the strike became known nationally, and donations and offers of help started pouring in from all over the country.

The economic impact of the strike on the Delano growers appeared relatively slight. They merely went farther afield to recruit workers, eventually extending their search for labor as far away as Oregon, Texas, and Mexico and sparking NFWA charges that they were using "illegal, foreign strikebreakers." By late November the field harvest was virtually completed. NFWA had found it almost impossible to keep the strikebreakers out of the fields. Much of the difficulty was simply the logistics of picketing over 30 ranches. As one civil rights activist helping the union commented at the time, "It's like striking an industrial plant that has a thousand entrance gates and is four hundred square miles large. And if that isn't bad enough, you don't know each morning where the plant will be, or where the gates are, or whether it

will be open or closed, or what wages will be offered that day."

The Boycott Begins

Seeking to make the strike more effective, Chavez developed a new tactic: economic boycott. With the support of the AFL-CIO, NFWA and AWOC announced a nationwide boycott of Delano grapes on December 18, 1965. The initial target of the boycott was Schenley Industries, Inc., because it grew wine grapes and marketed its products under nationally-known brand labels. Chavez explained: "It was a simple decision. In the first place, liquor is easier to boycott. And then it is usually the man who goes to the liquor store and he's more sympathetic to labor as a rule than his wife is." To implement the boycott, farm workers and volunteers were dispatched to major cities across the U.S.

Chavez received another boost in March 1966 when the U.S. Senate Subcommittee on Migratory Labor held public hearings in Delano. On the day the hearings ended, Chavez and over 60 strikers set off on a 250-mile, 25-day march to the state capitol in Sacramento. While the march was in progress, Chavez was informed by a Schenley attorney of the company's willingness to recognize NFWA.[8] The march, now part of NFWA's folklore, was described by one striker as follows:

Cesar told us that for a long time he had been thinking about a march of farm workers from the Mexican border to the state capitol in Sacramento to dramatize our problems. Then in January a priest came to Delano and we talked about the coming Lenten season and a lot of the older people began talking about Lenten pilgrimages they had made in Mexico. We began discussing if we should march from Delano to Schenley's head office in New York, or go to the Mexican border to protest the scabs, or to Sacramento to ask the governor to help.

We finally decided to go from Delano to Sacramento and arrive there on Easter Sunday. About 65 strikers volunteered to go. Chavez asked two Anglos to plan the route of the

[8]In later testimony before the California State Senate Committee on Agriculture, a Schenley vice-president explained his company's decision to settle as follows: "These reprisals [by the NFWA] and the publicity presented a threat of serious damage to our business on a nationwide scale. . . . Our sales department felt that even more damaging than any decline in our sales was the adverse publicity that accompanied the boycott and the NFWA organizing activities."

march and they set it up for us to go straight up Route 99 so that everyone could see us. Cesar kidded them that that was no way to reach the people and he said that we had to go through all the small farm worker towns and ask the people there to give us food and a place to sleep. With just a few days left, we changed the route to go through 53 farm worker towns and sent organizers ahead to tell people we were coming.

We planned to start the march on the day the Senate hearings ended so there would be a lot of publicity. Cesar said that we should assemble right at the end of Main Street [in Delano] and begin by marching right through the center of town. The police chief said that we couldn't do that since we had to have a parade permit and then sent a line of police with riot helmets and clubs to block off the street. We just stood there facing each other for an hour or so and all of the newspaper men and television cameras were on us. Finally, the mayor said that we could go ahead.

The pilgrimage was really beautiful, just like a religious procession. At the front, we carried a banner of the Lady of Guadalupe, the American flag, the Mexican flag, and the Star of David to show that we wanted dignity for everyone. Some nuns and fathers joined us along the way. In every town we visited, the farm workers came out to meet us with *huelga* flags and *mariachi* music. Every night we held a rally and a mass and sang *huelga* songs. The *Teatro Campesino* performed and Luis Valdez read the "Plan of Delano" to explain the purpose of the march.

When Schenley signed, we just couldn't believe that we had won. We changed our signs to read "Boycott Di Giorgio." Even though the Governor was too busy to meet with us when we got to Sacramento, we didn't care. There were 10,000 people there to greet us and I knew that from now on the growers were going to have to listen to the farm workers.

Immediately following its victory over Schenley, the NFWA called for a boycott of S&W Foods and Treesweet Orange Juice, the major products of the Di Giorgio Fruit Corporation. Di Giorgio responded by declaring its unwillingness to hold a union representation election. Negotiations between the company and the NFWA began, but repeatedly broke down in name-calling, charges, and countercharges. Apparently Di Giorgio had invited the Teamsters Union, which until this time had been a vigorous supporter of the NFWA, to organize their workers. On June 2, 1966, Di Giorgio announced that it would hold an election immediately under its own ground rules. NFWA and AWOC refused to participate and urged their members to boycott the election. The Teamsters emerged victorious, but from the vote it was apparent that almost half of the workers eligible to vote had not done so. Chavez denounced the election as a fraud; in a letter to Harrison Williams, the Chairman of the Senate Subcommittee on Migratory Labor, he charged that Di Giorgio had "reverted to every conceivable method of intimidation and coercion to force workers to vote for the Teamsters Union." The Mexican-American Political Association joined the fray, responding to an appeal from Chavez, and threatened to withhold its endorsement from incumbent Governor John Wilson, a liberal Democrat, in his upcoming reelection campaign against conservative Republican Douglas Patton. Responding to the pressure on him to act, Wilson brought in a nationally-respected labor arbitrator in an attempt to settle the dispute. Meanwhile the strike against Di Giorgio continued.

Imagine you are David Goldman at this point. What do you do?

Your personal goal is to provide legal assistance in a manner that helps organize the farm workers and thus gives them greater political power. That's why you took this job. You were impatient with the old models—legal aid and law reform. Your ideal is of a society in which farm workers, among other poor and powerless groups, gain enough political strength to alter the prevailing allocation of power in American society and thus enjoy the rights and opportunities open to other Americans.

Governor Wilson wants the Di Giorgio labor dispute settled quickly. You could help represent Chavez and the National Farm Workers Association in the upcoming arbitration, advancing their interests in the same way that any lawyer would represent his client, as in the legal aid model. Alternatively, you could look for ways to test the prevailing labor laws, defending the NFWA or a particular NFWA member against prosecution for violating the law, by raising Constitutional issues. This is the law reform model. But neither of these approaches solves the fundamental problem of the farm workers' lack of political strength. A quick settlement of the Di Giorgio dispute—even one that is somewhat favorable to the NFWA—would not mobilize the farm workers for future political action; similarly, a test case might change a particular law but would not alter other laws or future laws bearing upon farm workers, nor might the new law be enforced.

Assume, therefore, that you advise Chavez against arbitration. Perhaps you counsel some sort of confrontation that will gain publicity, such as having the farm workers block Di Giorgio trucks. Your logic runs as follows: In the ensuing showdown, Di Giorgio's employees are likely to overstep. They may even resort to violence, and surely the police will be summoned and there will be arrests. You will defend the farm workers in court, or you might represent them in a class action against the police. Whatever specific legal opportunities arise, your overall strategy will be to use the confrontation and subsequent legal actions as organizing devices, enhancing the visibility and solidarity of the NFWA and thereby gaining new members—an application of the "lawyer-organizer" model.

Think again. Remember that the California State Bar Association (two members of which sit on your board of directors) is opposed to any such political organizing. Moreover, under standard conditions applied to all grants made by the Office of Economic Opportunity, your California Legal Service program is explicitly prohibited from engaging in any partisan political activities. Finally, note that several special restrictions have been placed on your grant. You are expressly prohibited from acting as legal counsel or supplying legal representation to any labor union or political organization, and you cannot undertake or sponsor activities designed to encourage the formation of the poor into collective bargaining units.

Granted, your funders back in Washington—OEO's Office of Legal Services—seem generally supportive: Clinton Bamberger, Director of Legal Services, has stated that the War on Poverty requires advocacy on behalf of the unrepresented side of an economic struggle, and Sargent Shriver, Director of OEO, expects you and your colleagues to represent farm workers in suits against the growers. But Bamberger and Shriver are involved in political fights of their own. That's why they placed those restrictions on your grant, and why Shriver insisted that your headquarters be located far away from the NFWA headquarters. They do not want you to cross the boundary between providing farm workers with legal representation and helping organize them.

In fact, Congress has not authorized or funded the "lawyer-organizer" model of legal services. It has authorized you only to provide legal aid and perhaps to undertake some test cases on behalf of the poor. While some members of Congress may be sympathetic to your aims, most are not, nor are most members of the public. After all, if a majority of Congress and the President wanted you to pursue the "lawyer-organizer" model—and if a majority of the public shared your ideal—then presumably all sorts of laws would be changed and new ones enacted and all of them enforced, on behalf of the farm workers. The battle would already have been won. The reason you seek more political power for farm workers is to redress what you consider to have been an unjust allocation of rights and opportunities in the first place.

You might be able to get away with it, notwithstanding. Perhaps you can take precautions so that your board of directors remains unaware of your organizing activities—of the advice you were providing to the NFWA and your help in designing confrontations and legal strategies to mobilize the membership. You might be able to describe ensuing litigation in terms of legal aid or law reform. When questioned—by your board, by your supervisors in Washington, or by a congressional committee—you could be highly selective in your disclosures. That is, you might mislead them into thinking you have done nothing out of the ordinary.

Many of my students think that this is what David should do. They share David's ideals; they too want a more just society. Some of them worry that the strategy is dangerous—that David eventually will be found out and that his program may suffer in the long term as a result—but their concern is limited to the risk of discovery. If the risk is very low, they would agree to try.

Then I ask them to reverse the situation and assume that they strongly disagree with David's ideals. Perhaps David wants to use his office to promote white supremacy, by quietly helping to organize groups intent on blocking civil rights. Or David surreptitiously channels government funds to support various anticommunist (although dictatorial) regimes around the globe, because he believes that America must take a stronger stand against communism. Or David pursues any number of possible goals to which my students might object and which he has not been authorized to seek.

The thought experiment changes some of their minds. David is free to help organize the farm workers on his own, of course. But he is *not* free to use public authority in a manner that the public, and its representatives, have not approved, and probably would not approve were they fully apprised. That would be an abuse of trust. Our democracy would not long endure if public servants were free to pursue their own ideals regardless of what the public expected of them.

Such abuses of trust also undermine the public's confidence in government generally. The risk of discovery in this one instance may be small and the potential cost to this one program—were David discovered—relatively minor compared to everything else government does. But the cost would extend beyond this one program. The public's faith in public servants would decline ever so slightly, and as a result the next program may not be funded, even if its aim is widely supported. Or if it is funded, it will be accompanied by additional layers of review and oversight, the cumulative effect of which will be to stifle creative solutions to unforeseen problems and render the entire system less flexible.

Does this mean that public servants cannot act on their ideals?

Hardly. As I have said, most people enter the public service and find satisfaction there because of their ideals. The lesson here is that public servants must test their ideals against the public's ideals and be clear with their superiors and elected representatives about what they want to do. Public servants may try to persuade their overseers of the correctness and wisdom of what they intend: They may summon facts to bolster their arguments or they may appeal to higher-level principles. Public ideals are rarely static; usually they are in constant motion. And there is rarely "one" public, but usually many different publics, each adhering to different ideals or different versions of ideals. All this gives public servants reason to continue proposing and arguing.

In short, there is significant room for public servants to act in pursuit of their ideals. Used honestly and carefully, public authority permits some discretion. But the key words are "honestly" and "carefully." The public servant must always be aware of the limits of the mandate he or she has received. Does the same logic apply to an elected official? Consider the case of Stephanie McGrail.

Senator McGrail and the Death Penalty

In late March 1988, Senator Stephanie McGrail, a 25-year-old first-term Democrat from Saldon, voted to sustain then-Governor Frank Barnard's veto of a bill to restore the death penalty in the State of York. McGrail was against the death penalty although it had not been a major issue in her campaign. The vote was two short of overriding.

In the few days immediately after the vote, McGrail received what she called a "flood" of phone calls, mail and telegrams opposing her vote.

On the Friday before the Monday on which the senate was to vote on the veto again, McGrail announced that she would canvass the streets of her district to take a "fresh sounding" of public opinion on the issue. She and her associates found that nearly seven out of ten people whose views were asked favored the death penalty.

McGrail changed her vote, but the veto was still sustained by a one-vote margin.

Predictably, those favoring restoration classed her action a profile in courage and those opposed called it cowardice.

This is a slightly modified version of a case prepared by Martin Linsky for teaching purposes at the John F. Kennedy School of Government, Harvard University.

Copyright 1988 by the President and Fellows of Harvard College

---

Would McGrail have acted irresponsibly had she stuck to her original position and voted to sustain the Governor's veto of the death penalty? Remember: She has now contacted her constituents, a majority of whom are in favor of the death penalty. She was less sure of their position when she voted the first time.

Think back to David Goldman. The public did not authorize him to embark upon the lawyer-organizer model of legal services, and we concluded that he would abuse the public's trust were he to do so. At first blush, Stephanie McGrail would seem to be in the same position. Her constituents have not authorized her to oppose the death penalty—quite the contrary—and she is no less accountable to the public than is David Goldman. Thus, where there is a conflict between her personal ideals and those of her constituents, it would appear that she has an obligation to follow the dictates of *their* consciences.

But Stephanie McGrail, unlike David Goldman, is elected directly by the public, so the public has authorized her differently than it has authorized David. The public authorized David to undertake a specific set of tasks—to implement a particular law—and expressly instructed him not to do other things, like help to organize a labor union. The public has neither authorized nor prohibited Stephanie McGrail to vote for—or against—any specific piece of legislation. The authority conferred upon her by her constituents is more general, and more subtle: It is to *represent* them in the state legislature.

What does it mean to "represent" a set of constituents? Does it require that an elected official do precisely what a majority of them wants at any given time? If this were all there was to representative government, then it would be more efficient to install a system of two-way interactive video voting on each family's television set than to elect a representative—a system which would allow voters to express their views on each issue directly and merely tally up the results.*

Representation entails something else—a degree of reflection and deliberation, inevitably invoking whatever ideals the representative brings to her job. Voters do not elect automatons who simply advance the majority's unconsidered preferences. They elect whole people, replete with systems of values. They expect their representatives to weigh constituents' preferences, of course, but not to be totally bound by them. They expect her to bring to bear her own considered opinions. If they find themselves in fundamental disagreement with her over time—with her system of values and her approach to problems—they may choose someone else to represent them in the next election.

So how should Stephanie McGrail have voted? Not in favor of the death penalty solely because most of her constituents were in favor. Had she voted to sustain the Governor's veto she might owe her constituents an explanation, but it was still her choice, not theirs. On the other hand, her beliefs and values notwithstanding, a decision to vote against the Governor and in favor of the death penalty might reflect what she considers to be higher legislative priorities in the future; perhaps she does not want to risk the chance of losing the next election on this one issue. Or perhaps she has concluded that the death penalty will be enacted eventually regardless of her views or those of the Governor, and thus there's little benefit to be had in taking a visible stand against it at this point.

*See, for example, James C. Miller III, "A Program for Direct and Proxy Voting in the Legislative Process," *Public Choice* 7 (Fall 1969): 107.

_____ *chapter 2* _____

A Conflict
of Jobs

Much of the public sector is arranged hierarchically. A Bureau of Motor Vehicles, for example, might contain a number of divisions, each having responsibility for a particular type of motor vehicle (trucks, buses, passenger cars, motorcycles); each division might comprise, in turn, offices with responsibilities for particular kinds of regulations (licensing drivers, setting vehicle standards, monitoring and enforcing the standards). The Bureau of Motor Vehicles itself might be part of an even larger organization, the Department of Transportation, which also oversees highway construction, airports, and railways. And the Department, in turn, might be one of several departments under the broad supervision of the State's Secretary for Transportation, Communication, and Commerce.

"The decisive reason for the advance of bureaucratic organization," the German sociologist Max Weber observed almost a century ago, "has always been its purely technical superiority over any other form of organization."* This kind of arrangement can be highly efficient, for it allows specific functions (such as the granting of a driver's license) to be done uniformly and economically by a group of people who specialize in it, while also providing a means of coordinating related functions done by different groups (such as establishing safety standards for cars). And because the head of each unit of the organization reports upward to someone with wider responsibility for overseeing the unit's work, this

*Max Weber, "Bureaucracy," in H. Gerth and C. Wright Mills, *From Max Weber* (New York: Oxford University Press, 1946), p. 214.

31

form of organization also allows people at higher levels to set broad goals and hold subordinates responsible for meeting them.

No wonder that corporations and not-for-profit institutions are organized along roughly the same lines. Bureaucracies may be looser or tighter, with few or many layers of review, informal or strict reporting requirements, and more or less participation from below in setting goals. But the basic principles of specialization, coordination, and accountability remain the same.

Public bureaucracies are different from other hierarchies in one important respect, however. Accountability is not solely upward toward higher levels of executive authority. Public servants are accountable to the public, and the public (or its elected representatives) may intercede at *any* level, demanding all sorts of things, some of which may be inconsistent with one another. For example, the head of the state trucking association (a group of trucking companies) objects to the fees and weight limits proposed by the Division of Trucking, in a hearing organized by the Division's director. At the same hearing, a citizen's group dedicated to safer roads demands that trucks be held to even higher standards and pay higher fees. Elderly citizens who have been denied driver's licenses because of their poor eyesight, meanwhile, have lobbied state legislators, who in turn ask the head of the Bureau of Motor Vehicles to explain in writing why the sight requirement must be so high. And the Department of Transportation's efforts to improve the quality of its personnel notwithstanding, a disgruntled former employee of the Department persuades his local representative to the state legislature that he was improperly dismissed, prompting the representative to fire off a letter to the Secretary of Transportation, threatening to raise the matter at the next oversight hearing unless the employee is promptly reinstated.

Multiple directions of accountability for achieving sometimes inconsistent goals create dilemmas for public officials. To whom are they accountable and for what? Consider the dilemma facing Miles Mahoney.

Park Plaza

Miles Mahoney spread out the morning edition of the *Boston Globe*, Wednesday, November 29, 1972. The headline at the top of page 3 caught his eye: "Park Plaza plan revised; Sargent supports it."

Mahoney's eyes raced through the paragraphs:

Governor Francis W. Sargent said yesterday that new plans submitted to the state could lead to the construction of the controversial $266 million Park Plaza project in downtown Boston.

Expressing guarded optimism at a State House press conference, Sargent said the plans submitted yesterday by the Boston Redevelopment Authority to the Massachusetts Department of Community Affairs (DCA) "meet the

This case was prepared by Associate Professor Colin S. Diver for use in the Public Management Program at the Boston University School of Management. It is intended to serve as a basis for class discussion, not to illustrate either effective or ineffective handling of a managerial situation.

Copyright © 1975 by the Trustees of Boston University.

concerns" he had when the original plan was turned down by the state last June.

A few paragraphs later, Mahoney's glance was arrested:

Sargent also said that while he didn't want to prejudge DCA Comr. Miles Mahoney's final decision on the revised plan, "Park Plaza is now, in my view, finally on the road to reality."

As Mahoney turned to look out the window of his office on the fourteenth floor of the State Office Building, a mixed expression of disbelief and anger crossed his lean features. Turning to the telephone on his desk, he quickly dialed four familiar digits. "Hello? This is Miles Mahoney. Is Al Kramer there? . . . OK. Ask him to call me when he gets in. Thanks."

As he turned from the telephone, his eyes rested on the heavy Georgian facade of the State House, a few hundred yards up the hill, looming somehow like a fortress, impenetrable.

MILES MAHONEY

Miles Mahoney had served his political apprenticeship in Philadelphia. After obtaining a masters degree in community organization, he was hired by the city's Human Relations Commission as a housing specialist. Then he was appointed to a position in the Philadelphia Redevelopment Authority, as "area director" with responsibility to oversee the execution of a large residential-industrial urban renewal project. He later became director of the city's Neighborhood Renewal Program, a federally financed program of housing rehabilitation and housing code enforcement. In 1969, he was appointed chief executive officer of the Philadelphia Housing Authority, the agency responsible for operation, building, and leasing public housing for the city's poor. During Mahoney's tenure, the housing policies of the authority were often sharply criticized by conservatives in the city, led by Police Commissioner Frank Rizzo, who, in 1971, ran successfully for mayor. Shortly after Rizzo was elected, the housing authority board (including two Rizzo appointees) fired Mahoney. As Mahoney recalled:

His disposing of me and what he called the "commies" in the housing program was a campaign promise which he fulfilled within two months of his election. He disclaimed having

had anything to do with it—said it was a decision of the housing authority's board—the chairman of the board. Publicly the mayor had always disclaimed doing it, because legally he had no authority to do it. But the functional reasons were that he was—the same old stuff—looking for contracts, looking for jobs. . . . perhaps the major thing—the thing that became a major campaign issue—was our program to build public housing in the still all-white sections of the city. There was a major project called "Whitman" there, which he, as police commissioner, assisted in getting killed by refusing to enforce an injunction we got against the citizenry from tearing down the buildings as they were being built. He openly refused to enforce the injunction. The city ended up having to pay the developer $350,000 for breach of contract.

After his removal from the Philadelphia Housing Authority, Miles Mahoney began looking for a job. Boston was a natural place to look. Not only was he well known and respected by the professional "housing" community in Boston, but it happened that two of the most important housing jobs in the state were open: executive director of the Boston Housing Authority (BHA) and commissioner of the Massachusetts Department of Community Affairs (DCA). In addition, the mayor of Boston, Kevin H. White, was thinking of creating a new senior staff position of "development coordinator" to coordinate the city's fragmented housing and development functions.

Mahoney interviewed for all three positions. He was offered the position of BHA director by the authority's five-member board, three of whom had known and respected Mahoney for several years. He was not offered the development coordinator position. He was not told why, but wondered whether it had anything to do with his closeness to the three-member majority of the BHA board with whom Mayor White had had a long and extremely bitter feud.

At the state level, he met with several of Governor Sargent's top advisors, including his chief secretary, Jack Flannery, and his chief policy advisor, Albert Kramer. The discussions focused on Mahoney's past record and his views on housing policy. Mahoney was direct and outspoken in both defending his record at the Philadelphia Housing Authority and advocating an aggressive role for the state in housing development. Mahoney also met briefly with Governor Sargent and was impressed. Sargent, a Republican, had a reputation as a progressive, activist governor, with a particularly strong interest in the environment, public transportation and social services. Mahoney's encounter with the governor and his staff seemed to confirm the image.

When the governor offered Mahoney the position of commissioner of DCA, he accepted. The announcement was made on April 25, 1972. Mahoney took office on May 4.

THE DEPARTMENT OF COMMUNITY AFFAIRS

The Massachusetts Department of Community Affairs was created in 1968 under a reorganization that combined parts of three separate state agencies into a single department reporting directly to the governor. The reorganization gave the new department a very broad mandate to provide services to the 351 cities and towns in Massachusetts and consolidated the state's already extensive authority to supervise local housing and urban renewal activities. This authority included the power to appoint one of the five members of every local housing authority and redevelopment authority; to provide technical assistance to housing and redevelopment authorities; to approve all subsidized housing projects and urban renewal projects undertaken by local authorities; to review the plans of local and regional planning bodies; and to provide services, such as rental assistance and day care, for public housing tenants. At the time of his appointment, Miles Mahoney viewed the DCA enabling statute as "the best in the country. It made it possible to integrate urban renewal, housing, social services, and planning."

If the agency's charter impressed Mahoney, its past performance did not. DCA had a reputation for passivity. Although it had performed some useful services for the state's smaller cities and towns, it was not regarded as exercising effective supervision over their housing and renewal activities. In particular, it had shown no stomach for policing the activities of the state's largest renewal agency, the Boston Redevelopment Authority (BRA). During fifteen years of enormous redevelopment activity in Boston, often punctuated by bitter controversy, the BRA had never been seriously challenged by DCA. Mahoney recalled:

> There was a view that DCA was a patsy for the BRA. The department was scared to death of the authority, with all its architects and engineers and lawyers.

In addition to its timidity, the department was

drafting, haphazardly attacking what Mahoney called a "big and sprawling set of responsibilities" without clear priorities or policy direction.

After assuming the position of commissioner in May, Mahoney set about to strengthen both the capacity and the self-image of his agency. His first month was spent "trying to make some early-up organizational changes to make the agency more administrable." He began to assemble a small team of bright, aggressive associates as his personal staff. One of these, who was to play an important role in the Park Plaza controversy, was his executive assistant, Harry Spence, a young lawyer with a commitment to housing and social programs. At the end of his first month in office, when he was still very much preoccupied with "internal" administrative matters, Mahoney was confronted by an "external" issue that he couldn't ignore.

PARK PLAZA

Since the early 1960s, the city of Boston had been attempting to redevelop its commercial and retail downtown district. Although portions of the district were renewed by private investment, by 1970 there remained several major decaying or underutilized areas. One of the most prominent of these areas was located on the periphery of Boston's two large, adjacent downtown parks: the Boston Common and the Public Garden. This area centered around a confusing intersection of major streets, called Park Square. The area was characterized by small buildings crowded together on irregular lots, housing small retail and entertainment activities on the street level, and offices—many of them vacant—above the street level. There were several large vacant lots, created by the demolition of buildings and used as parking lots. The two major blocks at the northern end of the area, known locally as the "Combat Zone," housed the center of the city's thriving pornography industry—a neon jungle of girlie bars, burlesque houses, and "adult" bookstores and movie houses, colorfully garnished with streetwalkers of every persuasion.

The Park Square district lay precisely at the intersection of the two major commercial axes of downtown Boston. To the west lay the Copley Square-Back Bay district featuring converted townhouses, older office buildings and several new office towers. To the northeast lay the downtown commercial and financial district, housed in a mix of older office buildings and several new office towers. "Behind" Park Square (to the east and south) lay Chinatown (a residential-commercial-institutional urban renewal area) and Bay Village (an island of quaint brick townhouses).

Park Square, in other words, contained some of the potentially most attractive and valuable real estate in the city. And its low density, irregularity, general unsightliness, impossible traffic patterns and troublesome "entertainment" uses made it a prime target for redevelopment. The planners at the BRA felt that the area could not be redeveloped by private action alone. The large number of very small lots and crazy street patterns made it virtually impossible for a private developer to assemble a large enough parcel of land to carry out an economically feasible development.

This was, of course, a typical problem to which the federal-state "urban renewal program" had been addressed. The urban renewal program enabled a local renewal agency to assemble a large redevelopment parcel by taking the land within that parcel by eminent domain. After taking the land, paying the owners, relocating the tenants, clearing the structures and improving or relocating utilities and streets, the local renewal agency would then sell the land to one or more private developers, usually at a price considerably lower than the cost of assembling the land. This reduction in price ("write-down") was thought necessary to induce private development in a marginal urban area. The "net cost" of traditional urban renewal projects (the amount of the "write-down") came from public funds. The federal government contributed two-thirds of the net cost of an approved project. In Massachusetts, the state contributed one-sixth, and the city or town, the other one-sixth.

It had naturally occurred to the BRA, therefore, to use the urban renewal program to facilitate the redevelopment of Park Square. A plan to redevelop the entire central business district, including Park Square, was rejected by the federal government in 1965, however, and in the late 1960s it appeared less and less likely that the federal government would fund any new urban renewal projects in Boston. Boston had received a disproportionate amount of urban renewal funds during the early years of the program; and federal priorities were clearly shifting to new areas of the country and, to some extent, to new approaches to urban redevelopment. After failing to secure federal approval for the Central Business District Plan, the BRA then decided to see whether it would be possible to attract one or more private developers to undertake an urban renewal project in which the entire cost of the land assembly would be financed by private investors—that is, with no federal, state, or local financial participation.

On May 31, 1970, Mayor White publicly announced that the city was inviting proposals for redevelopment of the Park Square area, which he now officially designated the "Park Plaza Urban Renewal Area." In December of 1970, five companies submitted proposals for redevelopment of all or a portion of Park Plaza. After extensive review of the five proposals, the BRA announced, in March 1971, the award of redevelopment rights to Boston Urban Associates (BUA), a new company whose two principal partners, Mortimer Zuckerman and Edward Linde, each had extensive real estate experience, but which, as a company, had no track record.

The BUA proposal was, to say the least, ambitious. It called for the creation of a "new town intown," an integrated mixture of residential, retail, office, hotel, and entertainment uses. At an estimated total development cost of $260 million, BUA's Park Plaza project represented the largest urban renewal project in the city's history.

BUA proposed that Park Plaza be developed in two "stages." According to a "letter of intent" from BUA to BRA, stage I involved the phased redevelopment of the three parcels (designated as A, B, and C) adjacent to the Public Garden and Boston Common. The first step consisted of construction of an 800–1,000 room convention hotel and a 3,000-car parking garage. Subsequent steps called for the construction of three residential towers, containing 1,400 luxury apartment units and 150 units of low-to-moderate income housing for the elderly "if subsidized financing for the same can be secured," 50 townhouse units of luxury housing; a retail arcade containing 500,000 square feet of leasable area; and an office tower and low-rise office building containing 1,050,000 square feet of leasable space. The various buildings were to be built in sequence with the last step (the office tower) to be commenced not later than seven years after the first step was started.

With respect to stage II, covering parcels D and E—that is, the portion of Park Plaza located in the "Combat Zone"—BUA presented no concrete proposal and made no commitment, other than to express its interest and its intention of submitting a proposal as soon as stage I was off the ground.

CITY COUNCIL HEARINGS

On July 15, 1971, the BRA's governing board passed a resolution authorizing the Park Plaza Urban Renewal Plan, which was submitted to the Boston City Council for its approval, as required by state law. The city council hearings, which began on September 9, 1971, exposed the first real opposition to the project, led by the tenants and owners in the Park Plaza area. A number of environmental groups and neighborhood associations also raised questions about the project.

Opponents of the project made a number of charges, including the following:

1. With no track record in real estate development, BUA could not be trusted to undertake what was, in total cost, the largest urban renewal project in Boston history.
2. The plan represented a naked use of public eminent domain and bonding authority to enable a private speculator to make a potentially enormous profit.
3. There was no plan to redevelop the Combat Zone and little likelihood that there ever would be one since no other neighborhood would be willing to rehouse its current occupants.
4. Adverse environmental impacts (shadows, winds, and displacement of the water table) would damage the Public Garden and Boston Common.
5. The project was wholly for private benefit. There were no proposed "public purpose" uses other than a few units of low-income housing whose construction was contingent on uncertain governmental subsidies.
6. The financial plan for the project was weak. Except for the proposed hotel, there were no firm commitments from prime tenants or financial sponsors, and the legality of a proposed tax-exempt bond issue and real estate tax deal was dubious.
7. The city was selling its own land in the project area (the streets to be discontinued) at its "pre-assembly" value of $3 million, even though it would be worth perhaps $10 million after land assembly (since, as part of a broad tract, it would be much more usable).

After many often stormy hearings and executive sessions, the council, on December 6, 1971, approved Park Plaza in substantially its original form, by a vote of 7 to 2. During the period city councillors were re-elected—one having been defeated in his bid for re-election and three having left the council to run, unsuccessfully, for mayor against Kevin White, who was re-elected by a lopsided margin. The four lame-duck councillors all voted to approve Park Plaza on December 6.

On December 22, 1971, Mayor White approved the city council resolution; and on January 13, 1972, the BRA submitted the Park Plaza plan and supporting documentation to DCA.

DCA HEARINGS

The state urban renewal law requires that an urban renewal plan be approved in writing by the Department of Community Affairs before it may be undertaken. The department is required to hold a public hearing on the plan if so requested by certain specified persons or groups, including a group of "twenty-five or more taxable inhabitants" of the city. The Park Plaza tenants and owners, among whom were "twenty-five or more taxable inhabitants" of Boston, duly requested a public hearing. After two months of dispute over the ground rules for the hearing, DCA scheduled a public hearing for April 11, 1972. In three days of hearings, most of the same arguments were made as had been made before the city council. The hearings received little attention from the media or the public.

The responsibility for review and analysis of the Park Plaza submission within DCA had fallen to its Urban Renewal Bureau from the very start. The chief of the bureau, Edward Mangini, and several of his staff had been in the bureau for many years. They had reviewed and recommended approval of dozens of conventional federally aided urban renewal projects. But they, like virtually everyone else involved, had never seen anything quite like Park Plaza. And they didn't like what they saw. "Mangini," in Harry Spence's words, "just thought it was rotten. He just said it's lousy."

The urban renewal law required DCA to make six affirmative "findings" in order to approve an urban renewal project:

1. it could not be accomplished by private enterprise alone;
2. it was consistent with the sound needs of the locality;
3. the financial plan was sound;
4. the project area was blighted;
5. the plan was "sufficiently complete";
6. there was an acceptable plan for relocating tenants and owners.

After detailed review of the voluminous documentation and hearing transcripts, the Urban Renewal Bureau staff concluded that only the first of the six findings could be made. Underlying many of the objections and perceived deficiencies were two factors which the staff saw as particularly fatal:

1. there was no "plan" for the "Combat Zone" (parcels D and E); and

2. the financial underpinnings of the project, and particularly its proposed developer, were insubstantial.

THE COMBAT ZONE ISSUE

Although the official "Park Plaza Urban Renewal Plan" specified "land use and building requirements" for all five parcels, it was clear from the beginning that neither the BRA, the city, nor the developer (the BUA) had yet made any firm commitment to undertake redevelopment activities in the Combat Zone parcels. The "cooperation agreement" between the city and the BRA, whereby the city promised to make certain improvements (new street, etc.) in the project area, made no mention of parcels D and E other than the following:

> As soon as construction begins on A-1 [the hotel], the Authority will immediately advertise for redevelopment of parcels D and E. Unless the Authority shall select a developer for parcels D and E within three years from the date of approval of the Plan, parcels D and E shall no longer be considered part of the Park Plaza area.

The BRA, however, repeatedly asserted its "firm commitment" to redevelop parcels D and E.

It was strenuously argued by the BRA that the specifications in the "Plan" and the "firm commitment" were sufficient to satisfy the "completeness" test (finding #5). The authority argued that in conventional urban renewal, specific redevelopment plans (building configuration and occupancy) for individual parcels were never finalized at the plan-approval (DCA) stage. It was often many years before a developer was selected. Given the vast size of the Park Plaza project and the long duration of development activities, it was economically unfeasible to make commitments to develop D and E at such an early stage, the BRA contended.

The DCA staff was not persuaded. In their view, the Combat Zone was the portion of Park Plaza *most* warranting redevelopment—and indeed perhaps the *only* part of the project area sufficiently blighted to justify using urban renewal powers. By far the majority of substandard buildings in the project area were located in parcels D and E. Parcels D and E, with 49 of the 120 buildings in the project area, had 44 of the 73 buildings classified by the BRA as "blighting," including 22 of the 37 buildings clas-

sified as "structurally substandard." Under long-standing federal and state urban renewal regulations, an area could be considered "blighted"—finding #4—only if at least 20 percent of its buildings were "structurally substandard" and at least 50 percent of its buildings were "blighting." The "blighting" classification included "structurally substandard" buildings, as well as buildings with less serious but nevertheless blighting deficiencies. The "blight" criterion also required a finding that the blighting and structurally substandard buildings were distributed throughout the project area. In addition, parcels D and E housed nearly all of the most troublesome "entertainment" activities in the project area. Given the fact that parcels D and E were the most suited to urban redevelopment activities, the DCA staff found it ironic that they were the only parcels for which no concrete plans existed.

Focusing on BRA's analogy to conventional urban renewal, the DCA staff felt that the analogy broke down in at least two key respects. Although specific developers are rarely identified at the time of plan approval, a conventional renewal plan at least identifies every parcel to be acquired and specifies a financing and relocation plan for each. In the Park Plaza submission there were no financial or relocation plans for parcels D and E whatsoever. Secondly, there are more safeguards in conventional renewal, since the renewal authority must secure federal and state approval for the funding of each redevelopment activity actually undertaken within an approval plan. This gives the public the safeguard of continuing supervision of the project, even after the initial approval. Where there is no federal or state funding, as in Park Plaza, there is no further supervision because there are no further approvals required. DCA gets "one bite at the apple" only.

THE FINANCIAL PLAN

The Park Plaza plan contemplated that the acquisition of land, relocation of occupants and clearance of buildings would all be performed by the BRA, as the local renewal agency having statutory power of eminent domain and relocation responsibility. The cash to defray these expenses would come either from bonds issued by the BRA or directly from private investors lined up by BUA. It was anticipated that BRA bonds would be used, in particular, to assemble the land to be used for residential and parking developments. The reason for this is that under federal tax law it appeared that the interest on governmental bonds issued for such a purpose would be tax exempt, and that therefore the bonds could be sold at an interest rate considerably lower than interest payable on private bonds (about three percentage points less). The federal tax law had been recently amended, however, and all parties agreed that a satisfactory legal opinion and quite possibly a formal ruling from the Internal Revenue Service would be required before proceeding with a bond issue.

Wherever BRA bonds were to be used, the developer agreed that it would make all payments of principal and interest out of proceeds from the development. In other words, no public funds would be required to pay off the bonds. In respect to all other properties, the entire funding would come from private investors.

Land would be acquired in stages. The letter of intent stipulated that the BRA was not to acquire any property until it had "satisfactory assurance" that the total cost of acquiring the property and associated demolition and relocation costs were "available" to the BRA. Recognizing that staged acquisition and development might impose hardships on owners or tenants of property due for acquisition in later stages, the developer agreed to put up deposits of money to be used by the BRA for "early acquisition and relocation" where necessary to relieve such hardship. BUA had deposited $100,000 already and promised to increase it by $400,000 when BRA and BUA executed a "Master Land Disposition Agreement," permitting land acquisition to begin. When construction was completed on stages 1 and 2, the deposit was to be increased to $1 million, and then finally reduced to $500,000 when stage 5 was under way.

In support of its ability to attract the private investment necessary to make the project feasible, BUA offered the following evidence:

1. letters from three financial underwriters expressing an "interest" in underwriting the proposed bond issue, subject, in the words of one typical letter, "to all economic, financial, legal, and tax matters being resolved to all parties' mutual satisfaction";

2. a letter from the president of Western International Hotels Company, expressing its commitment to lease and operate the proposed hotel and to invest $5 million in furnishings and equipment;

3. 1970 market surveys by economic consulting companies, projecting a market demand for luxury apartments, office and retail space sufficient to occupy the proposed development at profitable rental levels; and

4. the commitment by the city of Boston to invest $6.8 million in public improvements in the area (including a relocated street).

All of this left the DCA staff singularly unimpressed. Part of the difficulty, again, was the utter lack of any cost estimate or financing projections for parcels D and E. But the bulk of the problem related to the project's complete dependence upon private funding, in general, and the identity of the BRA's preselected developer, in particular. In conventional publicly assisted urban renewal, the soundness of the financial plan was rarely a very difficult issue. No property could be acquired without federal and state funding approval. The consequence of such approval was a guarantee that all of the "front-end" site assembly costs (acquisition, relocation, demolition, and site preparation) would be met out of the proceeds of bonds issued by the renewal authority and backed by public funding commitments. Although the actual cost of erecting structures on the cleared site would be borne by developers using private funding (except in the case of a public facility or subsidized housing), it was felt that the land-cost "writedown" could be adjusted to make the development financially feasible. Also since the federal and state governments had to approve the public subsidy for each individual development within an approved urban renewal plan, the appropriate approving agency could examine the financial feasibility of a particular activity when the funding was requested to commence the acquisition.

In Park Plaza, however, there was to be no write-down, no front-end commitment of public funds. Except for a relatively small contribution of land by the city, the entire cost of site assembly as well as construction, and all the attendant risks, were to be borne by private investors. The identity of those investors, and the strength of their financial underpinnings, thus became of primary importance to DCA. And what they saw disturbed them. Boston Urban Associates was a partnership with no assets other than those of its two principal partners, Mortimer Zuckerman and Edward Linde. Their personal assets, Zuckerman reported, "exceeded $6 million." They intended, he said, to establish "joint ventures" to own the properties. Zuckerman and Linde would be the managing partners of each joint venture, which would also have the participation of unnamed additional investors. In addition, financing, presumably by mortgage, would be obtained from major financial institutions such as insurance companies—again unspecified.

Harry Spence reflects the prevailing view in DCA:

DISCARDED

Who the hell was Zuckerman? Did [he] really have the money to be able to carry this thing off? There was a sense that Zuckerman was a mighty weak reed to be hanging such an enormous project on. You had a broker, not someone who could ride out a tough construction period.

If you had the Prudential Insurance Company, you don't worry about those things. They can cover it. The John Hancock can go on with their thing forever. But when you've got a guy who basically has very shallow resources, do you commit thirty-five acres of the city to him?

In particular, DCA was concerned about the financing of the alter stages of the plan. The development seemed clearly arranged so as to give BUA the "cream" first (the low-cost, high-return portions of the development) with little assurance that it would proceed with subsequent stages. DCA feared that, if the early stages were successful, BUA might "skim the cream" and walk away, and if they were not successful, BUA would not be able to attract capital for the rest.

Another concern of the DCA staff was the issue of real estate taxation. One paragraph of the letter of intent from BUA made the entire project dependent upon "a satisfactory understanding with the City" concerning the level of future real estate taxes. This referred to the widespread practice in Massachusetts whereby the city tax assessors would agree to tax prospective commercial developments at a stated percentage of gross rentals. Such tax agreements, while questionably legal, were claimed to be indispensable to provide the predictability needed to attract major private investment. The trouble with Park Plaza, the DCA analysts felt, was that while BUA's market studies projected a gross annual rental income of $45 million, the city assessor predicted tax revenues of $4.5 million. This effective ten percent rate was less than half the usual rate in tax agreements.

THE DISAPPROVAL

Mangini and his staff drafted a long memorandum to Mahoney, outlining their objections to the plan. Mahoney reviewed the memorandum and discussed it with the staff. Park Plaza had received very little attention from the new commissioner up to that point. The staff recommendation seemed sound. He met with the BRA to discuss DCA's objections, but the meeting did nothing to dispel his doubts or meet his objections. The BRA seemed unwilling either to make changes or to offer significant new informa-

tion. Mahoney felt he had no choice. The project appeared to be so fundamentally flawed that further discussion was pointless. He would disapprove the project.

Late in May, Mahoney called Jack Flannery, Governor Sargent's chief secretary, and told him that he was about to make an important and controversial decision—to turn down Park Plaza. Flannery told him to come up and discuss it with the governor's staff first. On May 31, Mahoney met with Kramer, Flannery, and several other members of the governor's staff. Mahoney explained the statutory requirements and DCA's objections to the Park Plaza plan. With little disagreement or apparent concern for the implications, the governor's staff concurred. Then the inevitable question: How do we announce it? "Kill it as fast as you can," was Flannery's advice. "Don't give them any warning. If you do, they'll go straight to the press." It was agreed. Mahoney would issue his decision as soon as possible. Flannery would advise the governor. As Mahoney picked up his papers to leave the meeting, Flannery, in his patented laconic style, quipped: "Miles, you have no idea how heavy some of those people are who are gonna fall on you."

During the next week the DCA staff prepared a draft of the written statement of reasons for disapproval, as required by the statute. Mahoney called a press conference for the late afternoon of June 9. He put the finishing touches on the letter of disapproval and delivered it in person to BRA Director Robert Kenney an hour before the press conference. Kenney was bitterly disappointed and, though aware of Mahoney's objections, surprised at the suddenness and apparent finality of the decision.

Mahoney then went before the press conference and announced his disapproval of the Park Plaza Urban Renewal Project.

THE REACTION

The bombshell exploded. On June 13, Mayor White angrily denounced the decision, charging that it was the result of a political "conspiracy" by the Sargent administration. He accused Mahoney of seeking retribution for having been rejected as an applicant for a job on the mayor's staff. White demanded a meeting with Governor Sargent.

The meeting was held on the next day. Mahoney was called into the meeting for a short period:

I met with him briefly, just to have the governor have me explain directly to White why the thing was rejected and then have White ask me, would I reverse the decision, and for me to say, "No." That was the purpose of my being there.

Sargent seemed, as usual, very pleasant, anxious to please, perhaps embarrassed at the mayor's obvious anger. But he remained firm, summarily dismissing the "conspiracy" charge and insisting that the Park Plaza plan was "illegal." But he did make the concession that a second submission would be welcome if it dealt with the defects cited in the state's disapproval. White left the meeting "disappointed." Apparently taking little solace from Sargent's resubmission suggestion, he vowed to pursue unspecified "political" avenues.

In the next few days the chorus of opposition to Mahoney's decision swelled. In a rare display of unanimity, the three Boston daily newspapers attacked the decision and called for the city to press for a reversal. Lead editorials characterized the action as "brash presumption," "capricious and arbitrary," and "lint-picking negativism." Representatives of the building trade unions met with the mayor and promised to launch an all-out drive to save Park Plaza. The Boston business community echoed the cry. Governor Sargent had already antagonized the construction industry and its unions by the policies of his administration, including a moratorium on highway construction in the Boston area, his opposition to further growth of Boston's Logan Airport, and his outspoken support for new environmental controls. Park Plaza was, to many in the construction industry, the last straw.

The mayor filed a "home rule petition" (requiring passage by both the Boston City Council and the state legislature) to eliminate the requirement of DCA approval for privately funded renewal projects in Boston. The measure sailed through the council on a 7–2 vote and made rapid progress in the Democratically dominated state legislature.

The outpouring of support for Park Plaza took DCA and the governor's office by surprise. It appeared to them to be the product of a carefully orchestrated public relations effort by the mayor and Mortimer Zuckerman, the developer. Particularly surprising and troubling was the position of the *Boston Globe*. The *Globe* was not only Boston's biggest and most influential newspaper, but it had a reputation for strongly supporting liberal causes. It had consistently supported the governor in his policies on transportation and the environment, and its vehement criticism of Mahoney's decision seemed out of character. Mahoney called the paper to "complain bitterly," as he put it, about the *Globe*'s editorial position. A meeting was arranged for June 21, to be

chaired by Robert Healy, executive director of the *Globe*. The meeting, as Mahoney recalls it, was hardly productive:

Healy was really annoying as could be, with his preconceptions about so many things having to do with the project and his unwillingness to listen to anything other than what he seemed to have been spoon-fed by Zuckerman.

Healy was convinced that, on some issue, I had lied to him in that meeting, the issue having to do with whether or not similar developments had been built elsewhere—he saying, "This has been done, I know, in this place and that place and the other place"—and I saying to him, "No, it hasn't: what you're describing are projects that did not have the public auspices being asked for here" . . . but he somehow being convinced that everything I had to say on that score was a lie, just constructed for that purpose.

At one point, Mahoney charged the *Globe* with "being in the bag" on Park Plaza, a statement that drew a sharp expression of outrage from Healy:

I didn't mean financially, which he immediately took umbrage at. As soon as he did, I was surprised at his strong reaction. I said, "That's another one of my problems—I have not as yet come to understand the idiosyncrasies of language in the Boston area. In Philadelphia, that isn't so criminal a saying. I was really talking about your having been sucked in to what is a bad thing, rather than taking a buck for your editorial." At any rate, he didn't forget that.

The participants left the meeting in as much disagreement as before.

Organized labor—chiefly the Greater Boston Building Trades Council—moved into the vanguard of the effort to lobby for Park Plaza. Representatives of the GBBTC met with Sargent on June 20 to demand action on a number of stalled building projects, including Park Plaza. All they obtained from the governor was an expression of "hope" that BRA would work with DCA toward a solution. In response, labor took to the streets. On June 28, an estimated 20,000 construction workers from Greater Boston descended on the State House in a raucous and unruly demonstration. Called to protest Sargent's general anti-construction policies, the demonstration focused on Park Plaza. Signs could be seen in abundance, reading: "Free Boston from State

Rule," "Is Sarge in Charge?", "Who killed Park Plaza?", "Park Plaza: 3000 Construction Jobs." Sargent confronted the unruly mob on the State House steps. A newsman heard him shouting in a vain attempt to be heard:

> You want jobs, I want jobs. You want Park Plaza, I want Park Plaza; but the plans have to be right.

His words were drowned out by the crescendo of boos, catcalls, and insults. A hard hat tossed in his direction narrowly missed his head.

Retreating to the safety of his office, Sargent called a meeting with seven representatives of the workers and several members of the governor's staff. Mahoney was not present. In a press release issue later that day, Sargent's office summarized the meeting in these words:

> In his discussion with the labor leaders, the Governor stressed his support of the *concept* of Park Plaza. But he refused to grant approval for the project until it contains a full renewal plan for the Combat Zone area . . . and a firm financial agreement.

NEGOTIATIONS RESUME

The next day, Mahoney was called to a meeting with Kramer, Flannery, and other members of the governor's staff. "The governor has asked us," Kramer began, "to see if there isn't some way we can work this thing out—get what DCA wants and still get some kind of a project." Mahoney said it was "futile," reiterating his view that the plan submitted by BRA was fundamentally unacceptable. But Kramer persisted: "We're not asking you to approve this project. All we're asking is that you sit down with the BRA, talk to them, tell them what you want, and see what they can do." Mahoney could hardly refuse to talk—even *he* conceded that Park Plaza could be approved if enough changes were made, though he doubted the city's and the developer's willingness to make the changes.

Mahoney agreed to hold discussions with the city, but he demanded in return that no other discussions be held between the state and the city or the developer. He and his staff had become increasingly concerned about evidence that Zuckerman had been "cultivating" Kramer in an effort to win support for Park Plaza within the governor's office. Kramer agreed to Mahoney's conditions, but in turn insisted

that he, Kramer, sit in on at least some of the DCA-BRA meetings. As Mahoney summarized the understanding:

> I was being asked to go through this process at least to see what they [BRA] could do. Kramer's expressed intention in being at the meetings was to show that indeed the governor's office was interested in seeing things move along, he pledged not to be involved in any substantive matters at all. I had extracted a commitment that [the governor's] staff would not be dealing with the BRA and that recognition of Zuckerman as somebody to speak for the project would not be given. We were dealing with the BRA and not its developer.

As Harry Spence put it:

> Publicly, the agreement was that we'd sit down with them, and DCA would lay out where the problems were, and the BRA would go back and do their homework and come back with an acceptable, approvable submission. The purpose of those negotiations was supposed to be to develop an approvable submission, and that was under some pressure, certainly, from the governor's office . . . to take a positive approach and look like you're doing positive things.

In fulfillment of a promise made to the labor leaders by the governor, a meeting was held on June 30. The governor's office announced the meeting publicly, but the press was not permitted to sit in. In attendance were Kramer, Mahoney and his staff, Kenney and BRA staff, Zuckerman, and labor representatives. Speaking to the press after the meeting, Mahoney characterized it as "informational," but reported some progress. "In the sense that we're getting new information about the project from the city and the developer, we are getting closer to a positive finding on the Park Plaza Project."

The mayor continued to press for his home rule petition to exempt Park Plaza from state review in spite of the governor's publicly expressed opposition to it. Although it was passed by the legislature, the governor vetoed it on July 15, and its supporters could not muster the two-thirds vote necessary to override the veto.

In the ensuing months, Mahoney met regularly with BRA staff. Zuckerman sometimes attended. After the first two meetings, Kramer stopped attending, but the governor's office was represented by the governor's chief counsel, William Young. Mahoney and his staff found the meetings with the BRA extremely tiresome and frustrating for the most part:

> The negotiations went on, but they weren't real. They were just exercises. We went over and over the same ground. They [BRA] were just restating the arguments, trying to find the words that would satisfy me.

DCA's insistence on dealing with BRA—while in their view legally required—created major problems, as Harry Spence recalled:

> One of the problems with the process of negotiation was that when you were dealing with the BRA, you were negotiating with a ghost—and there were terrific tensions between Kenney and Zuckerman, tremendous tensions, personal tensions as well as programmatic ones. . . . Basically, we took the position that the public agency responsible for the plan was the BRA—we should not be dealing directly with the developer. But the BRA really had no positions, by and large. Or when they did have a position, if they found it differed with the developer, they would quickly be pushed, sometimes reluctantly, sometimes perfectly happily. They'd sort of go back to Mort [Zuckerman] and "What did Mort want?"

Simultaneously with the BRA meetings, Mahoney was called to meet repeatedly with Kramer and Flannery, to report on whatever progress was being made. From the very beginning, Mahoney and his staff were highly suspicious about Kramer's role and looked toward Flannery, technically Kramer's superior, for support. Harry Spence reflected on the prevailing view in DCA:

> I remember a great deal of concern at those first sessions about Kramer's role. Kramer came to one or two of those meetings—at one of the meetings I think he walked in with Zuckerman—and Kramer's role was equivocal very quickly. Now at the same time, we had some sense that Kramer's role wasn't necessarily the full governor's office role—that Kramer might be a stronger advocate for it than the rest of the governor's staff, particularly Flannery. Miles always felt much, much more comfortable in certain ways with Flannery than with Kramer, anyway—the style was a little more in tune, and there was the feeling, I remember, during that

period that Flannery was kind of the guy that we could depend on. . . . Basically, Flannery seemed to think Miles was a neat Irish kid and liked [his] guts. And there was a sense that Flannery was going to be our bulwark there with whatever games might be going on between Kramer and Zuckerman.

Flannery's role did not fully live up to those early expectations, however, as Mahoney recalled:

> At the outset, the way he regards so many matters, it [Flannery's role] was that of the humorist, trying to move something along, to get it out of the way. [It was] evident that he was more critical in dealing with the governor's position than was Kramer. Kramer being deferential to him. What kind of approach to use—whether to have a meeting—who should be in the meeting: all those things were by and large Flannery's.
>
> It seemed to me that he was not deeply involved in dealing with the city, the BRA, Zuckerman, what have you. But, by and large, he was a guy sitting at the table, half the time listening, half the time on the telephone, getting off the telephone to say, "Have we made any progress?," without discussing anything having to do with the project that approached substance, presumably because he wasn't claiming to have anything to comment on the substance—only the politics of it. I don't know whether he fancied himself as having opinions on the whole thing. He would lead you to believe that he didn't—couldn't be less interested.

Kramer, on the other hand, was very interested and characteristically aggressive in his friendly, witty, but persistent way. Mahoney recalled Kramer's role with decidedly mixed feelings:

> His actions, where intended for me to be known, were not involved in direct negotiations. He was deferential on the surface. It was a difficult thing, because I really like him very much. I have an awful lot of respect for particularly his social philosophy and his way of doing business—his attitude toward government. And it was really frustrating to try to maintain a friendly relationship with him while it was evident that increasingly he was assuming the role of an advocate—I don't think because of any special commitment to the BRA or Zuckerman or anything, but to the governor—to get out of

the governor's way a problem that was getting increasingly difficult to deal with.

I think he would argue that he was playing a very sophisticated devil's advocate, to make sure that arguments being presented to the BRA were of the best quality. It took on a flavor far more of an advocate than that, although they were sometimes amusing, sometimes useful grilling sessions.

Harry Spence, viewing Kramer's role from more of a distance, was less sympathetic:

He didn't take positions on the merits of the thing. That was one of the things that always disturbed Miles, and one of the reasons that Miles felt a certain distrust of Kramer was that Al would essentially say, "Now Miles, you're saying that it's not a blighted area. Well now, Miles, you could say without lying, couldn't you, Miles. . . ."

There was never an argument that the project had great merit or that Miles' actual findings weren't the right ones if one really came down to making a proper judgment on it. It was: "Miles, do you really have to be such a Puritan about it? Can't you really be more flexible about this thing? You don't have to be so hard-assed on the thing."

As discussions progressed into the fall, some progress was being made on at least some of the issues. Park Plaza had been out of the headlines for several months. Neither the city nor the developer had made any public statements. Kramer, however, was acting increasingly impatient and persistent in pressing toward a resolution. Others in the governor's office were for the first time exhibiting a similar tendency. For his part, Mahoney grew increasingly suspicious that Zuckerman was lobbying Kramer and making headway. Mahoney on several occasions asked Kramer about his involvement with Zuckerman, but Kramer, while conceding that they spoke from time to time, repeatedly denied any direct negotiations with Zuckerman.

Whatever Kramer's involvement with Zuckerman, it became evident to Mahoney that there was another reason for Kramer's increased advocacy. A massive restudy of transportation policy in the Greater Boston area, undertaken by the Sargent administration, was about to be completed, and the governor would soon face some momentous decisions about the future balance between the automobile and mass transit as modes of transportation in the metropolitan area. Nearly two years earlier, Sargent had called a moratorium on all major highway construction projects in the Boston region and had ordered a complete restudy of state transportation policy. The decision had attracted considerable attention, helping to accelerate the shift in national policy toward mass transit. The decision had also touched off bitter controversy within Massachusetts. While the restudy was in progress, Sargent had announced his decision to kill two pending highway projects outright. Given his strong anti-highway, pro-transit image, it was expected that he would kill the rest of the suspended highway projects once the restudy was completed. The principal architect of the Sargent policy had, from the very beginning, been Al Kramer.

Kramer on several occasions related to Mahoney his concern about criticism of a no-highway decision from the same groups that had criticized the Park Plaza rejection. He expected, of course, that business and labor would be unhappy about a no-highway decision, just as they had been highly critical of the moratorium and the two earlier no-build decisions. But he hoped to defuse their objections with a major construction program in mass transit. Since elements of a major mass transit expansion policy required state legislative and federal approval, he could not afford the kind of violent reaction that followed the Park Plaza rejection. Kramer's message to Mahoney was clear: if the state is still standing in the way of Park Plaza when the governor announced the transportation decision, "we're in serious trouble."

In spite of the increased pressure from Kramer, Flannery remained apparently neutral on the issues of substance and Mahoney heard nothing directly from the governor. The governor's legal counsel, William Young, began to assume a more significant role in the process. Young, who had left a prestigious Boston law firm in July to join the governor's staff, sat in on Mahoney's meetings with the BRA as well as his meetings with the governor's staff. In both contexts, he remained, for the most part, quiet, patient, and objective. Although he was clearly searching for legal arguments to facilitate forward motion on Park Plaza, he maintained a high degree of neutrality, occasionally rebuking Kramer mildly for his references to a "deal" or "understanding" with Mahoney that Park Plaza could be approved. In Young's view of the law, only Mahoney had authority to approve or reject an urban renewal project, and his independence would be improperly compromised by any pre-existing "deal" to approve a project.

Young suggested at one point that the BRA split Park Plaza into two or more pieces, feeling that an approvable plan might be developed for parcel A, or perhaps even parcels A, B, and C. The BRA was adamantly opposed to this idea, however. Young thought that a way out of the impasse might be some sort of conditional or staged approval of DCA, under the terms of which DCA would make its approval of each later stage contingent on satisfactory evidence of financing, a relocation plan, and whatever requirements for which satisfactory evidence was not currently available.

Mahoney was somewhat intrigued by the idea, but had reservations about both its legality and its acceptability to the developer. His staff expressed some concern, also, about its wisdom, and despite lengthy discussions with his staff about the idea, Mahoney reached no firm decision. Mahoney found himself very busy in November with other matters, many of which had suffered from inattention due to the demands of the Park Plaza negotiations. Mahoney was glad to turn his attention to them.

OTHER PRIORITIES

Throughout the summer and fall of 1972, Mahoney had been hard at work on the task which both he and Al Kramer had agreed from the very beginning was to be his priority—strengthening the capacity of DCA to supervise and assist local housing and renewal activities. In Mahoney's view, the state's local housing and renewal programs were marred by (1) a lack of professional planning and management, (2) excessive political influence of developers, and (3) insufficient participation in decisionmaking by the general public and "client groups" (e.g., public housing tenants). Accordingly, Mahoney's objective was to use the extensive controls and incentives at his command to induce cities and towns—particularly the smaller and intermediate sized communities lacking professional planning capability—to take a more professional, comprehensive, and client-oriented approach to housing and renewal decisions. At least four policies initiated by Mahoney were designed to achieve this objective. First, he ended the longstanding practice of passing federal planning funds through DCA directly to municipalities. He felt that these funds had been wasted on disjointed planning efforts, usually contracted out by municipalities to high-pressure and high-priced consultants. Instead, Mahoney used the planning funds to hire planners in DCA who could render professional service to municipalities on a continuing and comprehensive basis. Secondly, DCA undertook a statewide housing needs study which showed that, while municipalities were building many units of politically palatable housing for the el-

derly, they were neglecting a much more serious need for low-income family housing. On the basis of this study, Mahoney issued a regulation that DCA would not approve any elderly housing project until the applicant community began to meet its family housing needs as well.

The third element of Mahoney's program was to broaden participation in the governance of local housing and renewal authorities. DCA had the power to appoint one of the five members of the governing board of every local authority. Traditionally, these appointments had been dictated by the governor's patronage office. Mahoney instituted a new procedure whereby local authorities were required to establish a formal mechanism for participation by client groups in the referral of candidates to DCA and approval of appointments made by DCA. He went even further in the direction of "client participation" in public housing by promulgating regulations requiring formal tenant participation in public housing modernization and development programs. Finally, the fourth element of Mahoney's policy was his careful scrutiny of urban renewal applications. Park Plaza was really only one example—albeit the most spectacular—of this policy. On at least four other occasions Mahoney refused to approve urban renewal plans that struck him as unsound. Each case involved a proposal viewed by Mahoney as a piecemeal development motivated less by a comprehensive view of community needs than by the desire of influential developers to achieve a commercial success.

All of these policies, particularly the latter three, generated occasional tempests of criticism and protest which, on several occasions, swept up the governor's office in their fury. Mahoney was called repeatedly to meetings with Kramer and Flannery and others in the governor's office to explain a decision or action. But he always seemed to be able to convince them of the soundness of his policy. In all of these disputes, Mahoney was aided by the fact that the opposition was largely confined to private commercial and political interests, lacking broad public support. In fact, if anything, public support—particularly from tenants, community organizers, social service agencies and environmentalists—was with Mahoney. So as Mahoney approached the end of his seventh month in office, he felt a genuine sense of progress toward his goals for the department.

THE GOVERNOR'S ANNOUNCEMENT

It was then, on November 29, that Mahoney picked up the *Boston Globe* and first heard that the BRA had submitted a new Park Plaza plan and that the governor thought it "met his concerns." While Mahoney waited for Kramer to return his call, his staff looked for the "new submission." Sure enough, a letter was found from BRA Director Kenney to Miles Mahoney, date stamped "Nov. 28" in his office where DCA mail was received. That day, the 29th, a large package of supporting documents, referred to in the Kenney letter, was hand delivered to DCA.

A quick review revealed that the package contained most of the material submitted on January 13, plus several minor additions or revisions, none of which changed the essential nature of the plan. It was still inadequate, in Miles' view.

Imagine that you are Miles on the morning he reads in the newspaper of the Governor's basic acceptance of the revised plan for Park Plaza. What do you do now?

You could disapprove the revised plan. After all, you have the legal authority to do so; the law requires that any such plan must first be approved by the Department of Community Affairs. And the plan is still deficient, in your view.

Moreover, your job is to fortify the DCA against developers who, before your appointment, would often overlook the needs of the community. Were you to cave in now and approve a plan so obviously inadequate for the community, simply because the developers and their allies had applied political pressure, you would set the entire agency back. You'd be signaling to the communities and developers alike that you have no power to stop irresponsible development. You'd be telling your staff that their efforts and judgments are irrelevant. In short, by approving this plan you would undermine everything you have been trying to accomplish in the DCA.

On the other hand, the Governor clearly wants this plan approved. He and his staff were willing to give you time to work out a reasonable compromise, but their patience has ended. The Governor has a larger agenda—including shifting funds from highways to mass transit—which your obstinence is threatening. The cost to the DCA's mission must be weighed against these other goals. Be satisfied that you forced the developers to revise their plan even a bit; the result may not be perfect, but you got something for your efforts after all. You showed that the DCA has some clout, even if the agency is not yet as powerful as you would like it to be. Now be a team player and approve the plan, and do it quickly.

Which will it be?

Many of my students who are seasoned government bureaucrats feel that Miles should approve the revised plan. They regard him as stubborn and naive, moralistic and self-righteous. Some are surprised that the Governor and his staff have tolerated Miles this long. Miles's view of his job is far too narrow, in their opinions. His job is not only to enhance the power and integrity of the DCA but to promote the Governor's entire agenda, of which the DCA is but a part. It is for the Governor to make the necessary tradeoffs, not for Miles.

Miles should have understood the larger agenda (the Governor and his staff surely made their position clear long before it came to this) and his responsibility to that agenda. He is accountable to the Governor: The

DCA is part of the executive branch, the Governor appointed him, and he is part of the Governor's administration.

Yet this analysis is too simple. Miles is also accountable to the legislature which enacted the law instructing him to disapprove plans that do not meet specific legislative criteria. The law imposes obligations upon him directly, and by virtue of that law he is accountable to the public, which expects him to guard the community against irresponsible development. If the Governor wants Miles to disregard the clear requirement of the law, Miles has an obligation to disobey the Governor.

It depends, in part, upon how clear the law actually is. In a democratic society, a public servant's first obligation is to the law and to the Constitution which lies behind the law. But laws and Constitutional provisions are subject to interpretation. Language is rarely so clear, and the circumstances to which the language applies rarely so clear-cut, that there is not room for reasonable people to disagree about meanings. In this case, the revised plan might well have come within the broad criteria set out by the legislature. The Governor, as chief executive, has the prerogative to interpret the law, within these broad bounds, as he sees fit.

If legislators or community groups are unhappy with the Governor's interpretation of the law, they will apply political pressure in the opposite direction from that of the developers. They may change the law to render it more specific. More likely, they will threaten the Governor with opposition to some other goal the Governor wishes to achieve (much as the developers and contractors threatened the Governor's mass transit objective). The pull and tug of these opposing forces might induce the Governor to change his priorities somewhat in the future, giving the DCA a higher place on his overall agenda. But it is still for the Governor to determine these tradeoffs.

Miles could try to persuade the Governor of the importance of the DCA's mission and the damaging precedent this particular decision would establish. He might elicit the Governor's agreement to support the DCA the next time Miles takes on the developers, or to increase the DCA's budget.

Yet it would be inappropriate for Miles to solicit support for his position from community groups and friendly legislators, or to quietly ally himself with them in order to put pressure on the Governor. That is not his job. Nor should Miles threaten that unless the Governor relents he will disapprove the plan, forcing the Governor to fire him (Miles knows that the Governor doesn't want a noisy and embarrassing public scene). Again, this is not an aspect of Miles's job.

Obligations flow in both directions. Subordinates like Miles must continuously clarify their jobs by seeking repeatedly to understand the larger agenda and context in which they work. In this respect, Miles failed. But political superiors also owe people in Miles's position an ongoing hearing, in which subordinates like Miles can offer views about how they see their immediate agendas fitting into the larger scheme. It is through such continuous clarifications, arguments, and adjustments that jobs are defined and redefined and the system of political accountability maintained. It is by means of such explicative relationships—between subordinate and political superior—that what may otherwise seem like conflicting loyalties are managed. In this respect, Governor Sargent and his staff might have done a better job.

(By the way, Miles ultimately decided to disapprove the revised plan. He was fired by the Governor in a messy affair involving charges and countercharges that helped neither of their subsequent careers.)

_____ *chapter 3* _____

Leadership

Sometimes efforts to clarify jobs are not sufficient. Perhaps the public manager's political superiors have not focused on the issue or have no particular interest in it. Perhaps the public and its elected representatives and intermediaries are indifferent and uninformed, or both; and the relatively few members of the public and representatives who know something about the issue are divided with regard to the goal to be achieved or the best means of achieving it. Thus there is no clear mandate for the public manager to take action one way or the other. In these circumstances, public managers—even at rather low levels of formal authority—have opportunities to exert leadership on an issue.

Leadership is an attractive concept. Everyone wants to exert, or be capable of exerting, leadership. We admire strong leaders; in fact, many of us believe that public servants—particularly those in the highest offices of government—should be powerful, dynamic leaders.

But in a democratic society, leadership can be misused. The exertion of ''leadership'' can be an excuse for disregarding the public will. Or it can be used as a justification for manipulating public opinion in favor of some course of action that may not be in the public's long-term interest (were the public aware of the relevant facts and possessed of an opportunity to deliberate over the pros and cons of taking the action). Those who agreed with what David Goldman and Miles Mahoney were trying to achieve might think of them as courageous leaders, although, as I have suggested, both of them misunderstood their jobs by ignoring the sources of their authority.

A more precise notion of leadership, consistent with a public servant's responsibilities in a democratic form of government, involves an interactive process. Where mandates are weak or ambiguous, a democratic leader *engages* the public—sharpening the public's understandings of what is at stake, alternative courses of action for coping with it, benefits and disadvantages following from each course, and why one course is preferable. In other words, the leader promotes public deliberation, provokes a search for solutions, and thus—ultimately—creates a mandate for action.

Obviously, the relevant ''publics'' will differ, depending upon who is likely to be affected by the decision at hand. Necessarily involved will be people who act as intermediaries between the relevant public and the public servant—appointed officials, elected representatives, members of the press, leaders of organized interest groups. Often it will be necessary, in addition, for the leader to elicit the involvement of people who are not well organized but who nevertheless will experience some of the benefits or burdens of the proposed course of action.

The important point is this: Leadership in a democracy entails the creation of mandates which authorize the public servant to take action. Without awareness or involvement on the part of the relevant publics, there can be no such mandate. Nor is there a mandate where public support is based on half-truths; under these circumstances the public has been misled about what is at stake in the decision and about the alternatives for dealing with the problem.

Understood in this way, even lower-level public servants can appropriately exert leadership, especially where their political superiors are unable to provide a mandate for action one way or another. But because lower-level public servants are far less visible to the relevant publics than are elected or appointed officials, they may find it more difficult to engage the relevant publics and thus obtain a mandate directly from them. At the same time, and for the same reason, lower-level public servants may find it somewhat easier to manipulate the system in a way that *appears* to give them a mandate. The distinction between engagement and manipulation, rarely clear under the best of circumstances, can thus become quite ambiguous.

Consider Robert Hermann at the State Department's Bureau of Security and Consular Affairs.

Bureau of Security
and Consular Affairs

Robert Hermann was named acting administrator of the State Department's Bureau of Security and Consular Affairs (SCA) on March 6, 1966, six months after joining that bureau as deputy administrator.[1] He had come to the State Department from four years of appellate work on the staff of Solicitor General Archibald Cox in the Justice Department. Still earlier he had served as a law clerk for Justice Harlan of the US Supreme Court.

Hermann believed his new position afforded a number of opportunities to pursue a policy of increased freedom for Americans both to travel abroad and to encounter foreign visitors within the United States. Like his predecessor, Abba Schwartz, he wanted to promote an "open society" in terms of travel. He also had a strong desire "to do something, to make things happen, to make a record." His policy objectives included:

- Removing the restrictions on travel by Americans to places such as Cuba and Albania
- Issuing publicly announced regulations to replace the largely informal guidelines that controlled the issuance of passports
- Extending the period of validity of a passport beyond their current duration of five years
- Liberalizing the terms on which visas were issued to foreign citizens wishing to visit the US

This case describes the situation Hermann faced as he considered his prospects for achieving the fourth of these objectives.

[1]"The Hughes Passport Affair," a public incident in which Hermann became embroiled during his first month as acting administrator, is described in an appendix to this case. The appendix also sketches the history of the Bureau of Security and Consular Affairs and the circumstances under which Hermann's predecessor resigned.

THE VISA OFFICE

Visas were issued by SCA's Visa Office, which had been directed since 1965 by a career foreign service officer named Ted Zelenka.[2] The Visa Office, in charge of 300 American consulates abroad, employed around 900 Americans and several times as many foreigners. Requests for visas were relayed to the office through the consulates and were usually granted routinely. Visas for communists, however, required waivers granted by collaboration between the Visa Office and the Immigration and Naturalization Service of the Justice Department. In establishing the waiver requirement, Congress had presumably intended to exclude communists in most cases, but State Department practice made granting waivers the general rule and barring communists, the exception.[3]

In the mid-60s, the Visa Office issued between a million and a million and a half visitor's visas. According to the law:

A non-immigrant visa shall be valid for such periods as shall be by regulations prescribed. In prescribing the period of validity of a non-immigrant visa in the case of nationals of any

[2]Zelenka had joined the foreign service in 1946 after working in the Federal Bureau of Investigation for five years as a special agent. Since joining the State Department, he had worked his way up through the consular branch of the foreign service; his last post before assignment to Washington in 1962 had been that of consul general at the embassy in Manila. Zelenka's relationship with Hermann was largely a business one, but he had felt sufficiently intimate to ask that Hermann propose him for an ambassadorship. (Ambassadorships awarded to career officers usually went to those who had followed the political (diplomatic) career path in the service, rather than the consular path.)

[3]Most of the major controversies surrounding the Visa Office in recent years had concerned this policy of granting entry to known communists. These controversies were covered extensively by the press and provoked much anger on Capitol Hill.

This case was prepared by Jeanne Johns, research assistant, under the supervision of Professor Philip B. Heymann and Mr. Stephen B. Hitchner for use at the Kennedy School of Government, Harvard University. Funds for its development were supplied by the Alfred P. Sloan Foundation. The names of certain individuals have been changed.

Copyright © 1975 by the President and Fellows of Harvard College.

foreign country who are eligible for such visas, the secretary of state shall, insofar as practicable, accord to such nationals the same treatment upon a reciprocal basis as such foreign country accords to nationals of the United States who are within a similar class. (8 U.S.C. 1201)

Under the prevailing regulations, visas were issued for a maximum period of four years, after which period an alien had to apply for a new visa. As acting administrator of SCA, Hermann had the legal authority, delegated to him by the secretary of state as authorized by the McCarran-Walter Act, to prescribe the rules governing visa issuance, including those concerned with the length of time for which the visa was valid (i.e., the length of time during which the alien could, without reapplying to the state department, make visits of such duration as the Immigration and Naturalization Service allowed).[4]

THE IMMIGRATION AND NATURALIZATION SERVICE

The entry of aliens into the United States was controlled by a "two-key" system. While the Visa Office issued visas, the Justice Department's Immigration and Naturalization Service (INS) held a second key: they made the decision at the border as to whether the alien might actually enter. In practice, this later decision was almost always controlled by the issuance of a visa. INS was also responsible for determining how long the alien could stay in the United States.

There was constant interaction between the Visa Office and INS due to this "two-key" system. The Visa Office frequently asked INS to allow the entry of refugees to whom it could not issue visas. The Visa Office could reciprocate by doing favors for INS, such as including INS representatives in conferences concerning immigration, visits by aliens, and other matters of concern to them. INS and the Visa Office also cooperated in issuing waivers to commu-

nists and members of other classes denied admission unless there was waiver.

CONGRESSIONAL COMMITTEES

SCA dealt with Congress through four subcommittees. Appropriations hearings were held annually by the House appropriations subcommittees for the Departments of State and Justice, chaired by Rep. John Rooney. In anticipation of these hearings, Rooney took an annual world tour of consular posts with Visa Office Director Ted Zelenka and John Lynch, commissioner of the INS since 1962.

The policy-making subcommittees with which SCA dealt were the Senate Judiciary Committee's Internal Security and Immigration Subcommittees (chaired by Senator Eastland), its Refugee Subcommittee (chaired by Senator Edward Kennedy), and the House Judiciary Committee's Immigration Subcommittee under Representative Gaighan, who was particularly influential in SCA policy matters. It was he who had been instrumental in the ouster of Hermann's predecessor, Abba Schwartz. Immigration and security were his major policy concerns, and he had good relations and frequent communications with FBI Director J. Edgar Hoover and Passport Office Director Frances Knight, both of whom had a similar preoccupation with security.

SCA's dealings with Senator Kennedy's subcommittee were few, and Senator Eastland had many other concerns. As chairman of the full Judiciary Committee, Eastland handled an array of important matters, unlike Representative Gaighan, whose House subcommittee dealt exclusively with the immigration law. One of Hermann's first jobs upon succeeding Schwartz was to testify before Eastland on a restrictive passport bill prepared by the subcommittee's general counsel, Jay Sourwine. Hermann testified against the bill and heard no more about it. He concluded that Eastland did not consider the bill important enough to pursue if the administration was opposed.[5]

Hermann had been acting administrator of SCA for almost a year before he even met Gaighan. There was no occasion for regular contact with the policy-making committees. Annual authorization

---

[4]A federal agency that wishes to issue a new rule or regulation is generally required to publish a notice of proposed rule-making in the Federal Register at least 30 days before the new rule or regulation is to take effect. After this notice is published, the agency must give interested persons an opportunity to submit written information or arguments regarding its proposed action. These provisions for "notice and comment" do not apply, however, to regulations relating to a military of foreign affairs function of the government. Source: Section 4, Administrative Procedures Act.

[5]It is interesting to note that SCA's position on this bill was formulated by Hermann personally; the cursory nature of such clearance as was necessary indicated to Hermann that his superiors had little interest in SCA affairs or at least had little time for them.

was not required, and there was no legislation pending of interest to the bureau. The most frequent interaction between SCA and Congress took the form of requests from congressmen for favors from the Visa Office; specifically, the office could expedite the issuance of visas to friends and relatives of constituents of congressmen. Requests for such favors were handled by Ted Zelenka, who consequently had access to committee members, Representative Gaighan in particular.

HERMANN'S OBJECTIVES

Though he lacked detailed knowledge about many of the intricacies of the process by which visas were issued, Hermann had a general desire to liberalize US visa requirements, particularly since he knew that most European countries allowed Americans to travel without visas. Hermann knew that opponents of such liberalization would base their principal objection on a perceived threat to security. He did not, however, regard the visa as an effective bar to unfriendly agents, so he did not believe that a change in visa regulations would significantly affect US security. Moreover, a careful review of the security procedures for visa issuance and revocation established that substantially identical precautions could be incorporated in a scheme of permanent, but revocable, visas.

Many congressmen would nevertheless consider a more liberal visa policy a threat to security. Objections could also be expected from the FBI, the agency charged with monitoring the activities of likely agents of foreign powers. Reluctant to seek elimination of visas, since that would require legislation, Hermann began to consider an alternative—the creation of a permanent visa, valid for the owner's lifetime, by administrative action.

COMMITTEE ON BALANCE OF PAYMENTS

About one year after he had become acting administrator of the SCA, Hermann was still thinking about initiating a change in visa regulations. He had recently become aware that the president had set up a committee on balance of payments to deal with the balance of payments[6] "crisis," which had been exac-

erbated by the war in Vietnam. In early 1967, the committee had issued a general request to all federal agencies for suggestions of actions that could be taken to reduce the payment deficit. Hermann wondered whether this new development presented a good opportunity to move on the visa issue.

APPENDIX: THE HUGHES PASSPORT AFFAIR[1]

The Bureau of Security and Consular Affairs (SCA) in the US Department of State was created in 1952 by a provision of the Immigration and Nationality Act (66 Stat. 174; 8 U.S.C. 1104), also known as the McCarran-Walter Act after its sponsors, Sen. Patrick McCarran of Nevada and Rep. Francis E. Walter of Pennsylvania. An outgrowth of the McCarthy era's fervent anti-communism, SCA was established to monitor requests of foreigners wishing to visit the US and of US citizens wishing to go abroad to ensure that such travel would not undermine national security. It was also placed in charge of guaranteeing the in-house security of Department of State personnel.

The background of the controversial McCarran-Walter Act sheds light on the subsequent nature of the bureau. The heated debate on the bill and President Truman's veto message focused on the proposed retention of a system of immigration quotas based on the national origins of the United States population in 1920. Senator McCarran, the bill's fervently anti-communist sponsor, also had other objectives for the bill. He argued that the bill provided an effective screen against subversives intent on entering the country. (Presumably, one reason for also charging the bureau with controlling which Americans received passports was to keep those subversives already inside the US from leaving.)

The bill was passed over the president's veto in June of 1952. Six months later a further controversy arose relating to a special commission that President Truman had set up to study the bill: Senator McCarran accused three members of that commission of belonging to communist-front organizations. Such were the days of McCarthy.

The highly political nature of the McCarran-Walter Act destined the new office it created, the Bureau of Security and Consular Affairs, to be a center

---

[6] The "balance of payments" refers to the balance between money flowing into the US (e.g., for foreign purchases of US goods and services or for foreign investments in the US) and money flowing out of the US (e.g., for US purchases of foreign goods and services

or for US investments abroad). A balance of payments crisis may result if outflows are significantly greater than inflows over a period of time.

[1] This appendix was prepared by Jeanne Johns, research assistant, from a case study prepared by Susan Elliot, Martin Wishnatsky, and Philip Heymann.

of controversy, its administration and functions subject to differences in interpretation depending upon whether conservatives or liberals were running it. Thus, begun as the darling of the rabidly anti-communist senators and congressmen of the 1950's, it suddenly took on a very different coloration in the early 1960's when the Kennedy Administration came to power.

Organizationally, the new bureau was placed under the jurisdiction of the deputy under secretary for administration, and its administrator was to rank equally with assistant secretaries of state. One of the administrator's duties, specified by statute, is to "maintain close liaison with the appropriate committees of Congress in order that they may be advised regarding the administration of this chapter by consular officers." The McCarran-Walter Act also directed that the administrator of the Bureau of Security and Consular Affairs, along with the commissioner of immigration, "shall have the authority to maintain direct and continuous liaison with the directors of the Federal Bureau of Investigation and the Central Intelligence Agency and with other internal security officers of the government for the purpose of obtaining and exchanging information for use in enforcing the provisions of this chapter in the interest of the internal security of the United States." (8 U.S.C. 1105). These provisions clearly linked the administrator and the bureau to the congressional committees and to other security agencies at least as closely as to the secretary of state.

At the time of its creation, the Bureau of Security and Consular Affairs was divided into five offices: a Passport Office, an Office of Security, a Visa Office, an Office of Special Consular Services (dealing with Americans in trouble abroad), and an office in charge of the State Department's refugee programs. Each office was to have a director under the supervision of the bureau's administrator and his two deputy administrators.

The first administrator of the new bureau was Scot McLeod, a man whose political philosophy matched that of the legislators who had created the bureau. Chosen to head the Passport Office was Ruth Shipley who, according to a later State Department official, "combined the attributes of colossal incompetence with very strong anti-liberal, anti-communist sentiment." During Shipley's tenure, it took six weeks or more to get an ordinary passport. If she doubted your loyalty, she would simply ignore your request.

On May 1, 1955, Shipley was replaced by Frances Knight, who had been brought into the de-partment as an assistant to McLeod. When Knight took over, the efficiency of the operation increased substantially; today one can obtain a passport in three days to a week. Knight was also, compared to Shipley, a civil libertarian; she denied passports to communists, but not to all liberals.

From 1955 on, Knight maintained her position and consolidated her power while there was a constant turnover of bureau administrators and other State Department officials. She was particularly careful to build herself a solid constituency on the Hill by winning the friendship of those on the Senate's Internal Security Subcommittee and of other congressmen who shared her strong conservative bias. She also won the favor of congressmen in general by giving them special passport services; for instance, she would provide hand-delivered passports almost immediately.

During the '50s, Knight and those who agreed with her were in the majority in the State Department; with the advent of the '60s and the Kennedy administration, they began to confront some strong opposition. For Knight, direct conflict began with the appointment of Abba Schwartz to head the Bureau of Security and Consular Affairs in September, 1962. Schwartz was a staunch liberal, an early member of Americans for Democratic Action, a close friend of Eleanor Roosevelt, and later one of Robert Kennedy's most active supporters in his New York senatorial race. He also had one useful conservative tie: he was a close friend of Rep. Francis E. Walter, chairman of the House Un-American Activities Committee and a zealous congressional guardian of immigration policy.

Schwartz's first fight with Knight—and perhaps his most important one—was over the rights of confrontation to be given a person denied a passport on the grounds that he was a communist. Schwartz insisted that the person had a right to be confronted by those who accused him; Knight insisted that the statutory authority vested in the head of the Passport Office entitled her to deny a passport on the basis of her own interpretation of the FBI reports. In due course Schwartz won that fight, but it was just the first of many.

Meanwhile, Schwartz was developing strong enemies on the Hill, almost all of whom were strongly identified with the political right. One group involved the supporters of Knight on Senator Eastland's Internal Security Subcommittee; its general counsel, Jay Sourwine, began a vendetta that was to continue for years. Another group of enemies involved the head of the Immigration Subcommittee on the House side, Rep. Gaighan of Ohio, who, at least at that time, was a very conservative figure and a very important one to immigration legislation.[2]

Schwartz made some enemies among conservatives because of his strong support of liberal policies. However, an equally important cause of his failure to win strong support on the Hill—and in the State Department—was his individualism coupled with an independent operating style. Schwartz refused to play the political "game"; he neglected the courtesy calls and token requests for permission that encourage people to cooperate. This manner of doing things contrasted with that of Knight, and it cost him some potential friends in important places.

The man who had to mediate the Knight-Schwartz dispute was the deputy under secretary for administration, since the family quarrels within the Bureau of Security and Consular Affairs were within his jurisdiction. The person faced with this task was William J. Crockett, a former foreign service officer promoted to the post from deputy assistant secretary of state for budget and finance on January 25, 1961, at the outset of the Kennedy administration. His special contribution to the organization—and the probable reason for his appointment—was his close friendship with Rep. John Rooney of Brooklyn, chairman of the House appropriations subcommittee in charge of State Department appropriations.

Crockett had his own relationship with Congress to think about, while Schwartz evidently felt he had nothing to lose, and liberal support to gain, by declaring open battle with Knight. Also, there was again a difference in operating styles. Crockett's attitude can be summed up with the phrase "Don't rock the boat," and he tended to side with Knight, perhaps because she was such a seemingly permanent aspect of the bureau. On the other hand, Crockett saw himself as an administrator without ideology, and he was clearly puzzled by Knight's persistence in office in the face of her dissatisfaction with the prevailing liberal policy. At one time he remarked, "It is amusing, in a sense, to consider the many allegations Knight has made about the non-support she gets from the State Department. It is a wonder to me she stays around when she is so dissatisfied with her superiors."

Schwartz took the initiative in his battle with Knight by attempting to get her transferred from her job. In this effort he was backed by some top-ranking officials of the State Department. In addition, he was encouraged by Rep. Rooney, who also

had a running feud with Knight—to the extent that she consistently refused to appear at budget hearings because of alleged poor treatment.

Knight had staunch allies on the Internal Security Subcommittee, however, and they hurried to her defense. At one point, 10 influential senators wrote Secretary of State Dean Rusk urging that action against her be deferred pending a subcommittee report (which was never made). The subcommittee also conducted hearings in 1962, 1963, and 1964 which were, in effect, calculated harassment of Schwartz. According to a *New York Times* article of March 25, 1965:

Mr. Schwartz was obliged to reappear time after time to be questioned about an extraordinary range of matters. Mr. Schwartz was asked about his personal bill-paying habits. He was asked about homosexuality in his department. He was asked about a report that $15,000 had been paid for remodeling his offices—a figure later established at $3,100. He was asked whether his relations with Mr. Rusk allowed him to walk into the secretary's office without checking with the receptionist. . . . Miss Knight's testimony was occasionally punctuated by tributes from members of the subcommittee. It was devoted to detailing what she described as intensive bureaucratic harassment and measures whose effect was to isolate her department and reduce her powers. As examples, she cited delays of four to five months by the department in paying her office's telephone bills, numerous delays in furnishing supplies, and transfers of members from her office. She described the transfers as "hiring-away," a phrase that moved Mr. Crockett to protest that Miss Knight's department was, after all, a part of the State Department.

By 1965, the Department of State was being pressured, particularly by Rep. Gaighan, to do something about Schwartz. A secret set of meetings took place in the secretary's office with the decision finally made that a reorganization plan would eliminate the Bureau of Security and Consular Affairs and thereby eliminate Schwartz. Schwartz was placidly unaware of this since he had left his office in the hands of his newly appointed deputy, Robert Hermann, and was spending the fall and winter abroad in Geneva while attempting to do something about American prisoners-of-war in Vietnam.

The choice of ways to eliminate Schwartz was ill-conceived, at best. It involved secrecy, so when the

---

[2]Gaighan held strong views on security and did not hesitate to voice them; he was known to consider Eleanor Roosevelt a "dangerous communist."

decision was discovered observers would suspect that only bad motives could have been involved, and it was a secret that was not going to be kept. Even at best, removing Schwartz invited a public reopening of basic "liberal" versus "anti-communist" issues of the sort that had been lying somewhere under the surface since the 1950s. Under Schwartz, the bureau had completely reversed its reputation. It was now viewed as a citadel of liberalism and a strong defender of an "open society" in terms of travel, in spite of the conservative opinions of those heading the Passport and Visa Offices.

The decision to eliminate the bureau got out when Hermann was informed of what was in the wind by a close friend of one of the three or four participants at the "sack Schwartz" meetings. Hermann made a number of phone calls to Schwartz in Geneva and finally persuaded him of the reality of the threat. Schwartz returned and talked first to Crockett, then to the Secretary, who confirmed on March 4, 1966, that the plan was under way, although no reorganization plan had yet been sent to Congress. The following day, Schwartz resigned with a substantial flourish amid an array of front-page newspaper articles.

The issue, quite predictably, became defined as a victory of the most conservative elements in Congress over the most liberal elements in the administration. The problem was probably the more acute because the Johnson administration had taken over; Schwartz had been appointed by Kennedy, and a number of Kennedy appointees were leaving. Newspaper stories attacking Schwartz's surreptitious discharge were met by statements of Bill Moyers, the new presidential press secretary, defending the White House and staunchly insisting that no change was to be made in the liberal travel policy of recent years.

The person who appeared to have originated the reorganization plan to accomplish the ouster of Schwartz was Crockett. According to a *New York Times* story on March 9, 1966, "Some State Department officials feel the position occupied by Mr. Schwartz fell victim to Mr. Crockett and W. Marvin Watson, a special assistant to the President." The article continues: "Mr. Schwartz said he had been removed last year as head of the American delegation to two international conferences on Mr. Crockett's orders. Both times, he said, he was led by State Department officials to understand that Mr. Crockett had acted on instructions from Mr. Watson."

Clearly, then, Schwartz and Crockett were not getting along very well. Since the Schwartz-Knight controversy was a thorn in Crockett's side anyway, Schwartz's resignation was probably a relief for him.

The person destined to succeed Schwartz was Robert Hermann, who had served as deputy administrator of the bureau for the preceding six months. One of several possible candidates, Hermann was chosen when a more experienced candidate rejected the controversial and apparently thankless job. Before coming to SCA, Hermann had spent four years in the Justice Department doing appellate work, and his sense of government had been strongly influenced by this experience. He had left believing that most problems could be reasoned out and that compromises acceptable to all parties could be selected with good will and tolerance. This belief fitted well with Crockett's desire for harmony in the department, and on appointing Hermann to the position, Crockett expressed his hope that there would be a new era of good relations with the Passport Office. Hermann responded that he would try to produce that result.

Shortly after making this promise, Hermann faced an interesting dilemma. During the second week of March, a foreign service officer in the bureau showed him a telegram that had recently been sent to Paris with a very low classification: "Limited Official Use." In it, Prof. Stuart Hughes (a well-known historian at Harvard who had run against Edward Kennedy for the US Senate in Massachusetts in 1962 and who had already spoken out against the Vietnam War) was described as closely attached to communist beliefs. The US Embassy in Paris was requested to report anything of interest concerning Hughes' activities when he was in France (the *Harvard Crimson* had reported that he was planning to take a sabbatical in Europe the following autumn; he had not yet applied for a passport).

The message had been authorized in the name of Frances Knight. Hermann asked his aide to check the files to find out whether any investigative agency had requested this information on Stuart Hughes. This aide's check, and a subsequent recheck, did not turn up a request for the investigation.

The cable sent from Knight's Passport Office was a challenge to the new administrator. It represented the continuance of a restrictive policy toward travel and immigration which Hermann, like his predecessor, strongly opposed. Hermann, though not wishing actively to continue Schwartz's feud with Knight, decided that he had best make his position clear at the outset of his tenure.

On March 11, three days after the telegram, Hermann brought up the issue at his regular weekly meeting with Knight and her deputy, Bob Johnson. He told them he could find no record of an FBI request in the Hughes case and that he felt strongly that the Passport Office should not attempt to become an investigative agency. There was evidently some confusion, for Hermann recalls that "They did not seem aware of the particular telegram." (Later, Knight claimed that the cable had been signed by someone acting in her stead while she was away from the office.)

Hermann advised Knight and Johnson that he would follow up with a memo putting his views in writing, which he did on March 14. In part, the memo instructed Knight that members of the Bureau of Security and Consular Affairs should never request information from posts as to the activity of a traveler unless they were first asked to obtain such information by a federal agency duly charged by Congress with investigative responsibilities. The memo was classified "confidential" so that the possibility of renewed conflict within SCA would not be made public.

He recalls, "I explained my directive by saying that it is important right of Americans not to be subjected to governmental interest, observation, and reporting by anyone except a duly authorized investigative agency. I was well aware that I was not foreclosing requests by the FBI for information as to an American's activities abroad. My status as acting administrator of the bureau promised no support in a head-on battle with the director of the FBI. Beyond that, a case with an FBI request did not seem to be the issue. There was no indication that the FBI had made a request and, for all I knew, it rarely if ever did. My memo to Knight specifically authorized State Department inquiries at the request of the FBI although it directed that I must see each of these requests and each cable we sent out in response."

On March 16, the State Department officially announced Hermann's appointment as Acting Administrator of the Bureau of Security and Consular Affairs. The item in the *New York Times* noted, "In announcing that Mr. Hermann . . . will move into the top spot, Robert J. McCloskey, State Department press officer, said the shift would not affect United States policies in this field." As this announcement went to press, Hermann continued the policies and the battles of his predecessor; he cabled the Paris Embassy and cancelled Knight's cable.

Hermann assumed the issue was closed. He was wrong, for there was another player in the game, unknown to him, who was soon to change the stakes, the rules, and the outcome.

When Hermann first discussed the Knight telegram with the man who had brought it to his attention, there was a third person in the room. The fascinated eavesdropper was Sam Jones, another State Department employee, who had lived and worked through earlier battles between Schwartz and Knight. Jones evidently decided that he wanted to join the fray and, on leaving the office, obtained for himself a copy of the cable concerning Stuart Hughes.

Jones then did something taboo in bureaucratic circles: he took his copy of Knight's cable and delivered it to a correspondent of the *New York Times*. Clearly, the *Times* had a story on its hands: a well-known professor, a well-known critic of a war that was becoming increasingly unpopular, was being reported on, at Knight's instigation, by the embassy in Paris. Hermann recalls what happened subsequently:

> Pursuing a fuller story, the *Times* reporter presented the cable to the White House press office, which of course knew nothing about it, and in turn asked the State Department what the story was behind the cable. The under secretary asked me, and I responded that the matter was well in hand, that I had sent a memorandum to Frances Knight telling her that we were not again to make such inquiries without an investigative request; and that I had directed our post at Paris to disregard the earlier cable. Mr. Ball asked for a copy of the memo and he presumably furnished it to the White House press office. In due course, perhaps to polish the President's recently tarnished image as a liberal in the area of travel, both the classified memorandum and information that the Hughes cable had been cancelled were given to the *New York Times* to show what had in fact been done to right the situation.

If White House aides believed they were killing one story by giving a copy of Hermann's memorandum to the *New York Times,* they were blind to the new story they had created. As Hermann put it, "The *Times* now had the story that Knight, tigress in the Passport Office and recent devourer of Schwartz, had been reprimanded by her fearless young superior for acting like a policewoman without an FBI request."

At this point, press officials in the State Department realized the potential embarrassment of airing departmental dirty linen to the public and undertook a major effort to stall and then stop the story. Hermann advised Knight of its imminence, and she said that she was sure that an FBI request could be found. And while she searched, she protected herself by denying that she had sent the messages that prompted the memorandum; she asserted that March 8, the date on which they were sent, fell in a period when she was away from the office for five weeks.

The *Times* checked out her explanation and waited for her to find the FBI request. Finally, on March 22, the *Times* announced that the story was to go to press the following morning. Fifteen minutes or half an hour before the deadline, Knight came through. She had found the FBI request, dated February 7, which requested the surveillance on Hughes. It had, she said, accidentally fallen out of the file when it was first being reviewed in the Passport Office.

The front-page story in the *New York Times* on March 23 was headlined "Knight Is Given a Rebuke for Action sought by the FBI." The story included Knight's assertion that she had not sent the message, and continued: "After a thorough check, a State Department spokesman said that, while the messages bore her name as authorizing officer, they had not been signed by her but by someone acting in her stead. The spokesman declined to identify the drafter of the messages." A brief identification of Professor Hughes was provided and included the statement, "On two occasions, in 1935 and 1955, he experienced delays in getting a passport." The story concluded with a brief, provocative biography of Knight, to wit:

Miss Knight, who became director of the Passport Office May 1, 1955, has long been a controversial figure in the State Department.

She vigorously opposed the policy, initiated in 1962, of giving people who were denied passports because of derogatory security information the right to review the evidence and confront witnesses and informants. In testimony before the Senate Internal Security Subcommittee several years ago, she asserted that the regulation "in effect forbids us to protect ourselves" and questioned "whether there actually exists the will to defend the country" from "the inroads of Communism."

Miss Knight was involved in an almost constant feud with Abba P. Schwartz, who resigned as administrator of the Bureau of Security and Consular Affairs March 5 after he learned of a secret reorganization plan to abolish the bureau. His deputy, Mr. Hermann, was named acting administrator March 16, two days after he sent Miss Knight the reproving memorandum.

With the publication of the *Times* story on March 23, the lines of battle hardened: each party felt that he or she had been wronged, and now each was sure to be joined by others wishing to take sides. As Hermann recalls, "I felt that the message of the story was that I had badly botched by reprimanding Knight for something that she hadn't done. Knight took the story quite differently—as a direct threat to her power and her influence."

The *Times* story was followed quickly by an Associated Press story. Both not only referred to the FBI request but also quoted from Hermann's memorandum to Knight and had all the details of the Stuart Hughes cable. Hermann recalls, "I immediately went to see Knight and explained that I had nothing to do with the story getting into the press. Certain that I must be lying, she responded that she was sure that I was 'bleeding over the floor' and that she too knew how to play this game. . . . She referred to the fact that there were people in the State Department who were out to get rid of women in office, pointed out quite correctly that this was a classified memorandum that someone had given to the press (she was referring to my memorandum to her which I had classified 'Confidential') and reflected that the concern about Stuart Hughes seemed excessive to her at a time when men were dying to fight communism in Vietnam."

Knight then called her own press conference and set the record straight with rare candor—and a flair of colorful language. The stories which appeared in the *New York Times* on March 25 and 26 included the following comments:

In a report of an interview in *The Washington Evening Star* today, Miss Knight said Mr. Hermann had come to her after the *Times* story had appeared and asked her if she blamed him. "I sure as hell do," she was quoted as replying.

Miss Knight was in an almost constant feud with Mr. Schwartz over liberalization of passport policies. She wrote Mr. Hermann that she had "reliable information that Mr. Schwartz spent considerable time in his office following his resignation, calling reporters and peddling highly inflammable stories about me in the press."

"He is reported to have said," she continued, "he would drag me out with him if it was the last thing he did. Mr. Schwartz's antagonism to any cooperation or contact we had with the FBI is a matter of general knowledge."

In an interview today with a Scripps-Howard reporter, Miss Knight was quoted as saying: "This leak to the *Times* was not a leak;

it was a handout. Some creeps are out to get me.''

When asked by a *Times* reporter whether she had used the word "creeps," she said she could not recall, and then added, "I think it's a pretty good description. . . ."

In the *Star* interview, Miss Knight is quoted as saying: "I cannot see the sense of the United States government going all out in Vietnam and having our boys murdered and mutilated and then having lax security practices in the State Department. I make no bones about saying so."

"They are so concerned about Professor Hughes," she continued, "that no one has mentioned the leak of classified information to the *New York Times*. This is not the first time. There is a *New York Times* coterie in here which is virtually part of the State Department's staff."

Interviewed at her home today, Miss Knight referred to her present superior, Robert Hermann, as "a 32-year-old whiz kid." "I will issue a passport to a baboon if I can find out that that is the policy," she said. "Trouble is, I've had eight bosses in my ten years as head of the Passport Office. It's like a railroad station. They're here today, gone tomorow. I will follow instructions if I can find out what they are."

She vowed she would not be forced out of her job. She is under civil service and at 60 can stay on ten more years "Unless they prefer charges of inefficiency, which they haven't the nerve to do."

Her determination to stay is not based on her economic motives. She said that her $24,000-a-year job costs her and her husband money. This is because her salary puts her husband, Wayne Parrish, a publisher, into a higher income tax bracket.

As Knight was going to press, so was Sen. Edward Kennedy. Senator Kennedy had run against Stuart Hughes for the Senate in 1962. He addressed a pointed letter to Secretary Rusk asking what business the State Department had "shadowing" American citizens abroad and vouching for the integrity, the honesty, and the loyalty of Professor Hughes. Senator Kennedy gave his letter, or at least the substance of it, to the press. On March 24, the *New York Times* quoted it in an article headlined "Rusk Is Pressed on 'Shadowing': Edward Kennedy Questions Surveillance of Professor."

It was clear by now that the substantive issue was changing. It was now a question of whether the United States was "shadowing" its citizens abroad. As Senator Kennedy put it in his letter:

> The right to travel without harassment by our government is a fundamental right of American citizenship. The methods used in the past trenched heavily on this established right. I trust the [State] Department will take every step necessary to see that our citizens can travel with the guarantee of privacy.

In short, the debate was rapidly becoming distorted. As Hermann explains: "The implications of 'tailing,' following, investigating, or doing overseas police work were never true. At most, the request had been to report on any press stories or any other information that happened to come to the attention of State Department officers about the man's activities abroad. But by some Gresham's law, the false but sexier issue pushed aside the real one."

With Knight and Senator Kennedy both meeting the press, the burden of responding for the State Department fell first on Bob McCloskey, the State Department's press spokesman who regularly met with the press each day at 12:30. On March 24, he was pressed hard by a number of reporters, as the transcript of questions and answers reveals. First he admitted that a procedure had existed for many years whereby requests for information on American citizens had been made of the State Department by investigative agencies and forwarded to our posts abroad. He denied quite specifically that there had been any shadowing, tailing, or police work by our missions.

The questioning focused in on what, if any, control the State Department exercised over these requests. McCloskey's answers changed as the pressure built up. In the background was the fact that the press had available to it Hermann's memorandum to Knight asking to see each request from investigative agencies and each telegram sent out in response to such a request—a directive motivated by doubts as to whether a request had actually been received in the case of Stuart Hughes. The first time McCloskey was asked whether the State Department would screen requests from investigative agencies, he responded, "The extent of it is simply to see whether a specific request had been received from the investigative agency." Later he was pressed further: "Do you think the screening process is sort of a temporary measure to see whether what is going on is what ought to go on, or do you think that there is a permanent procedure for handling such requests?'' He responded ''I would expect that it will become permanent.'' He was pressed further, ''Well, Mack, if there never has been a single instance in which such request was made, except on an instigation of one of the investigatory agencies, why do you need a screening process?'' McCloskey responded, ''Let's just say in the judgment of the department it was felt desirable.''

It was obvious from the reporters' question that the entire procedure from top to bottom was a highly unpopular one and that keeping it secret had not helped. McCloskey was pressed again: ''Bob,'' he asked, ''is it contemplated under the present procedures that the State Department has, I mean the Bureau of Security and Consular Affairs may at times exercise its own judgment?'' The meaning of the question was clear: would the State Department, the Bureau of Security and Consular Affairs, sometimes say ''no'' to the FBI? This time McCloskey gave ground. He responded, ''I would think that it is entirely possible, yes.'' McCloskey's response became a front-page story of the *New York Times* the following morning, March 25. It was headed ''Department of State to Sift FBI Bids.'' It is impossible to tell from the transcript whether the question to which McCloskey responded as he did was asked by the *Times* reporter, but it seems extremely likely.

On March 25, Secretary Rusk had a long-planned news conference. He too was asked about the Stuart Hughes affair. The secretary stated that he found the practice of sending unconformed, libelous allegations about an American citizen abroad very questionable and indeed offensive. He stated that the entire process required a new review by the Departments of State and Justice and directed that such a review would go forward immediately.

Thereafter, the columnists on major newspapers and the editorial writers throughout the country took over from the daily reporters. They lined up on both sides of the question, which they recognized as one of basic civil liberties. On the Right, Knight was defended as the victim of persecution by the State Department. On the Left, she was attacked as a threatening resurgence of McCarthyism. Neither defense nor accusation had a great deal of truth to it.

Meanwhile, Secretary Rusk sent his friend and legal advisor Leonard Meeker to Attorney General Katzenbach to review with him the process of getting information about the activities of American citizens abroad. Acting on his own initiative, Meeker asked Hermann to accompany him. Hermann was acutely conscious that Rusk had not chosen to work through him on this matter and was left with the impression that the secretary, with whom he had never had a personal or regular business relationship, did not trust him.[3] In contrast, the meeting in the attorney general's office was the beginning of a warm friendship between Hermann and Katzenbach.

While Rusk's emissaries met with the attorney general, the director of the FBI, J. Edgar Hoover, wrote directly to the secretary of state, demanding to know why his judgment had come to be questioned and complaining about Hermann, demanding that something be done about him. Ironically, Mr. Hoover's letter landed routinely on Hermann's desk with a request that his office draft a reply. The Departments of State and Justice ignored the separate channel between the FBI and the secretary of state on a new procedure which took the Passport Office out of the business of forwarding investigatory requests by the FBI. It also produced channels that guaranteed considerably less public knowledge of any allegations that might be included in a cable asking for information about an American travelling abroad.

The FBI was ultimately left with a channel to obtain information that came to the attention of our posts in foreign countries. The director of the FBI was not, however, willing to use this channel. ''Without any announcement, requests for such information simply ceased. The result was not wholly surprising. Our posts abroad had never furnished much useful information to the FBI. The publicity given the practice and the largely unfavorable public reaction could only have been viewed as extremely undesirable from the FBI's point of view. Finally, Mr. Hoover must have taken the idea that the State Department would exercise an independent check on the validity of each request as a questioning on his competence and he was bound to resent it. Why, in these circumstances, should he risk further public embarrassment by continuing to send largely fruitless requests for information to what seemed to him a leak prone State Department? The major result of the debacle was thus a *de facto* end to the practice of reporting back to investigative agencies, at their request, any information that came to the attention of our missions abroad about the activities of Americans traveling in foreign countries.

The effects of the events on the participants are worth noting. Knight declared her form of warfare. She made available to right-wing columnists reports

---

[3]Under attack from Kennedy Democrats for his Vietnam policies and ''burned'' by the liberal backlash of the Schwartz affair, Rusk may well have mistrusted a successor chosen by Schwartz. On the other hand, what Hermann considered Rusk's aloofness may have resulted from the very low priority which SCA responsibilities held with the hard-worked Secretary.

of private meetings at which Hermann had questioned the efficacy of any use of our passport power as control on the activities of foreign or domestic communists. A short spate of articles suggested that Hermann was either extremely simpleminded about, or possibly sympathetic to, communist spies at a time when we were fighting a very bloody war in Vietnam. She must have made similar information available to her friends in Congress.

At the same time, Knight herself was not without troubles. Once again a serious effort was made to transfer her to another position. Under Secretary George Ball, outraged by her press conference, gave an independent fact-finder the job of assessing whether Knight could be removed under civil service regulations; the alternatives of transfer to another job were also present. These plans foundered on the hard rock of Secretary Rusk's unwillingness to take on what must have looked like an unnecessarily nasty battle with Knight's friends (and allies needed by the administration) on the Hill (Sen. Mundt, Sen. Hickenlooper, Rep. Gaighan, etc.).

Sam Jones, who had furnished the "Limited Official Use" message on Stuart Hughes to the *New York Times,* was less fortunate, for he did not enjoy political protection on the Hill and was accordingly treated far more harshly. Hermann was asked almost immediately to cooperate with an investigation by the security branch of the State Department as to the source of the leaks to the press, first of the cable on Stuart Hughes and second of the "confidential" memorandum addressed to Knight. Hermann refused, except to say that no one in his bureau was responsible. But eventually the pursuit of the informant focussed in on Jones' bureau, where each of its employees was asked to admit or deny the charge. Jones admitted what he had done and was asked to leave the State Department.[4]

[4]Note by Mr. Hermann: "I had been asked by Sam's boss what he should do in these circumstances. After some thought, I responded

For Hermann, the case was resolved in the following way:

A few weeks later I decided to check the truth of Frances Knight's claim that the FBI request had been lost by one of her subordinates for the weeks from the time when I first saw the Stuart Hughes cable until minutes before the *Times* went to press on its first story. It seemed to me entirely possible that a close personal friendship between Miss Knight and Mr. Hoover had resulted in a creation of a false or at least predated request. To check, I took a random sample of fifteen out of 100 or 150 inquiring cables that had gone off during the preceding year. I gave the names to the appropriate sections of the State Department's Bureau of Intelligence and Research and asked them to check their files to determine whether an FBI request had been received in each of these cases. Later I was informed that they could locate a request in 14 of the 15 cases and that the lack of one request was entirely consistent with less than perfect filing procedures. My somewhat surprised conclusion was that a request concerning Stuart Hughes had in all probability been received by the Passport Office from the Federal Bureau of Investigation before the cable asking for information on Hughes was sent and was indeed lost shortly thereafter.

---

that he should tell the secretary that he was quite happy to have his employee treated in whatever manner Frances Knight was treated for exactly the same offense of delivering classified information or 'Official Use Only' information to the press. If Frances Knight were to be punished, so could the man who gave the Stuart Hughes cable to the *Times.* I was of course aware that this was idle dreaming. Nothing happened to Frances Knight."

Imagine you are Robert Hermann. You have an opportunity to exert leadership on the visa issue by gaining a mandate for a more open visa policy. You have the formal legal authority to do so, yet (as with Miles Mahoney) this is not sufficient: You need political authorization as well. Your superiors at the State Department and in the White House have no clear position on the issue, nor do your congressional overseers on the House and Senate Judiciary subcommittees and the House Appropriations subcommittee, nor, finally, do other agencies, like the FBI and the Immigration and Naturalization Service, which share responsibility for determining whether a foreign national can enter the United States.

What's your problem? Many congresspersons and several agency officials are particularly concerned about national security—especially Herbert Hoover, director of the FBI; Representative Gaighan of the House Judiciary Committee's Immigration Subcommittee; and Senator Eastland of the Senate Judiciary's Internal Security Subcommittee. They might consider your proposal for a more liberal visa policy to be a threat to national security.

There is also Frances Knight, head of the Passport Office, who has ties to many of the conservatives in Congress who are most concerned about national security. You are (or should be) aware of the plight of your predecessor, Abba Schwartz, who tangled with Frances Knight and simultaneously antagonized the conservatives. Schwartz ultimately resigned, leaving behind him a residue of suspicion among the conservatives; the Bureau has gained a reputation as a citadel of liberalism and a strong defender of an ''open society.'' Thus conservatives and others especially concerned about national security will be keeping careful watch on what you do. And to make matters even more difficult for you, you already have had a run-in with Frances Knight.

How then do you gain a mandate to proceed with an open visa policy? My students usually see this as a traditional problem of political management—how to outmaneuver the opposition and gain sufficient support to do what you want. You must carefully use all the resources at your command to leverage your position.

For example, Ted Zelenka, head of the Visa Office, wants you to propose him for an ambassadorship. You know that the Visa Office has done many favors for members of Congress in the past—expediting the issuance of visas to friends and relatives of key constituents. Zelenka is thus on good terms with many members—in particular, Representative Gaighan (who was instrumental in ousting Abba Schwartz and is in frequent contact with FBI Director J. Edgar Hoover and Passport Office Director Frances Knight). Zelenka also has toured world consular posts with Representative John Rooney, chair of the House appropriations subcommittee for the Department of Justice. Here's an obvious opportunity: Get Zelenka to run interference for you with the conservatives. They trust him; he'll assure them that you are concerned about national security and that you would do nothing to jeopardize it. (By the way, it won't be necessary for you to make an explicit deal with Zelenka—his cooperation on open visas in exchange for your cooperation on his ambassadorship. He knows that he needs you, and he knows that you know that he does.)

How do you ''neutralize'' J. Edgar Hoover? Think for a moment about formal lines of authority. Hoover and the FBI report to the Justice Department, and the Attorney General of the Justice Department happens to be Nicholas Katzenbach, whom you befriended during the ''Frances Knight affair.'' (Katzenbach and you get along well, probably because you share similar backgrounds—elite law schools, Supreme Court clerkships, work in or with the Solicitor General's office.) Moreover, Katzenbach's liberal values are similar to yours. Maybe you could enlist him, at least to keep watch over Hoover and subtly let Hoover know that he would have to pay a price for interfering in your proposal.

Senator Eastland, another potential opponent, is less worrying than Hoover or Gaighan. As chair of the full Judiciary Committee, Eastland has many other matters on his mind. Recall that you testified before Eastland against a restrictive passport bill prepared by the subcommittee's general counsel and subsequently heard nothing about it. Visas and passports must be quite low on his agenda.

Dean Rusk, the Secretary of State, seems somewhat suspicious of you. You've had little contact with him; he did not ask you to help determine the administration's policy on collecting information about the activities of American citizens abroad. Under attack from liberals for his Vietnam policies and for the Schwartz affair, he may distrust anyone chosen by Schwartz to be his successor at the Bureau. Better play it safe: Rather than asking Rusk expressly to approve the open visa policy, send a memo informing him of what you are planning to do. This will force him to take the initiative in opposing it, if he objects. He has so many larger issues to contend with (such as the Vietnam War) that he's unlikely to want to spend any time or political capital on this one.

These steps may help guard your flanks, but you will need more positive support for the open visa policy if you want to avoid being trapped by the national security issue. To the extent that the open visa policy is perceived, even by moderates in the administration or in Congress, as a potential threat to national security—or something to be traded off against national security—you will lose.

The balance of payments crisis presents an opportunity for you to change this context. The White House is soliciting ideas for improving the nation's balance of payments, and the open visa proposal could fit right in. As more foreign visitors enter the United States, they spend more money here, thus reducing the deficit. By getting the open visa plan onto the White House's list of means to solve the balance of payments problem, you change the way the plan is perceived; you alter its apparent logic and supply a ready answer to the implicit question (otherwise raised in the context of national security): Why seek to liberalize visas *now*? You thus give your proposal a meaning and context apart from the old battle between civil liberties and national security.

Assume that you succeed and initiate an open visa policy without opposition. (In fact, Robert Hermann *did* succeed by following a strategy very similar to this.) All these strategic steps—leveraging of your allies, forestalling potential adversaries, changing the "face" of the issue by placing it in a different context—required careful diagnosis in advance. You had to map all the formal and informal relationships among potential allies and adversaries. You had to understand the history of analogous battles over national security in which the Bureau had been involved. You had to scan the environment for opportunities. You had to be acutely aware of timing.

But even if you are ultimately successful, you must still ask yourself: Am I doing my job? Am I being accountable to the public, or am I simply arrogating to myself the decision about what is best for the public? Have I asserted leadership on an issue previously lacking a leader or have I just manipulated the system?

Return now to our definition of leadership. A true leader creates mandates for action through engaging relevant publics in a deliberation over the nature of the problem and possible solutions to it. Robert Hermann, however, sought to remove the issue from the normal channels of deliberation—the congressional committees with direct oversight responsibility and the Secretary of State. He thus disengaged it from those who had a particular interest in national security. In so doing he failed to create a new channel of deliberation, or to engage a different or additional group of people in thinking through the problem and its possible solutions.

Hermann might argue in defense that by placing the open visa proposal on the White House's list of ways to reduce the balance of payments crisis he fulfilled his responsibility for provoking deliberation. But this justification won't work. His interest in promoting an open visa policy had nothing to do with the balance of payments, which he regarded as a pretext for changing the way the issue was perceived. People who subsequently might have discussed his proposal as a means of reducing the balance of payments but who had no knowledge of the larger controversy over national security were hardly engaged in a meaningful deliberation over it.

Hermann convinced *himself* that his open visa proposal posed no threat to national security, but he never made the argument to anyone else. In fact, he organized his strategy so that he would never have to test his argument against arguments raised by people concerned about national security. He thus never made himself accountable to a democratic process. Robert Hermann did not lead; he manipulated.

_____ *chapter 4* _____

Neutral
Competence

In the textbook version of American democratic institutions, the legislature has responsibility for enacting laws, the executive for implementing them. This separation of powers ensures that each branch checks the possible excesses of the other. In a pinch, the third branch—the "least dangerous," in Hamilton's words, "lacking power over the sword or the purse"*—umpires any conflict and imposes a check on both of its more potent partners. Each of the three branches also constitutes a different form of representation: legislators, representing their geographic constituents; the chief executive, representing the entire body politic; the highest court, representing past generations who drew up and interpreted the original compact, future generations who are not otherwise represented, and citizens in the minority whose rights might otherwise be overlooked. Such is the theory. And for two hundred years at the national level (and for varying lengths of time at the state level) the basic framework has stood up remarkably well.

In practice, relationships are less well defined. Legislators continuously negotiate with officials in the executive branch (elected, appointed, or civil servants)—threatening, cajoling, making deals. Members of the executive threaten, cajole, and counteroffer in response.

*Alexander Hamilton et al., *The Federalist,* No. 78, B. Wright, ed. (Cambridge, Mass.: Harvard University Press, 1961), pp. 103–10.

Public intermediaries—the press, organized interest groups, other departments and levels of government, companies, and not-for-profit institutions—are involved as well, proffering their own subtle (and not so subtle) deals.

In this fluid system, there is no clear demarcation between enacting and enforcing laws. Executive-branch employees may work with sympathetic legislators to draft a law (say, to limit the noise levels of various products) whose detailed provisions, in turn, are subject to debate and compromise among legislative staffs, lower-level bureaucrats in the executive branch, key legislators, and representatives of particularly powerful constituencies. (What products? What limits? Under what circumstances?)

Where compromise is difficult, the law might be left vague, to be filled in by executive-branch officials as they subsequently decide how to interpret it. Even at this stage there is apt to be ongoing bargaining—sometimes overt and formal (as in regulatory proceedings and congressional hearings), often covert and informal (a phone call from a legislator, a breakfast with an interest-group representative). And here, too, the courts broadly monitor the process, setting limits to how informal and secretive these relationships can be. (Regulatory commissioners, for example, may not engage in off-the-record, private meetings with industry representatives to discuss a proposed regulation.)

The *final* products of this system are not laws and regulations. They are particular governmental decisions *pursuant* to laws and regulations, to penalize certain people or to reward others. (Acme Machine Tool Company, for example, is to be fined $25,000 for selling a product that violates the rule setting limits on machine tool noise pollution.) Regulators, program managers, or prosecutors—all of whom interpret the laws and regulations, often with the help of many other players in the system—then apply their interpretations to specific cases. That is, they match their interpretations and the resulting criteria to particular factual situations.

What is the public entitled to expect from this fluid system of law making and law enforcing? In what ways should public servants who match laws and regulations to particular factual circumstances be held accountable, and for what?

Consider the case of Phil Heymann at the U.S. Department of Justice.

Oversight of the Criminal Division

On April 23, 1980, readers of Jack Anderson's widely syndicated column learned that the foreman of a grand jury investigating the Robert Vesco[1] affair had made allegations of improprieties against the head of the Justice Department's Public Integrity Section (PIS), Tom Henderson. Specifically, readers were told that

- The grand jury foreman said he had to "fight, fight, fight" for 17 days to get critical transcripts of the proceedings released for the grand jury's review.
- "There was a concerted effort by the Department of Justice to prevent the grand jury from obtaining a quorum at times," the foreman charged. On many occasions, he said, "jurors were given conflicting times as to when the jury was meeting."

Also, according to Anderson,

Ulmer claimed, "Henderson refused to answer questions by the grand jurors [and] refused to obtain information requested by the grand jurors," telling them they'd have to get it themselves. Seeking help in the issuance of subpoenas, the jury foreman was instructed by Judge William Bryant to ask the prosecutor for the proper forms. "Ralph Ulmer says he went to Henderson's office," the Senate report states, "and was in effect thrown out by Henderson." Ulmer said he had "never been talked to that way before."

That same morning, the Senate Committee on the Judiciary opened hearings on the Department of Justice's authorization bill. Chaired by Senator Joseph Biden (D-Del.), the hearing was attended by Senators Strom Thurmond (R-S.C.) and Orrin Hatch (R-Utah). Halfway into the hearing, in fact, Senator Hatch brought up the Anderson column:

this article of Jack Anderson's this morning is the most interesting one and I have to admit that these things in the article are true. Are true as far as I have been able to ascertain. I have met with Mr. Ulmer, who, of course, does not want to divulge what really happened within a grand jury proceeding without a subpoena from this committee or any other committee for that matter, and I have investigated it personally very much.[2]

Senator Hatch went on to say that he was interested in a "whole variety of matters" under Tom Henderson's direction that went "to the very integrity of the Chief of the Public Integrity Section."

The man whose integrity was being questioned before the Senate Judiciary Committee had just a few months earlier been nominated by the Carter Administration for the post of Special Counsel to the Merit Systems Protection Board (MSPB), the agency newly created to protect the rights of government "whistle blowers" (federal employees who expose corruption). Henderson's nomination, submitted to the

---

[1] Vesco, who made frequent appearances in Anderson's column, had fled the United States in 1973, during a grand jury investigation of allegations that he had made a $200,000 cash contribution to the 1972 reelection campaign of Richard Nixon in exchange for favorable treatment before the Securities and Exchange Commission. In his absence, Vesco was also indicted on charges that he looted more than $224 million from a mutual fund complex which he had headed. In 1978, the Justice Department had convened a grand jury to investigate allegations that Vesco had, through intermediaries, attempted to bribe White House aides to drop extradition proceedings against him. Because of conflicts between the grand jury foreman and Henderson, the Justice Department had elected in August of 1979 to transfer handling of the case from the Department's Public Integrity Section to the U.S. Attorney's Office for the District of Columbia. On April 1, 1980, the grand jury decided against returning any indictments in the matter.

[2] To some staff in the Criminal Division of the Justice Department (of which the Public Integrity Section was a part), Hatch's "interest" in the article on Henderson was unsurprising, since it was widely suspected that the Senator's office had leaked the information to Anderson.

This case was prepared by Nancy Dolberg under the supervision of Stephanie Gould for use at the John F. Kennedy School of Government, Harvard University. Funds for the development of this case and supporting documents were provided by the U.S. Office of Personnel Management and Departments of Commerce, Defense, Health and Human Services, Housing and Urban Development, and Labor through OPM contract 61–80. This material may be reproduced by or for the U.S. Government pursuant to the copyright license under DAR clause 7-104.9(a).

Copyright © 1981 by the President and Fellows of Harvard College.

Senate Committee on Governmental Affairs, would languish in that Committee for several months, while the Judiciary Committee and the Criminal Division of the Justice Department engaged in an increasingly heated battle over their mutual prerogatives.

BACKGROUND: THE "CASE" AGAINST PIS

Mistrust of the Public Integrity Section had been brewing among a small group of Washington journalists several weeks before it surfaced in Anderson's column. On March 10 a group of these journalists met with Senator Orrin Hatch and his assistant minority counsel, Kim Pearson, to express displeasure over Henderson's nomination to the MSPB post. Included in the group were Clark Mollenhoff and Greg Rushford, independent Washington writers who had made a specialty of investigating the federal judiciary; and Shiela Hershow and Inderjit Badwhar, reporters for a small Washington weekly, the *Federal Times,* read primarily by federal employees. According to Pearson, the journalists said that

> "We don't think that Henderson has been rigorous in prosecuting or following up many cases while he has been Chief of the Public Integrity Section. We have written about several of these cases and have found that the final resolution is always to have them dropped by the Public Integrity Section."

The journalists cited a number of cases of alleged misconduct involving federal judges, as well as a prolonged course of civil and criminal litigation involving a man named Nard, whom newspapers said Senator Hatch had once represented and who had lost in the civil cases and had been convicted criminally. Nard had been seeking since 1972 to have the conduct of judges, prosecutors and witnesses in this litigation investigated and prosecuted. Portraying himself as the victim of a judicial conspiracy, he had (according to June 25 and June 26, 1979 articles published in the *Pittsburgh Post-Gazette*) enlisted the sympathies of Mollenhoff and Rushford, who incorporated Nard's grievances into their own investigation of the federal judiciary.[3] The Nard case alone, however, did not ac-

count for the presence of the two journalists in Hatch's office. A member of the Senate Subcommittee on Improvements in Judicial Machinery, Hatch was a sponsor of the Judicial Conduct and Disability Act of 1980, which proposed the establishment of councils to effect the removal of errant judges without having to rely on the ordinary impeachment process. Hatch's concern for judicial performance had also been previously recorded by Mollenhoff and Rushford in a *Reader's Digest* article of February 1980, where they quoted him as saying that he had "seen certain federal judges controlled or influenced by special interests . . . and others become arbitrary, capricious."

According to Kim Pearson, after the meeting of March 10, Senator Hatch asked him to look into the allegations made by the journalists. (Pearson had joined Senator Hatch's staff right out of law school and had been working for the Senator for about ten months when the matter arose.) As Pearson recalled,

> We had some familiarity with some of the cases, although we had not identified them as Public Integrity cases. We did a little checking around and then it came to me that the Public Integrity Section was responsible for looking into allegations of judicial misconduct.

In addition, Pearson said, someone had called from the Justice Department to say that Henderson had handled the Vesco grand jury. According to Pearson, Senator Hatch realized that he could not question Henderson's nomination as MSPB Special Counsel because that fell within the jurisdiction of the Senate Governmental Affairs Committee. The Senate Judiciary Committee was, however, under Senate Standing Rule XXVI (8)(a), charged with the responsibility for examining the application, administration and execution of laws within its jurisdiction, including those creating the Department of Justice. Reporting of the Department's annual authorization bill, required since 1976, had become something of an oversight mechanism. According to Pearson, Senator Hatch decided, then, to "attempt to hold an oversight hearing during the authorization process which was coming up in April; to get Mr. Henderson to come up and explain some of the processes of the Public Integrity Section."

Meanwhile, the journalists proceeded with their own investigation. On March 16, Hershow, Badwhar and Rushford came to meet with Tom Henderson in his office, at their request. At that meeting, according to Henderson, Hershow informed him that she had been investigating his tenure as Chief of PIS and

---

[3]According to the same article, the ties between Nard and the two journalists went deeper than sympathy: The *Gazette* went on to say that Nard had actually contributed to the two Washington foundations that supported Rushford and Mollenhoff's efforts; that these journalists stayed with Nard when they visited Pittsburgh; and that they had brought Nard to meet with Senator Dennis DeConcini (D-Ariz.), Chairman of the Subcommittee on Improvements in Judiciary Machinery.

had discovered a dozen cases (the Nard case among them) that he had mishandled or had covered up for political reasons. A PIS staff member present at the meeting recalled that Rushford added that he had wanted to support Henderson's nomination, but when he looked at his record he simply couldn't.

Henderson recollected responding to the accusations by explaining that

> We brought more than 125 indictments and prosecutions during the past four and one half years. We probably handled five hundred or more substantive investigations where we actually did affirmative investigative work. And there would be several thousands of cases that did not require investigation, that for one reason or another do not rise to the threshold level of the criminal investigation on its face. Something that happened beyond the statute of limitations or something that doesn't violate federal law.

According to Henderson, Congressional referrals, as many of those mentioned by the reporters had been, were often "quick declinations"—those that did not contain enough potential leads to warrant the expenditure of scarce resources.

When it came to discussing specifics of the cases, though, Henderson drew the line because, as he said, "The Federal Privacy Act forbids me to talk about the specifics of a closed criminal case." PIS staff present also felt that whatever information he might divulge would not be received fairly. Speaking of Hershow, a senior PIS attorney who was also present recalled that

> Essentially, Tom was not in a position to respond, because she wasn't being open about it. . . . She made it totally explicit that she was going to print [an] article no matter what we said. I think it was clear to all of us that she wasn't amenable to the truth.

In fact, according to the attorney, although a lot of cases "were very good stories . . . and did have scandals in them, they just weren't prosecutable for the most part." Furthermore, "In all but one or two [cases], Henderson had virtually nothing to do with them, other than having them pass through his Section." In fact, as Tom Henderson described his and PIS's involvement in the Nard case, it consisted of responding to a U.S. attorney's request for help in locating the existing file on the Nard allegations

within the Department. The documents found by the attorney assigned to the task proved not to be those in question, and Henderson referred the U.S. attorney to the Deputy Attorney General's office.

On March 17, Sheila Hershow and Inderjit Badwhar's story, entitled "Sensitive Cases Let Hanging," appeared on the front page of the *Federal Times* and took up two and a half pages of the tabloid. At stake with Tom Henderson's nomination, the authors suggested, was "the most sensitive investigative job in the federal bureaucracy—special counsel to the Merit Systems Protection Board." In reviewing Henderson's performance, the authors spoke with members of the law enforcement system who had criticized "Henderson's lack of judgment . . . and prosecutory zeal." The piece continued:

> In a series of interviews, FBI, agents, U.S. attorneys, assistant U.S. attorneys and congressional investigators complained that, under Henderson, Public Integrity was slow and slipshod in its conduct of major investigations. Others with first-hand knowledge of his operation said that Public Integrity is a lightweight outfit, staffed by novice lawyers, and, in one well-respected prosecutor's words, "long on public relations, and short on legal analysis."

Although the *Federal Times* piece went on to say that, "None of the sources suggested that Henderson is corrupt or venal . . . [that] one assistant U.S. attorney described him as 'polite, personable and charming,'" it also ascribed mishandling of the dozen cases subsequently named to a "willingness to back away from politically sensitive issues." Concerning the Nard case, the authors wrote,

> A new U.S. attorney in Iowa, James Reynolds, is now presenting evidence in the Nard case to a grand jury in that state. According to reliable sources, Reynolds, like his predecessor, was pressured by Justice Department officials to drop the case when he insisted on interviewing Thornburgh. Even though Henderson maintains he had nothing to do with investigating the Nard case he participated in the meeting during which the alleged pressure was put on Reynolds to back off. . . . The curious twist in this case, according to sources, is that after assurances by Henderson . . . that the investigative file would be turned over to Reynolds, Public Integrity did not hand over the appropriate files.

OUT OF THE PRESS AND INTO THE CONGRESS

The date for the Justice Department's annual hearings had been set for April 23. The fact that the Department had annual authorization hearings was in itself something of an anomaly, representing a "tradition" only five years old.

For the past five years, the Department of Justice's enabling legislation has required that an authorization bill be passed annually. (Some federal agencies—the Commerce Department, for example—have permanent authorizations; others, multi-year [the Federal Trade Commission, for example, has three-year authorizations].) Alan Parker, Chief Counsel to the House Subcommittee on Civil and Constitutional Rights from 1973–1977, explained the movement towards annual Department authorization which began in the House:

It started with my experience during the Watergate years, when we were doing the impeachment inquiry. That was about the same time that we found out about COINTELPRO, the counterintelligence program which had gone on within the Federal Bureau of Investigation. We decided that we had to have more careful oversight over the FBI . . . so the Subcommittee on Civil and Constitutional Rights started looking into some of those things. We found that the FBI and the Department of Justice were not as forthcoming with information as we thought they should be. We wondered what we could do to enhance our capability with respect to our oversight responsibilities and I got to thinking that if we had power over their purse they would certainly pay more attention to us. Until that time the appropriations for the Department of Justice would simply go directly to the appropriations subcommittee that did their work; there was no authorizing process. I looked into it and found that the legislative committee with jurisdiction over the State Department had actually altered the law to provide for prior authorization of its appropriation. We had drafted a bill to achieve the same purpose and had the support of all the subcommittee chairmen when Representative Conyers decided to add it to the LEAA authorization bill. So it passed in 1976.

According to staff of Senate Judiciary members, under the Chairmanship of Senator Eastland (pre-1978), the Committee's oversight of the Justice Department was "*pro-forma*": "The kinds of investigations that were routinely done were nominations. Most investigations were legislatively oriented; when specific things came up, a group would form *ad-hoc*." With the accession of Senator Edward Kennedy to the position of Committee Chairman (1978–1980), however, the authorization process acquired more of an oversight character.

Although authorization bills were handled at the full Committee level ("that way," according to one staff member, "no subcommittee involvement was encouraged, and every Senator worked as a Senator for the full Committee"), in fact, the chairman for any particular authorization hearing would probably be at least a member—and, more likely, the chairman—of the subcommittee which ordinarily had jurisdiction over the subject area and relevant Department, Division or program.

In 1979, Senator Biden, chairman of the Criminal Law Subcommittee, had chaired the authorization hearings over the Criminal Division of the Justice Department, and, according to a member of Biden's staff, had enjoyed a cooperative relationship with the Division. According to a Judiciary Committee staff member, the authorization hearings were "not adversarial if you define adversarial as hostile. But it was not friendly, if you define friendly as not questioning." According to a staffer for Kennedy, who had held hearings on FBI undercover operations the same year, "We could work things out with Phil Heymann [Assistant Attorney General in charge of the Criminal Division]. He had no problem with us talking to strike-force chiefs or U.S. attorneys; most of that was information-gathering."

Requests for hearings witnesses were generally channeled through one Senate Judiciary Committee staff member to the Department of Justices Office of Legislative Affairs (OLA). OLA, headed by an Assistant Attorney General in charge of Legislative Affairs, was responsible for relations between the Department and Congress on matters involving legislation, as well as processing Congressional inquiries and arranging hearings. Although much informal and sometimes formal communication took place between other Department and Congressional staff members, one OLA representative said that initial requests from Congress usually go through the Office; while later contacts are often made directly to the Division in question, although OLA will be apprised of events. The same OLA representative said that the Department chooses spokesmen on a topic of interest for a Congressional hearing, rather than responding to a request for a given Department member.

Although Senator Hatch technically had a right to hold a hearing himself as part of the authorization process (since all members of the Judiciary Committee technically have that right), according to Pearson he was asked by the Committee staff member who usually dealt with OLA to make the request through Senator Biden's office. Hatch was a member of Biden's subcommittee. According to Pearson, "Kennedy deferred to Biden because he was chairman of the subcommittee which had jurisdiction over the Criminal Division." Kim Pearson wrote in a memo to Senator Hatch dated mid-April, 1980:

> Because of the runaround we've been getting from the Biden staff, I called them this morning and asked them for a copy of their letter to the Department of Justice requesting witnesses for the hearing next Wednesday. They told us that we would be having a hearing on the Public Integrity Section on April 23, and we asked that Henderson testify.

According to a member of Biden's staff, the Senator was not enthusiastic about the hearing. He was concerned, for example, about

> the difficulty of investigating cases that were recently closed and some of the problems of getting into essentially what would have been prosecutorial discretion. The second set of problems were whether it was really our jurisdiction or whether it should have been in the Governmental Affairs Committee.

The staff found from speaking with staff of other Senators, though, that it was clear that some "Democratic Senators were going to do something regardless of what Senator Biden did." According to Pearson, Biden's staff indicated that they had placed a phone call to OLA requesting Henderson's appearance on the 23rd.

The View From the Criminal Division

No one in the Criminal Division, it seemed, had ever heard of the *Federal Times* before the paper's March 17 issue was released. According to one PIS attorney, members of the Division found the allegations "ludicrous, so that nobody really thought much of them." Although few of the Division personnel were familiar with the cases in question, they uniformly considered Tom Henderson to be, in Heymann's words, "an absolutely honorable guy."

Henderson had joined the Department of Jus-

tice in 1966, right out of law school. He served in various organized crime and labor racketeering sections as well as on Department strike forces until 1973, when he moved to a subcommittee of the Senate Judiciary Committee, chaired by Senator Edward Kennedy (D-Mass.) as Deputy Chief Counsel. A year later, Henderson returned to the Justice Department and, in 1976, he was named the first Chief of the Public Integrity Section of the Criminal Division. As Chief, for the next four and a half years, Henderson and a complement of up to 30 attorneys provided oversight of and litigation support to U.S. attorneys involved in the prosecution of government officials and employees, as well as directly handling Washington-based corruption cases. It was clear to Heymann that during this period Henderson had earned the respect and confidence of his PIS deputies. Heymann further received assurances from his own deputies and from Henderson himself that there had been no wrongdoing in the handling of the cases.

During the next few weeks, Heymann also spent 8–16 hours—a significant amount of time—reviewing the Department's files on the cases named. His judgment after reviewing the files was that

> it doesn't seem to me that there's any impropriety in any of them. Nothing like impropriety. Just plain as a whistle. You could disagree with three or four, just as reasonable people could disagree on either side. With the rest you couldn't possibly have prosecuted, and there's no indication of anything but good faith judgment being exercised.

Heymann concluded that, in general, the cases were weak candidates for prosecution, and that, in any event, none of them were sufficiently important to have occasioned political pressure. Finally, from a reading of the files Heymann saw that in all cases a recommendation to decline prosecution had been made by line attorneys under Henderson.

Heymann's own view of the cases cited in the *Federal Times* article was that they were "to some extent matters in which Henderson opposed the views of Senate or House staff people who thought there was something wrong, and had wanted a criminal investigation." As Heymann had told PIS attorneys, "They [the attorneys] are in a tough position, because they really are the barrier, in a sense, that prevents political people or press people from getting charges they want brought against someone."

Heymann was not alone in his concern for protecting the independence of Criminal Division litigation. Just a year earlier, in the aftermath of the Watergate revelations, Attorney General Bell had acted to insulate the Assistant Attorney General, Criminal Division, from political pressures by ordering that

1. No member of Congress or the White House could contact the Assistant Attorney General or his staff about pending prosecution.
2. The decisions of the Assistant Attorney General about whether or not to prosecute would be final unless overturned by the Attorney General or the Deputy Attorney General in a written opinion, giving reasons for the reversal, which would be made public consistent with the privacy rights of the parties concerned.

This hard line got harder to hold in mid-April, when Phil Heymann was asked to have Tom Henderson testify at an authorization hearing of the Senate Judiciary Committee on April 23. On April 16, Heymann followed what has been described by many Criminal Division attorneys as his common procedure for deciding major issues. According to one attorney,

> Cases generally get worked out in the sections, but when something is very important it goes to Heymann. If he agrees straight out with the attorney's recommendation then there is no meeting and Heymann just signs off on it. If he think that it's close or if he disagrees or if he just wants to learn more about it, he will call in the Section Chief and sometimes the attorney involved.

One of Heymann's assistants described these as "large meetings, and long ones, where everyone went around and gave their opinion . . . and Phil tried out a lot of ideas." In this case, by Heymann's own description, he wanted "to have all interested parties" at a meeting to decide whether or not he should permit Henderson to appear. "I'd particularly want to have Alan Parker on a question like this . . . and one of my senior deputies."

Alan Parker had become Assistant Attorney General in charge of Legislative Affairs in 1979, after spending the prior two years as General Counsel to the House Judiciary Committee. Having been involved with the Watergate impeachment and the Department of Justice authorization processes, Parker felt that Congressional oversight "had been neglected for a long time."

> Watergate has probably left us with a legacy of the fact that the legislative branch is an investi-

gative tool as well as a legislative tool. And that is correct and it should be correct. But oversight needs to be done in a very thorough way. Oversight is as much gathering information as it is just going public. Oversight is looking at how an institution really works over a long period of time.

Parker felt that from his experience, the House of Representatives, because it's the larger legislative body and its committees have to function as collegial groups, had a "purer" attitude toward oversight than did the Senate. According to Parker,

> I think in the Senate you'll find more of a tendency for individual Senators to use the power of oversight or their subcommittee for whatever whim or purpose strikes their fancy at the moment. Some of it I'm sure is rational and good, but an awful lot of it will be purely political or purely for the sake of media exposure or purely on the basis of some staff person's idea of what they ought to be doing.

By the time Parker had arrived at the Department of Justice, he was used to saying "no" to the Senate. At the Department, Parker said, he was "somewhat surprised by the Department's willingness to accede to Congress where I felt institutionally it did not make sense." In part, too, Parker saw it as his job to say no; "and then Phil, or the Deputy or the Attorney General could be good guys and say, well you know how Parker is. Forget about him. Sure, we'll agree to do such-and-such." Of the meeting on the request for Henderson's testimony, Parker said, "If there was a range of 1–10 in terms of softness to toughness, I was a 10, and others were a 1, and everybody else was in between!" Although Parker did not recall precisely how he became aware of the situation, it was clear to him that the Senate Judiciary Committee was not planning "to do oversight over the Public Integrity Section," but rather "that they were really interested in delving into the allegations in these articles in the *Federal Times* about Tom Henderson." In addition, Parker's office had had previous contact with staff of some of the Senate Judiciary Committee's members who were interested in the allegations; staff members witin OLA had actually received threatening phone calls from one of them. Parker felt that certain Senate staffers "saw this as a great opportunity to really raise some hell."

It seemed highly unfair to subject Tom Henderson to their oversight, prior to his being able to go to the Governmental Affairs Committee and defend himself in the proper setting, which was in the context of his nomination, rather than backdooring it by doing this so-called oversight of Public Integrity.

Parker thought it a mistake, then, to send Henderson on the 23rd, but another long-term attorney in the Criminal Division concluded just the opposite: that it was entirely appropriate for Tom Henderson to testify before the Committee. Between these positions, recalled one participant, "every position on the spectrum was represented." Heymann remembered "Tom indicating that he didn't want to appear . . . maybe on the grounds that he thought it wouldn't help him to appear at that session and be beaten up." One senior PIS attorney remembered "the main topic of discussion" revolving around the argument that Section Chiefs, such as Henderson, who organizationally were two layers below the Assistant Attorney General, shouldn't appear before Congressional Committees; that they and the attorneys below them must be insulated from political pressure and second-guessing, so that they will continue to make decisions to prosecute or to close a case strictly on merit. One PIS attorney commented:

> There might have been twenty different reasons for not wanting Tom to appear, but only some of them were ones you'd want to make. We can't say to Congress that it will never be fair to Henderson. So you pick your most presentable arguments . . . and I think we all felt that it was a sound argument that Section Chiefs shouldn't appear.

Heymann's own feelings were mixed. He didn't regard the possibility of having a Section Chief appear before a Congressional committee to be "an awful thing," although he felt that he could make a strong argument that the practice would be extremely disruptive if it became regular. Heymann also felt

that Henderson would be hurting his chances for confirmation if he did not appear. Yet the principle expressed during the course of the Department meeting seemed right to him. As one participant described Heymann's attitude:

> He always had an open mind; he viewed it primarily as Henderson's fight in terms of who had something at stake. He was willing to do whatever he thought would help Henderson, in whatever way people thought was a principled way of dealing with it. I think Phil didn't have any history to go by in the Department as to how to handle these things. And I think he had an extremely open mind and was also extremely offended by the way the Senate was acting.

The same day Heymann and Parker, and Heymann's Deputy, were visited by a friend on Senator Biden's staff. The planned authorization hearing was Biden's responsibility; furthermore, the offices were friendly. According to the staffer, "We had been somewhat critical of the Criminal Division but Biden and Heymann got along quite well." Although the staffer didn't "question Henderson's integrity," he advised Heymann to have Henderson appear. For one, he felt that because Tom Henderson was a policy-maker and not simply an attorney who made recommendations on single cases, perhaps he should be called. Secondly, he felt, "To stand on principle here was actually the most impolitic thing to do." He told Heymann,

> To diffuse this issue . . . the thing to do would be to have Henderson prepped to answer any possible question. . . . You can be there with him and you can help him out or whatever. . . . The more you resist on this, the more resistance will become an issue. As long as you don't send Tom Henderson up there is still an issue, because you can't ask the question of the man who made the decision.

Imagine you are Phil Heymann. Do you agree to send Henderson up to the Hill to be grilled by Senator Hatch and to provide confidential files on investigations that never led to prosecution?

There are good reasons for doing so. First, by supplying Henderson and the files you avoid a major confrontation with several senators and possibly the entire subcommittee, which could mushroom into a highly visible contest over senatorial prerogatives. You thus avoid stories in the press which suggest you are covering up incidents of executive wrongdoing, or withholding politically embarrassing information. A cooperative response will alleviate suspicions and reduce tensions. Moreover, the proceedings will be over quickly, soon to be forgotten; thus you need not worry that you are setting an unfortunate precedent for congressional oversight. And thus Henderson's own career ambitions—particularly his wish to become Special Counsel of the Merit Systems Protection Board—need not be jeopardized. Besides, you are on friendly terms with Senators Kennedy and Biden; they will help ensure that the hearings do not get out of hand and that the files are handled carefully and confidentially.

In addition, you might reason that Congress is entitled to oversee the workings of the Department of Justice to ensure fairness and impartiality. This is particularly important with regard to investigations of possible government corruption. There have been suggestions in the press that Henderson's unit has not followed up on politically sensitive investigations. The public has a right to know what's going on, and Henderson is accountable to the public's elected representatives. The best antiseptic, Louis Brandeis once said, is sunshine. (Of course, before you were to act on the basis of this analysis, you must first check that the Attorney General agrees with you.)

Most of my students find these arguments persuasive, at least at first. But as discussion continues, they begin to have doubts.

Decisions about whom to prosecute should not be influenced by concerns about how members of Congress might react (nor, for that matter, should decisions about who should be penalized for violating an environmental regulation, or even about which firm should receive a government contract). These decisions should be made on the basis of criteria *other* than political preference: for example, the nature of the evidence, the seriousness of the alleged offense, or the proven dependability of a contractor.

Why *shouldn't* elected representatives play an important role in making such choices? Shouldn't prosecutors, regulators, program funders, and contracting officers be accountable to the public? The public and its elected representatives are entitled to decide upon broad objectives (deterring murder, penalizing noise pollution, building a new aircraft carrier) and criteria for achieving such objectives (the death penalty, a $50,000 fine, a ship that supports 100 aircraft and costs no more than $2 billion). But the public and its representatives have no particular expertise in applying these criteria to individual facts. Indeed, there is a danger that were the public's representatives to try, the official criteria might be subordinated to implicit criteria having less to do with the stated objectives than with political influence. Under these circumstances, for example, prosecutors might focus their investigations on outspoken opponents of politically powerful figures; regulators might harass firms that have failed to provide hefty campaign contributions to leading politicians while benignly ignoring firms that have been more politically astute; contracts might be awarded to companies unqualified to build first-class aircraft carriers but whose executives are friendly with political leaders. In other words, were legislators to involve themselves in the investigative process, power and influence might be more determinative than objective criteria, openly defined. As a result, the process would be *less* accountable than before.

The problem of illegitimate criteria is not limited to interference by legislators. Elected and senior appointed officials in the executive branch must also keep their distance. There is as much danger of abuse of power and violation of public trust through high-level executive interference in decisions about whom to prosecute (or, more generally, to penalize or reward) as through legislative interference.

The more onerous the penalty, the greater the danger that political interference will result in the use of illegitimate criteria. Public servants responsible for commencing criminal investigations and deciding whether to seek an indictment, for example, must be careful to avoid any hint of political influence upon their decisions. The potential for abuse is particularly troublesome—and public trust especially fragile—with regard to investigations of possible government corruption. Both the choices of whom to investigate and subsequent decisions to commence formal prosecutions on the basis of evidence gathered should be made on the basis of objective criteria.

Public servants authorized to make these sorts of choices are thus accountable to the public in a special way. They are accountable for applying laws and regulations according to neutral criteria directly related to the purposes of the laws and regulations, and they are accountable for doing so in a neutral way—employing their professional judgment.

Allowing Henderson to testify and confidential investigatory files to be examined thus sends a dangerous signal, both to the public at large and to public servants with investigatory responsibilities. Even if the congressional inquiry were to be purely informative, with senators expressing no opinions about the targets of investigation and with Henderson's career prospects unimpeded, the mere fact that it occurred once suggests that it can occur again. Prosecutors and investigators would assume that they might be in Henderson's position one day, with no guarantees that future legislators would be as restrained. In addition, the public would lose confidence in the independence and neutrality of the public servants engaged in ferreting out government corruption.

Heymann also should worry about leaks. Reputations are at stake. Senatorial inquiries about specific investigations could find their way into the press, as could specific files. Even if the investigations have been closed for lack of evidence of wrongdoing, the targets of the investigations might suffer. A decision to investigate someone is not evidence of culpability, but the public (and the press) might not make the distinction.

So what is Heymann to do?

One possibility is to negotiate with the subcommittee the terms of accountability—that is, define more exactly what is legitimate for the subcommittee to oversee. Surely the legislators have a role in reviewing the *criteria* guiding Henderson and his staff. And they also have a role in reassuring the public that high-level officials in the executive branch are not improperly influencing how these criteria are applied (or substituting their own, illegitimate criteria).

Thus an agreement with the subcommittee might be structured this way: Heymann will appear with Henderson (but without files) to answer questions about the criteria used for choosing targets of investigation and for seeking indictments. But neither Heymann nor Henderson will answer questions about specific investigations. Should the subcommittee have reason to believe that specific investigations have been improperly influenced, Heymann and Henderson will provide specific information. A majority of the subcommittee's members, however, must first request the information, and the subcommittee must give reasons for its request.

Note that this kind of arrangement provides a check on improper legislative influence and yet also preserves a legitimate oversight role. It thus serves to reassure the public that public servants are accountable on both grounds—accountable to the law *and* accountable for applying the law in a neutral and objective manner.

(In fact, Phil Heymann negotiated an agreement very much like this, which served as a basis not only for the subcommittee's review of Henderson's work but also for reviews of other work of the Criminal Division. Henderson's Public Integrity Section continued to enjoy a high degree of public trust.)

The lesson here: Public servants must understand the difference between authority based on political accountability and authority based on neutral, professional competence. Both sources of authority may operate simultaneously. Part of the public servant's responsibility is not to mix them up—and, where necessary, to devise ways of enhancing each.

chapter 5

Accountability for Basic Rights

In a democratic society, public servants are accountable not only to the majority of voters but to the minority as well. Their accountability extends even to those who do not vote: to children, the retarded, generations yet unborn. It is a special kind of accountability, having less to do with what the minority of voters or nonvoters might wish for on a given issue than with their basic rights as members (or future members) of society.

Where should public servants look to discover these basic rights? In the United States, basic rights are enumerated in the federal Constitution, especially in the Bill of Rights. State constitutions contain similar guarantees. These broad provisions have been interpreted and reinterpreted by judges, who have applied them to specific cases. Judges' interpretations, in turn, have provided guidance to other judges who deal with analogous cases. Over time, and under the overall guidance (and ultimate authority) of the Supreme Court, these cumulative interpretations comprise a richly textured codification of our society's basic standards of justice. Most other democracies around the world also have systems of judicial review to guard the rights of minorities against the majority. Public servants—elected, appointed, and career—are accountable to judges who intepret the Constitution. Judges' interpretations take precedence over any law or policy that might be in conflict with them.

Potential conflicts are brought to a judge's attention by people who feel that their rights have been abridged by the elected representatives who enacted a law, or by those who interpreted and applied it. Sometimes such people are defending themselves against prosecution by the government, claiming that they have a constitutional right to do what they are being prosecuted for doing or claiming that their rights were violated by the way in which government investigators or prosecutors sought to convict them. Or such people might be suing the government for failure to give them a constitutionally protected benefit, or for imposing on them a constitutionally impermissible harm.

Public servants need not—and should not—await a definitive court ruling to uncover such potential conflicts between constitutional standards and laws or policies. Indeed, public servants should be on the alert for such conflicts or potential conflicts even before the courts become involved, and when they find them, they have a responsibility to seek a change in the law or policy to bring it into conformity with the Constitution. This is what it means to be accountable for upholding the basic rights of membership in society: being accountable to the Constitution itself.

What happens when public servants fail to recognize and avoid such a conflict? Consider the case of Pendleton State School.

Pendleton State School

Dr. Abram Steinberg, commissioner of the York Department of Mental Health, couldn't believe it. Residents of one of York's five institutions for the mentally retarded had sued Steinberg and other mental health officials for violating their constitutional rights, by allegedly subjecting them to inhumane conditions of confinement. They were asking the court to issue an order requiring wholesale changes in the institution's operations, staffing, facilities and practices. And the state's lawyer, Assistant Attorney General Neil Greene, was telling him that they just might win.

"Good heavens!" said Steinberg. "Where will it all end? Are the courts going to run the entire government?"

"I don't know," said Greene. "But right now, we'd better figure out who's going to run Pendleton State School."

THE DEPARTMENT OF MENTAL HEALTH

The historic mission of the York Department of Mental Health (DMH) had been primarily one of operating several large-scale, isolated institutions for the care, custody, and treatment of the state's most severely mentally ill and retarded citizens. By the 1960s, most mental health professionals had come to look with disfavor on such institutions. They were too impersonal, bureaucratic, monotonous, remote, artificial and congested to provide effective care, they said. What was needed, they claimed, was a wider array of community-based and community-supported treatment options in smaller settings. Following this line of thinking, a law was enacted in 1966 to reorganize DMH and redirect its programmatic focus. The law required DMH to divide the state into regions and to establish a "comprehensive

This case was prepared by Associate Professor Colin S. Diver, of Boston University's Public Management Program, with the help of Jo-An Kilgore, Research Assistant. The case is intended to serve as a basis for class discussion, not to illustrate either effective or ineffective handling of a managerial situation.

Copyright © 1978 by the Trustees of Boston University. Rev. ed. 1984 program in mental health and retardation services" in each. Community involvement was to be provided by citizen participation in three regional advisory councils: a mental health advisory council, an advisory council for community mental health services, and an advisory council for mental retardation services.

The 1966 law also reorganized the department, replacing the old "Mental Health Board" with a single commissioner assisted by a deputy commissioner and five assistant commissioners, one each for the Divisions of Community Programs, Mental Retardation, Research, Planning & Training, Administrative Services, and Children's Services (see Exhibit 5-1). Each region was to be headed by a regional administrator for Mental Health and a regional administrator for Mental Retardation, both appointed by the commissioner and reporting to the deputy commissioner.

The commissioner of Mental Health in 1972 was Dr. Abram Steinberg. Steinberg was a psychiatrist with an extensive background in clinical psychiatry and the administration of clinical psychiatric research. An adjunct member of the faculty of the York Medical School, Steinberg had published many scholarly writings in the field. Despite his interna-

tional reputation as a scholar, he was not regarded as a particularly effective manager. While he had sponsored many innovations at DMH, particularly in his area of greatest interest—research psychiatry—he shared little inclination or ability to exercise control over the day-to-day functioning of the department. The management responsibility tended, therefore, to devolve upon his deputy commissioner, Dr. Susan Isaacs. Isaacs, also a psychiatrist, had until recently been regional director of the largest region in the mental health department of a neighboring state. A strong believer in community-based treatment programs, Isaacs had been hired by Steinberg in 1970 to accelerate DMH's lagging efforts to effectuate the goals of the 1966 legislation.

By 1972, largely due to Isaacs' leadership, DMH had made considerable progress toward those goals. A progress report published by the department stated that the number of facilities and services offerd by DMH had grown from approximately 50 in 1967 to more than 560 in January 1972. The number of mental health clinics had grown from 39 to 120; the number of day care programs from zero to 77; the number of community clinical nursery schools for the retarded from 59 to 115; and the number of community residences for the mentally ill and re-

EXHIBIT 5-1

Pendleton State School *Organization of DMH*

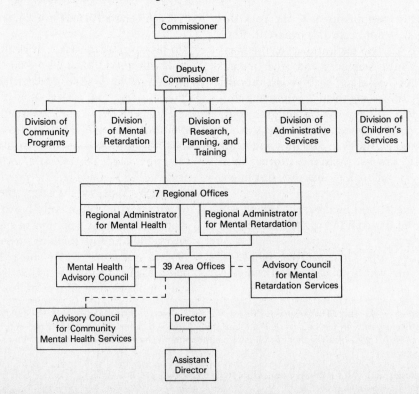

tarded from zero to 20. This same report concluded with the following statement about DMH future plans:

> The greatest unmet needs are for comprehensive programs for children, including in-patient services in each region; day programs for the mentally disabled and retarded of all ages; more community residences; and more specific programs for adolescents and the aged. A greater emphasis must be placed on research into the basic causes of mental illness and retardation and the development of new programs of prevention, treatment and rehabilitation.

MENTAL RETARDATION SERVICES

The Division of Mental Retardation (MR) was responsible for the programs and policies, although not directly in charge of operations, of the various state institutions for the retarded. In 1972 these included five residential "state schools" (see Exhibits 5-2 through 5-5 for data on expenditures and populations). In addition, there were three treament centers run primarily on a day rather than a residential basis. Finally, the MR division aided the various areas in developing some day care programs and workshops which served retarded people, and was in charge of programs and policies at the community clinical nursery schools throughout the state.

Many people involved with mental retardation felt that the MR division was the "stepchild" of DMH. They pointed to the much larger appropriations for mental health services (see Exhibit 5-6). In addition, the commissioner of DMH was required by law to be a psychiatrist, and the top management of the department had traditionally been much more interested in problems of mental health than mental retardation. As a former assistant commissioner for MR explained:

At every level of this department there was a vast distinterest in mental retardation . . . because it was a totally psychiatric department. . . . There were no rewards in the psychiatric system for being interested in retardation . . . and the feeling was there was nothing you could do for them (the retarded). God, nature or something doomed them to nothingness, so what's the difference? . . . They're retarded . . . what's the difference how they feel?

Until 1946, DMH had had no responsibility for mental retardation whatsoever. In that year, the five state schools were incorporated into the department. Prior to that time, the schools had existed as autonomous institutions of state government, each governed by a board of trustees appointed by the governor. The first state school, Flagstaff, had been founded in 1860, as a temporary boarding school for "idiotic and feeble-minded children." It was built during an early wave of optimism about the prospects of "curing" the retarded, based upon the pioneering efforts of Dr. Samuel Howe of Massachusetts.

By the turn of the century, however, attitudes toward the retarded had changed. Optimism gave way to pessimism. Those who had come to expect complete and rapid "cures" became disenchanted with the performance of the schools. The retarded came to be viewed as either incurable and helpless innocents requiring indefinite protection from society or as dangerous menaces from which society must be protected. Both views led to the construction of facilities in isolated rural areas, far removed from civilization. More and more parents were encouraged to institutionalize their children. As a result, institutions grew rapidly in size and number. It was during this period (1890–1920), that York built the remaining four of its five state schools.[1]

The rapid growth of institutional populations

[1]Warren in 1891, Danville in 1898, Morristown in 1913 and Pendleton in 1920.

EXHIBIT 5–2

Pendleton State School
Appropriations for State Schools 1967–1972 (in $000's)

Institution	1967	1968	1969	1970	1971	1972
Pendleton	3,623	4,097	4,509	4,549	6,179	6,443
Flagstaff	6,193	7,069	7,775	8,175	9,832	10,241
Warren	4,853	5,625	5,965	6,044	7,233	7,393
Danville	4,538	5,234	5,487	7,489	7,278	7,279
Morristown	3,751	4,397	4,550	4,733	6,040	6,526

EXHIBIT 5-3
Resident Populations at State Schools 1961-1971
Resident Population

Fiscal Year	Pendleton	Flagstaff	Warren	Danville	Morristown
1961	1413	2320	2095	1618	1504
1962	1424	2325	2092	1646	1504
1963	1550	2600	2200	1658	1550
1964	1536	2463	2060	1698	1554
1965	1554	2364	2027	1737	1550
1966	1560	2267	1932	1817	1552
1967	1562	2209	1849	1834	1546
1968	1477	2083	1726	1787	1527
1969	1405	1965	1685	1740	1501
1970	1356	1832	1606	1656	1473
1971	1290	1782	1536	1596	1448

generated inevitable fiscal pressures to reduce per capita expenditures. By reducing staffing, amenities, and living space, and by utilizing uncompensated resident labor to an increasing degree, institutional administrators were able to balance increased demands for institutional care with political resistance to expanded appropriations. Although attitudes toward the retarded began to soften somewhat in the 1920s, very little real change occurred in the structure of public programs for the retarded. The model of institutional care deeloped in the nineteenth century continued to dominate the service delivery system well into the second half of the twentieth century.

Many state schools had been organized on a "medical model," in which a dominant professional staff (physicians, psychiatrists and nurses) would preside over a subordinate lay staff of ward attendants, office workers and maintenance workers. The medical model, transplanted from the hospital setting, reflected a view of mental retardation as primarily a medical condition, a kind of congenital illness, requiring "treatment." A growing frustration with conventional medical and psychological technologies, coupled with chronic difficulties in attract-

ing competent professional staff, led to a withering of the medical model and a shift of de facto power to nurses and nonprofessional ward attendants. While the rhetoric of "treatment" persisted (or was replaced by the rhetoric of "habilitation"), the role of most state schools was almost purely custodial.

In most states the physical isolation of the state schools was mirrored by their political autonomy. Even after their incorporation into DMH, the York state schools continued to be regarded as "feudal baronies" surrounded by a moat of public indifference. Their principal political allies were local state legislators whose constituents they employed in great numbers. For the most part DMH administrators made little effort to exercise control over the state schools. Although the schools' superintendents formally reported to the regional MR administrators, there was little substance to the relationship. Their relationship to the MR Division was even more attenuated. Dr. Franklin Williams, first assistant commissioner of MR, made some efforts to improve the state schools, but soon abandoned these efforts in favor of planning new community-based programming. His frustration with institutional inertia and depart-

EXHIBIT 5-4
Pendleton State School
Distribution of Residents of State Schools, by Type (1972)

	Children (%)				Adults (%)			
	Trainable		Educable		Trainable		Educable	
Institution	S.N.*	St.*	S.N.	St.	S.N.	St.	S.N.	St.
Pendleton	17	6	13	6	27	9	7	16
Flagstaff	12	9	1	1	23	33	3	19
Warren	19	3	2	2	39	19	8	8
Danville	25	6	7	1	28	11	9	14
Morristown	12	3	—	3	43	18	8	13

*S.N. = Special Needs (i.e., with additional physical or emotional handicaps)
*St. = Standard Care

EXHIBIT 5-5
Pendleton State School
Direct Care Expenditures, Per Resident, by Type of Resident (1972)

| | Children | | | | Adults | | | |
| | Trainable | | Educable | | Trainable | | Educable | |
	S.N.	St.	S.N.	St.	S.N.	St.	S.N.	St.
Pendleton	$5750	5263	7121	4536	3655	2186	3686	2500
Flagstaff	6198	3866	4382	1214	5104	1912	4527	1612
Warren	4166	3795	4755	2993	2929	1643	3042	1745
Danville	3533	4059	3525	3101	2899	1725	1920	1810
Morristown	5605	3761	5749	3822	4515	1808	5363	2772

mental inattention to mental retardation led, ultimately, to his resignation in 1971.

In January 1972, after an eight-month search for a successor, Steinberg appointed Paul Boudreau as assistant commissioner. Boudreau had a Ph.D. in psychology and extensive experience in clinical psychology, with particular experience in the counseling of children with emotional problems and their families. As a consulting psychologist to the Wisconsin Mental Health Department for many years, he had worked with mentally retarded children housed in state institutions. During this period Wisconsin closed its largest state school and set up a network of innovative community programs for the retarded. His experience with this reform convinced Boudreau that traditional large, remote institutions for the retarded were inherently destructive and should be abolished. The philosphical premise for this belief was the "normalization principle"—a school of thought gaining increasing currency among mental retardation professionals. Adherents of this view believed that even the most severely retarded person could learn to achieve an acceptable level of "normal" behavior if given the chance to emulate "normal" people and participate in "normal" life situations, and if given sufficient support services

(therapy, counseling, education, training) to overcome the physical or emotional handicaps which often accompanied severe retardation. "Normalization" was considered impossible to achieve in an institutional setting, precisely because institutions presented their residents with such abnormal role models and living conditions. What was needed, instead, according to this school of thought, was a hierarchy of community-based settings, ranging from group homes to "normal" individual apartments, supported by social services tailored to individual needs, through which retarded persons would move in their journey toward "normalcy." Boudreau came to his new position as assistant commissioner for MR convinced that this was the proper direction to take.

PENDLETON STATE SCHOOL

By the 1960s disaffection with the old institutional models was beginning to spread beyond the confines of the professional community. Physical deterioration, overcrowding and understaffing were attracting increasing public attention. In York, the first spark of public concern was kindled in Pendleton, a rural community in the rolling hills of northern York,

EXHIBIT 5-6
Pendleton State School
State Appropriations for Mental Health and Retardation, Selected Years (in $000's)

| | Fiscal Year | | |
	1965	1969	1971
Administration	4,861	5,682	8,275
Community Mental Health & Retardation Services	—	6,421	9,160
Mental Health Institutions	54,048	73,619[1]	89,422[3]
Mental Retardation Institutions	22,365	31,162[2]	40,253[4]
Total, DMH	82,547	116,884	149,932

[1]Total number of patients served: 15,666

[2]Total number of residents/patients served: 8,780

[3]Total number of patients served: 13,569
  (6 institutions had populations greater than 1000; 6 others had populations between 500 and 1000.)

[4]Total number of residents/patients served: 7,831

which was the home of Pendleton State School (PSS).

In 1968, a Special Legislative Commission investigating complaints of inhumane conditions at Pendleton reported that "residents are forced to live in situations far below minimum standards [of the state Department of Public Health]." The report also stated that there was "complete inadequacy of the basic medical care and supervision" of the residents and cited the "flagrant lack of social service workers, psychologists and psychiatric personnel," the "desperate need for doctors, nurses, licensed practical nurses" and shortages of other essential personnel. In addition it called the educational rehabilitation programming at the institution "totally inadequate."

In January 1969, Dr. Williams spent a 24-hour period at PSS and recorded some of his impressions in an eloquent report to the commissioner:

> I saw several nude women eating food from a metal bowl using a spoon. Others were on the floor. Some parts of the walls and floors bore evidence of feces. The smell of urine was strong. . . . See the woman partially nude, restrained by cotton tapes, walking around the pole, slowly turning about in a circle, endlessly walking. . . .

> *Question:* Could you partition the room and give them some privacy?

> *Answer:* Oh no, that will never do.

> *Question:* Why not?

> *Answer:* Why you lose the ability to control them. You cut off the fresh air and sunshine and they really need space to walk off their frustrations. If you do that, we'll need more manpower because you'll make them into smaller groups.

> See fifty nude men huddled together in the shower room. Two shower heads go full blast. The cleaners wash the men. . . .

> "The laundry complains that because the men in K ward soil their clothes, they are overworked. This is why we keep them nude," said the attendant. The laundry is now very happy with Ward K.

> *Question:* There's no partition between the toilets. Why not?

> *Answer:* The men destroy them. We need a rubber mat in the shower. The men keep slipping on the wet tile floor.

> *Answer:* I'll try to get you one.

> *Says an attendant:* But the men will eat it up.

After Dr. Williams' visit, he wrote a series of letters to Robert Lowry, the superintendent of PSS, recommending changes in operational practices. Three months later, he received a reply from Lowry blaming DMH "red tape" and budgetary limitations.

In 1970 the state Public Health Department reported that its recent periodic inspecton revealed serious deficiencies in health care services, staffing and facilities at PSS. In 1971, the American Association on Mental Deficiency, a private association constituted to promulgate standards for institutions for the mentally ill and retarded,[2] evaluated PSS at the request of DMH. Later that year a local newspaper ran a series of sensationalized stories entitled "The Tragedy of Pendleton," charging, among other things, that "death is the only escape from Pendleton" and that "rehabilitative services are all but nonexistent."

According to his associates, Superintendent Lowry was "deeply wounded" by this rash of attacks on "his school." During his 26-year tenure as superintendent, Lowry had come to regard PSS as a tranquil and happy community which, despite its faults and obvious needs, had made steady progress. Most of the staff would probably have agreed. They regarded Lowry, whom they always referred to as "the Doctor" (Lowry had once been a practicing physician), as a stern, distant, but eminently fair administrator. Most of the staff had worked at PSS for many years and felt a strong attachment to the school. Many lived on the grounds, paying minimal rent for comfortable quarters. It was common for several members of a single family to be employed at the school. Staff frequently attended social events at the school. Like Lowry, most of the employees took the rash of recent criticism as a personal affront. Lowry did what he could to respond to the school's critics, issuing a steady barrage of responses, corrections and defenses. For example, he issued an "in-patient census" and a "progress report" in an effort to respond to the newspaper series, but they received little attention.

---

[2]AAMD standards were both quantitative (e.g., staffing ratios, square footage per resident) and qualitative (e.g., "adequate" nutrition, recreation, medical care). The quantifiable standards tended to exceed the performance of most state institutions by a considerable margin.

THE LAWSUIT

Much of the inspiration for the recent attacks on PSS had come from a single source, Richard Carter. Carter, an anthropologist, was the father of a 34-year-old retarded man who had been a resident of PSS since childhood. In 1968 he had been asked to join the board of directors of the Pendleton School Friends Association, a volunteer group founded, at Superintendent Lowry's suggestion, in 1952. As Carter put it:

> They bought the soap and the toothpaste and the toothbrushes that the state never bought. . . . They were basically a very conservative group of people with a great fear of the state. . . . At that time, they asked if I would join the board, and I said sure, and so I . . . was on the recreation committee. Recreation is not my cup of tea, but they asked me next year if I would run for president, and I said, "Sure, with one condition—that we become a bit more forceful in our approach." And they said, "Fine." I don't think they understood what it was that I wanted to do. . . .
>
> Well we talked to the superintendent, we talked to the commissioner of Mental Health, we talked to the governor, we talked to the legislators. Everybody was nice. The governor would say, well we'll get around to it. He didn't tell us when, but he'd get around to us. . . . They were dishonest answers, but nevertheless they were still answers. So we learned that the executive branch of government didn't work too well. The legislative branch responded by forming the legislative commission because of my dissatisfaction. The governor put me on that commission and so we investigated. . . . But nothing ever came of it. We saw, for example, maggots crawling out of bandages. We saw women using urinals for males, you see, because they were put into an inappropriate place. It was a horror story. And it's all well documented in Special Legislative Commission reports, but it's gathering dust.

Understandably, Carter—a feisty, acid-tongued bundle of nervous energy—made himself increasingly unpopular with the people at DMH. One high official in the department referred to him as a "self-seeking liar who had made himself completely obnoxious." Another DMH official stated:

> I can't believe that his motivations were noble, to clean up the institutions. . . . He set himself up as a pious leader of righteousness and rectitude. But according to what I have been told by the staff out there, he didn't visit his son very often. He didn't see him very often at all. They lived in the same town, or the next town over . . . I don't think he really gives much of a damn about a lot of these things. He wants to teach some people a lesson—he's mad. How much he cares about improving things, I'm not sure. And if they're going to be improved, they're going to be improved only his way. That is, he won't admit that there are going to be lots of improvements and lots of people have ideas about it. You're going to do it his way or it's not considered improved.

Carter had recently been to Norway doing research, and while there he had visited some Scandinavian institutions for the retarded. He was very impressed. In his words there were "light year differences between what they were doing and what we were doing." In addition, he had "a feeling that there were some constitutional deprivations, without being able to pinpoint what they were." He began to feel that the only way to get any action was through the courts. Carter enlisted the aid of a local attorney, Joseph Harrington, who agreed to take the case. The two of them worked together on documenting the evidence, and, on February 18, 1972, filed suit in the United States District Court for the Southern District of York.

The plaintiffs in the suit were eight named residents of PSS, represented by their nearest relatives or guardians. They filed the suit on behalf of a "class" consisting of all "present and future" residents of PSS.

The named defendants were: Abram Steinberg, M.D., commissioner of Mental Health; Susan Isaacs, M.D., deputy commissioner of Mental Health; Paul Boudreau, Ph.D., assistant commissioner for Mental Retardation; and Robert Lowry, M.D., superintendent.

The suit was brought under the Civil Rights Act of 1871, which forbids any state official, acting "under color of state law," from depriving any citizen of the United States of the "rights, privileges and immunities" secured by the United States Constitution. The Civil Rights Act had once been used primarily by blacks in southern states to obtain damages for, and injunctive relief from, acts of discrimination, but had been used increasingly by other groups in other regions to secure protection against unconstitutional state action. The theory of the Carter complaint was that conditions at PSS violated two constitutional rights of the plaintiffs: (1) freedom from "cruel and unusual punishment" guaranteed by the Eighth Amendment and (2) protection against being deprived of "liberty" without "due process of law" under the Fourteenth Amendment.

In support of these claims, the plaintiffs made over 100 factual allegations taking up some 36 pages of the complaint.

As relief, in addition to asking the court to declare that various legal rights of the plaintiffs had been violated, the complaint asked the court to make the following orders:

1. Permanently enjoin the defendants from operating and maintaining the Pendleton State School in a manner infringing upon the constitutional rights of the plaintiffs and the class they represent.
2. Order the defendants to submit for the court's approval a comprehensive plan for the maintenance of an adequate facility or facilities for the treatment and maintenance of the plaintiffs and the class they represent which will protect their rights and privileges or exceed standards set forth by the Accreditation Council for Facilities for the Mentally Retarded, AAMD.
3. Order defendants to prepare within a reasonable time for the court's approval a comprehensive constitutionally acceptable plan to provide adequate treatment for all patients confined to Pendleton State School.

DEFENSE STRATEGY

Under York state law, the exclusive authority to defend a lawsuit against state officials is vested in the elected attorney general. The attorney general in February of 1972 was William Flanagan. Flanagan, elected to a four-year term in 1970, was something of an enigma. Long active in Democratic politics in York, Flanagan had never been part of the Democratic Party establishment. His support came primarily from a group of small businessmen with conservative leanings. Flanagan was a highly successful criminal defense lawyer with a magnetic personality and a brilliant mind. York liberals had at one time fiercely opposed Flanagan because of his stands on capital punishment (supportive) and abortion (opposed), but their opposition softened somewhat in

1970 when he ran against an arch-conservative blueblood Republican.

After his election, much to everyone's surprise, Flanagan appointed several extremely liberal young lawyers to important positions in his office. One of them was Neil Greene, a prominent civil rights attorney in York, whom Flanagan appointed as head of the attorney general's "Government Division," the unit responsible for defending suits against state agencies and officials. It was to Greene that Flanagan assigned the responsibility for defending *Carter v. Steinberg*.

The attorney general's control over defense strategy meant, as a practical matter, that he could decide whether to contest any claim, attempt to negotiate a resolution, or concede it. If he contested a legal claim, he had complete discretion to decide how strenuously to fight and the terms of any settlement. It was for the purpose of planning defense strategy that Greene called a meeting with the defendants shortly after the complaint was filed.

The meeting was held on February 23 in Commissioner Steinberg's office. In attendance were Greene, Steinberg, Isaacs, Boudreau and Lowry. Greene began by explaining that the plaintiffs' claims were based primarily on two legal theories that he called the "freedom from harm" theory and the "right to treatment" theory. The "freedom from harm" theory derived from the context of prison law: subjecting a convict to conditions which offended "prevailing standards of human decency" amounted to a "cruel and unusual punishment" in violation of the Eighth Amendment to the U.S. Constitution. On the basis of this theory, federal courts had recently condemned conditions prevailing in several prisons, such as overcrowding, brutality, inferior food, and inadequate protection, recreation, ventilation or other environmental conditions.

The second, or "right to treatment," theory was based on the due process of the Fourteenth Amendment ("no person shall be deprived of . . . liberty . . . without due process of law"). This provision had been used by courts in several recent cases to require state mental hospitals to provide treatment to involuntarily committed patients. The courts' reasoning was that a person not guilty of a crime could not be committed to a mental hospital ("deprived" of his "liberty") without being given treatment[3] so that he might eventually be released. While this legal theory had been used mostly by individual patients seeking treatment or release, a federal court in Ala-

[3]"Treatment," the courts had said, included not only decent living conditions (also guaranteed by the "right to freedom from harm"), but also individualized diagnosis and therapeutic services.

bama had recently used the theory, in a "class action" brought by all patients of a mental hospital, to require drastic improvements in staffing and services at the hospital.

Greene was careful to point out that the reach of both legal theories was very uncertain. The Supreme Court had never expressly approved either, and neither theory had been applied to state schools for the retarded. It was not clear, for example, whether the "cruel and unusual punishment" clause applied outside of the criminal context. Nor was it clear that a "right to treatment" would be extended to voluntarily admitted patients (only about 21 percent of Pendleton residents had been committed to PSS by courts; the rest had been "voluntarily" admitted by their families). The problem with this voluntary-involuntary distinction was that a court might find that from the *resident's* point of view, the admission had not been voluntary. Or a court might find that in a state without meaningful community-based treatment alternatives, institutionalization could never be considered truly "voluntary."

"It's a tough one to call," concluded Greene. "I'd figure the odds of winning an argument that the 'freedom from harm' theory doesn't apply to state schools to be about 30 to 40 percent. I'd give us an even chance to win an argument that only those residents who were court-committed have a "right to treatment."

"What happens if we fight?" asked Isaacs.

"The case will go to trial eventually. Preparation for trial will take a long time. The plaintiffs will want to interview lots of employees and residents at Pendleton, bring in a lot of experts to look the place over, that sort of thing."

"Can they do that? We can't run a school with people crawling all over it," Lowry protested.

"Yeah, within reasonable limits, they have a right to get access to people and places necessary to build their case."

"What happens at trial?"

"They'll put a lot of people on the stand—expert witnesses, parents, maybe some sympathetic staff, maybe even some residents—who will all swear that the place is a disaster area. We'll cross-examine them and put on our own witnesses, including, I suppose, you people, who will swear that the place really isn't so bad, that we're making various improvements, etcetera."

"Then what?"

"Well, the judge makes rulings on the facts—there's no jury in a case like this—and on the legal questions. If he finds in favor of the plaintiffs, then he'll have to decide what to order us to do to fix the place up. I expect that the first thing he'll do will be to give us something like 60 days to draw up a plan showing how we propose to remedy all the things he's found wrong with the place. Then the plaintiffs will tear the plan apart, and we'll do a lot of negotiating, with the judge breathing down our necks. Finally, we'll either negotiate a plan and get it approved by the judge—that's called a 'consent order'—or the judge will write his own order. If this case ends up anything like the Alabama case, the final order may have all kinds of specifics in it—like how many nurses you gotta hire, how many hours of recreation you gotta provide each week, how many square feet are required per resident, and so forth."

"How can we agree to that sort of thing if we don't have the money in our budgets?"

"Easy. You basically agree to try to get it. The implicit—or sometimes explicit—threat is that if you don't, the judge will close the place down. And just to make sure that you are doing whatever you *can* do, the judge may appoint what's sometimes called a 'monitor'—some outside expert who has complete run of the place, who goes around and checks up on what's going on."

"Has a judge ever really closed down a state institution?"

"Not really. They often threaten to but they tend to be pretty lenient, especially if the hang-up is money. On the other hand, if a judge catches a defendant refusing to carry out an order that *is* within his power—such as requiring a doctor's approval before drugs are administered to patients, or discontinuing 'gang showers'—he may slap a contempt citation on him."

"You mean throw him in jail?"

"Unlikely. More likely a civil fine. And even that's rare. Courts usually forgive the fine if the defendant shapes up quickly. In some school desegregation cases, the courts have put up with incredible foot-dragging!"

"How long could this whole process take?"

"Well, if we fight them all the way, it'll probably be at least a year until the case is tried, then maybe six to ten months before a final decree is entered. Then we can take an appeal to the Court of Appeals. That may take another year."

"Who's paying for this lawsuit? Can these guys afford the legal fees?"

"I don't know. A case like this could cost $25,000 to $100,000 in legal fees, easy. The Friends organization has some money, but those folks aren't well-to-do. I know Carter had trouble finding a lawyer to take the case. The guy who finally took it, Harrington, has a small office and needs business. I bet he's taken the suit just to get publicity—he probably realizes that if the thing drags on, he'll be working for nothing.''

"Maybe we can outlast them.''

"That's hard to say. Of course, I can't speak for Flanagan, but our office is pretty busy. And if the court things we've been guilty of 'bad faith'—dragging our feet—he may award attorney's fees to the plaintiffs' attorneys. Another problem is that the U.S. Justice Department sometimes intervenes in these cases on the plaintiff's side and helps out with the costs of trial preparation.''

"Do we have to go through a long drawn-out trial if we think these legal theories don't apply to this situation in the first place?''

"Well, we could file a 'motion to dismiss' which challenges the legal theory of the lawsuit. The judge would probably schedule an argument on the motion within a few weeks and make a decision within a few weeks after that. That way, we would at least find out what he thinks about the *legal* theory. Of course, he might just reserve ruling on the motion until the evidence is in, since it's sometimes hard to decide legal issues without seeing all the facts.''

"If he rules against us on the motion to dismiss, do we automatically lose the case?''

"No. Even if the judge rules that these legal theories do apply to this kind of institution, the plaintiffs still have to prove that this institution does *in fact* fail to meet minimal constitutional standards.''

"How likely is that?''

"I don't know. I haven't seen Pendleton first-hand. And anyway, the 'harm' and 'treatment' standards are so fuzzy that the trial judge has almost limitless discretion in applying them to complicated fact patterns.''

"What do you know about the judge? How is he likely to handle this?''

"Hard to say. The case has been assigned to Judge Morgan. Morgan's been on the bench about ten years—he's regarded as quiet, tough, competent, a good trial judge—likes to move cases along, pressure the parties to settle. No big judicial activist or social reformer. A liberal Republican before his appointment. I can't say how he'll go on this one.''

"So you want our recommendation on whether to defend and how to defend?''

"Yeah, generally. I've got to decide whether we're gonna fight this one all the way or go for a quick settlement, and, if so, on what terms. Specifically I've gotta decide how to answer the plaintiffs' complaint. The usual practice is to file a general de-

nial, denying all of the plaintiffs' claims. The basic alternative is to 'confess error' on either or both of the legal claims and let the court enter a judgment against you. Then, we've gotta decide whether to file a motion to dismiss or not. We can also offer various procedural objections at an early stage. For example, in order to bring suit as a 'class action,' the plaintiffs have to get the court to 'certify' that the class is appropriate. Among other things, the named plaintiffs have to be representative of the class as a whole. Superintendent Lowry tells me that all eight plaintiffs are severely retarded adults who were involuntarily committed to Pendleton and who live in the so-called 'back wards' where conditions are worst. The children and less severely retarded residents—mostly 'voluntary admits'—have better living conditions, get more services, and have a far better chance of being transferred out. We can say that they wouldn't support the suit because their living conditions are okay and because they'd rather see the department spend money on community programs than on the institution.''

"What do we gain by opposing certification of the class?''

"Well, time, for one thing. Technical defenses can take time to resolve. Second, if the plaintiffs can't sue on behalf of a class, they'll have to be content bringing suit just on their own behalf. It might make it easier to settle if we can just agree to take better care of a small group of residents than all twelve hundred. Besides Carter might not get much outside support if it's just him and a few friends suing.''

"Is that all?''

"Oh, one other thing. The plaintiffs have filed a motion for a preliminary injunction which asks for the court to order three things immediately. The first is to forbid any new admissions to Pendleton pending final resolution of the lawsuit. The second is to forbid the superintendent from transferring any resident *out* of Pendleton without the court's approval. The third is that, within 30 days, DMH conduct a medical and psychiatric examination of every resident and develop an 'individualized treatment plan' for each one. I need your advice on how to respond to these motions.''

"My God, do you realize what it'd take to do a complete medical and psychiatric work-up on every resident? We don't have the manpower,'' said Steinberg. "And what about all the other state schools. How are they affected by all this?''

"Not directly, since this suit involves Pendleton only. But who's to say what might happen next.''

How should the Pendleton State School respond to the lawsuit? Should it confess error and settle, or fight it? If it decides to fight, should it fight on procedural grounds, arguing that the class is improperly constituted, or should it go directly to the substance of its defense? And when and if it gets to a substantive argument, should it take issue with the plaintiffs' claim about what the Constitution requires (under the "due process" clause of the Fifth and Fourteenth Amendments, and the Eighth Amendment's bar against cruel and unusual punishment) or should it contest the plaintiffs' factual assertions about treatment at Pendleton, or both?

These are the kinds of questions that must be answered in developing a litigation strategy. There are advantages and disadvantages to each decision—involving tradeoffs between risks and returns, immediate costs of settlement versus costs of a prolonged trial, and the potential costs of an adverse judgment on future litigation involving Pendleton School and other state institutions.

How to answer them? I often ask my students to take on the roles of Neil Greene (Assistant Attorney General), Paul Boudreau (Assistant Commissioner for Mental Retardation), Susan Isaacs (Deputy Commissioner of Mental Health), Abram Steinberg (Commissioner), and Robert Lowry (Superintendent of Pendleton School).

As they debate their litigation strategy, it soon becomes apparent that they cannot agree because they have sharply different stakes in the outcome. Greene is concerned about the cost to the state of capitulating to the plaintiffs, and he is also worried about a damaging precedent that might encourage other potential litigants in other state institutions. Boudreau wants Pendleton State School to be closed. An adverse judgment in this case, which would require the state to spend large sums of money to upgrade the institution if it wished to continue to keep it open, is just what Boudreau would like. Isaacs wants more resources from the state legislature but does not want the institution to close; for her, an ideal solution might be a settlement in which the state committed more funds. Steinberg is probably concerned about negative publicity, suggesting that he has not run the Department of Mental Health as he should. As the one closest to elected politicians, he wants to avoid embarrassing the Governor or putting too much pressure on the legislature (unless, of course, such pressure is part of the Governor's overall legislative agenda). Lowry, the Superintendent of Pendleton, wants to maintain the independence of his institution—free from meddling judges, bureaucrats, and politicians.

This lawsuit—like most lawsuits—brings into the open these conflicting goals and differing perspectives. It forces the participants to clarify what they deem to be the mission of the institution and of the agency that oversees it.

After extensive debate, my students discover something else. Neil Greene, and Assistant Attorney General, is in a particularly powerful position. He understands the formal legal process better than the others (I usually ask a law student or lawyer to take his role), and he is thus able to demonstrate the wisdom of his recommended strategy more persuasively than anyone else. He also is cloaked with more authority than the others for protecting the state's interest, now that the litigation has begun. None of the others can effectively weigh the costs of a damaging precedent to the state; none of the others is accountable for minimizing such costs.

There is a final discovery. None of the participants, with the exception of Paul Boudreau, is interested in fundamentally changing the system of custodial care. Indeed, this is the reason why Pendleton School became the object of litigation in the first place, and why it has proven so resistant to investigations and exposes over the years.

Care for the retarded is neither professionally nor politically popular. Mental retardation has been the poor stepchild of the Department, which is dominated by people who are more committed to the provision of mental health services. Pendleton School, like the other custodial institutions for the retarded, is not even directly linked to the Division of Mental Retardation; supervisors report to regional administrators with responsibility for both mental retardation and mental health services.

Mentally retarded adults do not constitute an important political constituency. Their parents could be a force for change, but thus far they have been unorganized and their efforts diffuse. The broad public is relatively unaware of the problem and relatively uninterested; most voters probably want mentally retarded people to remain out of sight; their presence on the streets can be disturbing. The public wants them to be treated decently but also wants to spend no more than is absolutely necessary on their upkeep. The major political constituency in favor of keeping Pendleton School open, and in much the same condition as it has always been, comprises citizens who live in the area of the school and are employed directly or indirectly in maintaining it.

In other words, there is no political mandate for change. The system is stable: The public, its elected representatives, appointed officials, and key constituencies are all content to let things continue as is. This is the type of situation in which courts typically become involved. Only judges can provide a mandate for change, because they are accountable for protecting basic rights. Public servants like Paul Boudreau are relatively powerless to effect change when politics and administration are so closely aligned against it.

Under these circumstances, the litigation can also serve as a device for organizing the one political constituency that could keep pressure on for change in the future: the parents. Just as David Goldman understood the power of a lawsuit to mobilize a previously dispersed group, Richard Carter (the instigator of the Pendleton suit) may understand the real role of his class action. Thus, he will not want to settle the case for the sake of achieving short-term improvements in the school; his litigation strategy is probably to gain as much publicity as possible and to focus the energies of many other parents of the mentally retarded on the long-term goal of achieving better care (inside and outside the institution). Thus a protracted lawsuit, in which the facts of custody at Pendleton State School are fully aired, could help mobilize political pressure for change. Were the state to pursue a litigation strategy based on procedural or legal objections, Carter's own strategy might never get off the ground.

This situation presents an interesting contrast to that of Robert Hermann in the Bureau of Security and Consular Affairs, or of Phil Heymann at the Criminal Division of the Justice Department. In those instances, part of the challenge was to create a sustainable mandate for action where there was no mandate to begin with. Here, as Paul Boudreau discovers, there *is* a strong and sustainable mandate. The challenge he faces (as does Richard Carter and the court) is how to *reverse* that mandate—how to destabilize the system and create a new mandate for accomplishing something very different.

chapter 6

The Media

The public gets most of its information about government from journalists. Like judges, journalists are in the business of interpreting what public servants have done—giving their actions meaning and context, deciding which facts are most relevant, and shaping a story around these interpretations. Journalists thus perform an important oversight function, but they do more: By choosing to write about certain events and not others, highlighting particular facts and downplaying others, analogizing what has occurred to other events, and suggesting why the public should want to know about these occurrences, journalists implicitly pass judgment. Even the most seemingly neutral of news reports carries with it subtle normative judgments about whether public servants have done their job appropriately, and why the public should care.

So important are journalists to the democratic process, in fact, that the media has been dubbed a "fourth branch" of American government, keeping careful check on the other three. It is difficult to conceive of a democratic system of government without a free and uninhibited press. Like participants in the three official branches, journalists engage in continuous bargaining over political agendas and policies—threatening, cajoling, and trading information with their compatriots in the three official branches. But journalists understand their constituents' needs differently from government officials who occupy the other branches, and journalists thus seek different things. Above all, they want *news* and they want it quickly and accurately. By "news" they mean new information relevant to an issue about which the public is likely to care. Speed is essential, for the information may otherwise become irrelevant, and the facts supporting it must be accurate if the public is to continue to trust journalists as overseers of public servants.

Public servants want from journalists accurate reporting on what government is doing. But public servants' definition of accuracy may be somewhat different from the definition used by journalists, who understand accuracy in terms of particular facts—when, where, and how. Public servants understand accuracy in terms of providing the public an accurate *impression* of what has happened and what is at stake. These different perspectives on accuracy can cause no end of trouble, because both are founded, ultimately, upon subjective judgments. Particular facts are meaningless without a context to which they are made relevant, but the context is always a matter of opinion. A public servant who disagrees with the way a journalist has described a given program or policy may feel that the journalist has been inaccurate, when the journalist has simply seen things differently.

Given these inherent tensions, how should public servants and journalists treat one another? What do they owe one another? Consider the case of the neutron bomb, and imagine that you are the Secretary of Defense, Harold Brown, on the morning that the story breaks.

The Press and the Neutron Bomb

PRELUDE TO THE STORM

At 5:30 a.m. on June 6, 1977, Major General Joseph Bratton was awakened by a phone call that marked the beginning of a series of extraordinary events for him and other officials concerned with the production of the "neutron bomb." Bratton, who was Director of Military Applications for the Energy Research and Development Administration (ERDA)—the successor to the Atomic Energy Commission—was, as he put it, "responsible for all the research, development, and production of nuclear weapons in the United States." Although Bratton was accustomed to pressure, he was "totally taken by surprise" by the call he received that morning from his chief aide, Major Andrews. "I thought I'd wake you," Andrews began, "and warn you." Have you seen today's *Washington Post*?" "No," Bratton replied, "mine hasn't even been delivered yet." "Well,

there's a front page article," Andrews continued, "on neutron warheads being buried in the ERDA budget. Undoubtedly, you're going to get a call from General Starbird [the ERDA Assistant Administrator and Bratton's boss] on it any minute now." Within the hour, "an extremely upset" Starbird had called. Starbird's congressional testimony earlier that year on upcoming production in the atomic stockpile had not been "scrubbed" (when declassified) of a reference to enhanced radiation (ER) warheads—the so-called neutron bomb—which the *Post*'s reporter, Walter Pincus, had picked up as the first public disclosure of the production of neutron weapons. Neither Starbird nor Bratton thought the existence of ER technology to be classified, and as they hadn't disclosed the technical characteristics of the weapons, Starbird "couldn't imagine," Bratton recalled, "why this had come out as a front page story. Starbird was extremely security conscious and said the Defense

This is a summary introduction for a case written by David Whitman under the supervision of Jonathan Moore and Martin Linsky at the John F. Kennedy School of Government, Harvard University. Support was provided by the Charles H. Revson Foundation.

Copyright © 1984 by the President and Fellows of Harvard College.

Department was going to be very upset about this— which indeed they were.''

Before, however, a year had passed, Starbird's concern about a classification slip-up had been dramatically eclipsed. As Zbigniew Brzezinski, President Carter's National Security Advisor, later put it: "The *Post* article touched off a political explosion that reverberated throughout the United States and Europe." In April 1978, following mass protests in several West European nations against the neutron bomb, and heated internal debate within the North Atlantic Treaty Organization (NATO), President Carter decided to defer deployment and production of neutron weapons. It was subsequently reported that Carter's controversial decision was due partly to his reluctance to embrace a bomb that the public understood to ''kill people but leave buildings intact.''

That eerie impression of the neutron bomb is a paraphrase of a description of it by Walter Pincus from the first of a series of articles he wrote during the summer of 1977. Several members of Congress and most quarters of the journalism world hailed Pincus' stories as outstanding examples of investigative reporting that had brought a worrisome weapons development to the attention of the public. His critics, on the other hand (at the Defense Department and elsewhere), lamented the stories as errant sensationalism that had pried upon the Pandora's box within the NATO alliance, leading to a weakening of the U.S. nuclear deterrant. But both his supporters and critics within the federal bureaucracy did appear to agree on one thing. As Harold Brown, the Secretary of Defense, later summed up: ''Without the Pincus articles, they [neutron warheads] would have been deployed and nobody would have noticed.''

After the appearance of Pincus' story, the tale of Carter's decision to defer deployment of the neutron bomb—and the role that the press played in that decision—breaks down roughly into four brief periods. First, there was the initial shock of the story in June and July 1977, during which time the question of producing the neutron bomb received substantial attention in the U.S. press and the U.S. Senate. Second, between August and December 1977, the controversy over the weapon shifted from the question of production to one of deployment and expanded to West Europe. During this period, U.S. officials pursued quiet diplomacy with the West Europeans and sought to develop a more aggressive public relations campaign to respond to public perceptions of the bomb. The third stage occurred between December 1977 and March 1978, when U.S. and European officials privately negotiated a deployment plan,

while implementing several actions to quiet European hysteria over the bomb and counter Soviet propaganda on the weapon. Finally, at the end of March, President Carter unexpectedly rejected the deployment plan, prompting leaks from administration officials who were apparently seeking to influence the President's decision (or the coverage of the decision) when it was announced on April 7, 1978. Throughout the administration's handling of the issue, administration officials explored, but never pursued vigorously, a wide variety of avenues both to influence press coverage of the bomb and to counter public misperceptions of the weapon that the coverage reportedly had provoked.

TIDINGS

Despite ERDA's conviction that ER weapons were noncontroversial, Pincus' was not the first such story to grace the *Post*'s front page. That honor, the first public account of ER weapons, went to a relatively mild story published in July 1959, relating that

> A radically new type of weapon . . . is being discussed in military circles. . . . The new weapon is a bomb that would produce as much man-killing radiation as a large weapon yet have the destructive blast of a small weapon and the radioactive fallout of an even smaller one.

A flurry of coverage about ER weapons—which were then being developed but had never been exploded— followed in major publications. Not surprisingly, the vision of a ''man-killing'' bomb that left property intact stirred some moral consternation. On the one hand, the neutron bomb was defended as being more ''moral'' than other nuclear weapons because it was more likely to restrict injuries to combatants; on the other hand, it was condemned as a ghastly capitalist invention by religious figures and Soviet leaders (Nikita Krushchev himself spoke forcefully on the subject.)

In strictly military terms, the advantage of ER weapons was felt to be that they would be a more credible tactical deterrent than ordinary battlefield nuclear weapons (intended, generally, for use in Europe against Soviet tank forces) which were dirtier and less ''surgical,'' and thus perhaps less likely to be employed when needed. As the *Post* story put it,

> It is a bomb that would be capable of killing an enemy force without too much physical damage

to an area without the fallout that would make the region uninhabitable after the attack. . . . Since the physical damage and fallout from such a weapon would be small, it would open up the possibility of fighting a war on friendly or home soil.

The attraction of ER weapons was such to spur some troublesome opposition from scientists and Congressmen to Kennedy's nuclear test ban treaty, but Kennedy and his Secretary of Defense, Robert McNamara, resisted and eventually overcame it. The neutron bomb—tested successfully just before the treaty was signed in 1963—was put on the back burner, and disappeared entirely from the public eye.

THE STORY BREAKS

Pincus was singularly qualified to bring it back. In 1969, as staff head of a Senate Foreign Relations subcommittee, he's participated in a groundbreaking examination of the role of theater nuclear weapons. The unclassified subcommittee report, co-authored by Pincus, stated:

It was clear [from our trips] that many years had passed since the political implications of the placement of these weapons has been so considered. . . . In almost every one of these countries a veil of secrecy hides the presence of such weapons. Nowhere is this veil stronger than in the United States. Most people here are unaware of the fact that United States tactical nuclear warheads have been and are stationed in countries all around the world.

Pincus was not only disturbed by the secrecy surrounding tactical nuclear weapons but also by the apparent mindlessness with which they had proliferated. As he wrote in the *New Republic* (of which he became Executive Editor in 1973), "within the military services over the past 20 years, tactical nukes have become accepted as if they were just another bomb, shell, or mine." He later pursued the issue at the *New Yorker*, where he wrote on the effects of nuclear tests, before joining the *Post*'s national staff in 1976. Like other journalists, he was unaware that the military had once again decided to press on with ER weapons, and he was both surprised and excited when he read Starbird's 1977 testimony referencing the ER warhead for the Lance. After a handful of calls to public affairs spokesmen and weapons experts, he wrote his June 6 story. Cast very much in

the mold of the 1960s accounts of ER weapons, it was the most important and controversial of all he wrote on the subject, and was set off by *Post* staffer Robert Williams' striking headline: "Neutron Killer Warhead Buried in ERDA Budget."

The United States is about to begin production of its first nuclear battlefield weapon specifically designed to kill people through the release of neutrons rather than to destroy military installations through heat and blast.

Funds to start building an "enhanced radiation" warhead for the 56-mile range Lance missile are buried in the Energy Research and Development Administration portion of the $10.2 billion public works appropriations bill now before Congress.

The new warhead is the first practical use of the so-called neutron bomb theory which government scientists have been working on for many years. According to one nuclear weapons expert, the new warhead "cuts down on blast and heat and thus total destruction, leaving buildings and tanks standing. But the great quantities of neutrons it releases kill people."

A heavy dose of neutrons attacks the central nervous system, according to "The Effects of Nuclear Weapons," published by the old Atomic Energy Commission. There is "almost immediate incapacitation" with convulsions, intermittent stupor and a lack of muscle coordination. "Death is certain in a few hours to several days," according to the book.

In testimony March 17 before a House Appropriations subcommittee, Alfred D. Starbird, assistant ERDA administrator for national security said that with the new Lance warhead, "You reduce the blast effect and get the kill radius you want through enhanced radiation."

The Lance warhead is the first in a new generation of tactical mini-nukes that have been sought by Army field commanders for many years. The leading advocates: the series of American generals who have commanded the North American Treaty Organization theater.

They have argued that the 7,000 nuclear warheads now in Europe are old, have too large a nuclear yield and thus would not be used in a war.

With lower yields and therefore less possible collateral damage to civilian populated areas, these commanders have argued, the new mini-nukes are more credible as deterrents because they just might be used on the battlefield without leading to automatic nuclear escalation.

Under the nuclear warhead production system, a President must personally give the production order. President Ford, according to informed sources, signed the order for the enhanced radiation Lance warhead.

That Lance already has regular nuclear warheads and is deployed with NATO forces in Europe.

The new Lance warhead is one of a half-dozen nuclear devices on which production is scheduled to start next year.

ERDA, as successor to the Atomic Energy Commission, finances and supervises research and production of nuclear warheads; the Defense Department pays for the delivery systems.

Thus funds for nuclear warheads is in the public works ERDA money bill that is to be taken up by the House Rules Committee today. Since the ERDA authorization has yet to pass Congress, a special rule is needed to permit voting first on its appropriation which is due to come up on the House floor June 13.

THE REACTION AT HOME

The making of neutron warheads into a major news story in June was catalyzed through the persistence of Pincus and the *Post*'s editorial board. On the day that Pincus' first story appeared, Jack Robertson, one of Senator Hatfield's (R-Ore.) aides, brought the story in to show it to Hatfield. Hatfield read the story, was "very alarmed" by it, and two days later introduced an amendment to strike funds for ER weapons from the appropriations bill. At the same time, other senators and several members of the House privately wrote angry letters to the Pentagon in which they asserted that DOD officials had attempted to conceal the development of neutron weapons from the Congress.

On June 7 Pincus wrote a follow-up story containing the White House's denial of involvement. The next day the *Post* editorialized that the President should reject the neutron warhead, likening "radiation kill" to chemical warfare. The following day Pincus reported that Senator Hatfield was seeking to bar funds for "the new neutron killer warhead" and two weeks later Pincus reported that the President and DOD were opposed to the Hatfield amendment,

and were pressing instead for the Senate to approve funds for the new "killer warhead."

Pincus' stories finally began to draw substantial attention in the national media when NBC News, where Pincus was also employed, ran a film clip on June 17 (obtained from the Armed Forces Radiology Research Institute) showing monkeys irradiated with a heavy dose of neutron radiation, with gruesome results. On June 22 Pincus ran an article on the film clip, and the next day he received a call from someone "who felt the switch to neutron weapons was much broader than had previously been portrayed and that that development ought really to be questioned." Pincus' source informed him that the Lance ER was only part of a plan to shift all nuclear artillery to an enhanced radiation basis and that the budget included funds for production of an ER 8″ shell and research for an ER 155 mm shell. Fitting an ER capacity into an 8″ shell was something of a technological marvel, which was classified and which officials at the labs and DOD felt confident the Russians hadn't figured out how to do yet.

On June 24 the *Post* led the paper with Pincus' story on the 8″ and 155 mm ER shells. The next day the *Post* ran another front page Pincus story on Pentagon efforts to keep the development of ER warheads secret and the following day the *Post* ran a second editorial, urging Congress to support the Hatfield amendment and asserting that "the whole thing [DOD's handling of the issue] has the look of a black bag job." Coming only days before the floor debate on Hatfield's amendment, the *Post* coverage helped galvanize an onslaught of press coverage in every medium.

PRESS INTEREST

In addition to keeping the issue alive, Pincus' articles had a definitive impact on the character of subsequent coverage. In particular, it is difficult to overstate the frequency with which neutron warheads were described in the media as "the bomb that killed people but left buildings (or property) standing." All AP and UPI stories employed the description during June and July and virtually every major newspaper in the country used it as well. On radio and television the reaction was similar. The nation's leading broadcasters, reporters, and talk-show hosts—Bruce Morton, John Chancellor, David Brinkley, Floyd Kalber, Walter Cronkite, Dan Rather, David Hartman, Tom Brokaw, Phil Jones, Bettina Gregory—were among the many who described neutron weapons in such terms. At the same time, the repulsive effects of radiation poisoning that Pincus had described in his first story were also widely quoted, usually in similarly clinical language. The moral indignation that this news coverage spurred was expressed most forcibly in the op-ed columns, where writers like Mary McGrory, Jake McCarthy, Mike Royko, Claude Lewis, Gary Wills, Louis Blumenfield, Russell Baker, and Art Buchwald treated the bomb as a sign of the warped mentality of the munition makers, a kind of twilight zone invention that had been designed to leave place settings intact (surrounded by the skeletons of the diners).

A number of other columnists, chiefly conservative ones (e.g., George Will, Peter Reich, James Kilpatrick, C.L. Sulzberger, Patrick Buchanan, and Jeffrey Hart) took the view that killing by radiation was no more immoral than killing by blast and, that if anything, neutron weapons were more "moral" than other nuclear weapons because they limited collateral damage. There were also a number of columnists who didn't treat the neutron bomb primarily as a moral issue (Carl Rowan, Herbert Scoville, William Rusher, George Will, Edward Teller, Richard Rovere, C.L. Sulzberger among them) but rather as one that raised questions about how to best prevent nuclear war. Was the bomb more likely to raise the "nuclear threshold" by deterring the Russians from moving into Western Europe, or was it more likely to lower the threshold by blurring the distinction between conventional and nuclear weapons, feeding the notion that a nuclear weapon could be used "surgically" in a limited nuclear war?

These accounts—news and editorial alike—treated the neutron bomb *sui generis*, as vastly different from other nuclear weapons. There was, for example, no discussion of the fact that low yield fission weapons also killed by radiation, or that many of the tactical nuclear weapons already deployed in Europe had both more blast and radiation than the neutron warheads. There was also little mention that the neutron bomb would be a small part of the theater nuclear arsenal.

THE SENATE DEBATE

The media coverage of the neutron bomb helped fuel a contentious debate in the Senate, and, not surprisingly, was hailed by opponents of neutron weapons and derided by its proponents. Senator Sam Nunn (D-Ga.), who was a staunch supporter of neutron weapons, stated on the Senate floor that "what we are really saying [in this debate] is that Congress is overwhelmed with technical information on matters and that unless it [information of neutron weapons] appears on the front pages of the newspaper it does not get the attention of Congress. This is an unfortunate state of affairs. . . . the misperceptions regarding this particular weapon are more widespread than those surrounding any other weapon I have seen since I have been in the Senate." Opponents of the bomb, like Senator Hatfield, took the contrary view, arguing that "the only time we found out the full impact of what this kind of weapons system would do is when we read the newspapers. . . . I want to commend the news media for extending the knowledge—what little we have of it—to the citizens of this country in a relatively short time."

On July 13, the Senate defeated the Hatfield amendment 58–38, approving instead an amendment by Senators Robert Byrd (D-W.Va.) and Howard Baker (R-Tenn.) that prohibited funds from being used to build ER weapons until the President certified to Congress they were in the national interest; following that notification Congress would have 45 days to disapprove the weapon, but could do so only by a concurrent resolution of both houses.

THE REACTION SPREADS TO EUROPE

Passions over the neutron bomb began to subside in the U.S. after the Senate vote, but the debate over the bomb in Europe was just beginning to heat up. The immediate response to Pincus' stories in Europe during June was similar to what occurred in the U.S.; i.e., not much attention was devoted to the subject either by the government or the press. Pincus' story reportedly stirred some suspicions on the part of the West German Chancellor, Helmut Schmidt, whose poor personal relationship with Jimmy Carter had already been established. Lou Finch, the NATO desk officer in the PM bureau, recalled,

> Sometime after the Pincus story broke, a German general, who was a close confidant of Schmidt's, told me that when Schmidt first read the story his reaction was that the White House—and not a lowly White House staffer but the President or Brzezinski—had leaked the story as part of a continuing vendetta between him and Carter. Schmidt suspected Carter was hyping the threat and trying to do so in a way that would embarrass him.

In early July, when the U.S. Senate began its debate on the Hatfield amendment, the communist media and West European press started editorializing about the subject. On July 15, two days after the Senate had approved ER funding, Carter's ambassador to the U.N., Andrew Young, told correspondents in Geneva that "were I a member of Congress I would have certainly strongly opposed and worked against the development of [the neutron] weapon. It does not make sense to spend all that money for killing folks." Although Young's comments threw some kindling on the fire, the debate was not really ignited in Europe until July 17, when the German weekly *Vorwaerts* published an article by Egon Bahr under the headline "Is Mankind Going Crazy?" Bahr had a reputation for innovative, sober analysis and was a pivotal figure in the liberal wing of the SPD, the ruling party of the tenuous coalition government headed up by Schmidt. Bahr's article picked up the themes of Pincus' initial story, stating: "Reduced to a simple formula [the neutron] weapon causes no, or only slight, material damage, but 'cleanly' kills man. This is to be the final progress. Is mankind about to go crazy? . . . The neutron bomb is a symbol of the perversion of thought." Bahr's view of the neutron bomb as "a symbol of mental perversion" soon became a catch phrase for the burgeoning anti-neutron bomb movement and a focus of editorial debate, particularly in West Germany. His article tended to portray the neutron bomb along the lines of a "Real Estate Bomb," and his piece, along with those of Walter Pincus, was widely quoted and set the tone for much of the European press coverage.

Now, imagine that you are Harold Brown, Secretary of Defense, on the morning that the story about the neutron bomb appears in the *Washington Post*. What do you do?

There are tactical issues you must deal with immediately. For example, certain members of the press are already on the phone. Do you want to take the calls? Probably not, at least for now. You haven't yet thought out how you should respond. Nor have you coordinated your response with other officials who will be called as well—the chairman of the Joint Chiefs of Staff, the President's National Security Advisor, the President himself, other officials in the Department of Defense.

You will need to develop a coordinated response quickly. In addition, you must decide the form the response should take. Should there be a press conference? If so, who should preside? When should it occur—before you have contacted congressional leaders, European leaders, and others who will be substantially affected by the likely public response to this? If you do it before, they will be confused or insulted. If you do it after, you may be too late.

And what is to be the substance of the response? You and other members of the administration cannot deny that the United States is preparing enhanced radiation warheads, although you are deeply troubled by what you regard as the deceptive way they have been described in the *Post*'s story. The journalist—Walter Pincus—has been technically correct in stating that the neutron bomb would reduce the blast effect and kill people through radiation. But he failed to note that the radius of radiation is smaller than that of nuclear bombs, or that many of the tactical nuclear weapons already deployed in Europe have more blast and more radiation than the neutron warheads. Indeed, the whole point of the neutron bomb is to impose less damage upon civilian populated areas, so that it can be used on a battlefield without running the risk of nuclear escalation. And Pincus has emphasized the gruesome effects of neutron radiation while neglecting to mention the equally gruesome effects of low-yield fission weapons, which also kill by radiation.

Thus, in your view, Pincus has distorted the purpose of the neutron bomb, making it appear to be designed to kill civilian populations while saving buildings and factories, and he also has suggested a false distinction between the neutron bomb and other bombs. But how to inform the public of the truth, when this story has framed the issue in such a misleading way?

After pondering these tactical and substantive problems, my students usually decide that the administration's best approach is a quick and forceful repudiation of Pincus's article in a press conference that morning, hosted by the President. Then we role-play the press conference and the students discover some problems with this approach. First, the press corps is "loaded for bear," and all they want is for the President to confirm or deny the factual allegations contained in the Pincus story. They are not particularly interested in hearing what they consider to be the administration's "version" of the story. They may report the President's explanation for why the neutron bomb was developed but not the very different way in which the administration conceived of the project from the outset. Pincus's story has established the framework—the "news"; the remaining information involves the details.

Moreover, a presidential news conference suggests that the story is as important as Pincus and the *Post* think it is. It increases the stakes and alerts editors all over the nation that this is the big news of the day. It may also suggest defensiveness on the part of the administration. (What do they have to hide? Why are they so upset by this revelation?) And it puts the onus of responsibility directly on the shoulders of the President, where (especially if the administration comes out looking bad) the President may not want it to be.

Think again. Every news story with the potential for "catching on" in this way confirms to the public something that the public already suspects, or about which the public already is vaguely concerned. The administration would have less difficulty conveying its side of the story and thus shifting the public's understanding of the neutron bomb away from the way Pincus has portrayed it were the public not already suspicious. Pincus's story is powerful because it represents part of a larger story—the story *behind* the story—which the public (both here and in Europe) already believes. The story behind the story is about costly and diabolical weapons systems, conceived and developed in secret, designed to further an ill-defined and ill-considered military strategy. Pincus's revelations confirm this more deeply embedded story, building upon the distrust already in the air.

Whatever tactic Harold Brown or the entire administration embarks upon here must be responsive to this larger failing. The public cannot understand the real purpose of the neutron bomb unless or until the public (and its intermediaries within the press)) understands the context in which the neutron bomb is considered to be an appropriate weapon. And *this* understanding requires that the public first have a better appreciation of—and stronger commitment to—the nation's overall military strategy. Harold Brown and the Carter Administration have not yet given the public (or the press) a sufficiently compelling story behind the story. Instead, there have been vacillation, ambiguity, and tensions among high-level military advisors, amid rising costs. *This* is the context in which Pincus's story has taken hold.

The normal reaction of public servants to what they see as a deceptive or unfair account in the press is to lash out: Sometimes they resort to public criticism of the press; sometimes they try to stop unfavorable leaks to the press by individuals within their agencies; sometimes they fire the person in charge of press relations and hire someone who they believe can elicit more favorable press coverage; or they go on the offensive with their version of the facts. These responses, while understandable, often fail to deal with the heart of the matter.

Public servants should listen carefully to what the media are telling them. An unfavorable story represents important feedback; it signals that public servants (or their superiors or subordinates) may not be doing their jobs as the public wants and expects the jobs to be done. Or it suggests that the public does not adequately understand the purposes of these jobs or the constraints within which they are undertaken. In either case, the lines of accountability already are under severe strain.

chapter 7

Of Heat Conductors and Heat Shields

Most organizations—public or private—insulate themselves from what they consider to be too much outside interference. While they must be responsive to their clients, customers, or constituents, they must also have a certain degree of day-to-day autonomy if they are going to get anything done. Were their personnel continuously responsive to every demand coming from the outside, they would have no time to formulate and implement larger policies designed to respond to long-term needs. They would have no capacity to develop priorities and allocate their limited resources accordingly. They would always be putting out brush fires.

Public servants, in particular, are apt to expend energies putting out brushfires. As we have seen, they are accountable in so many different ways to so many different institutions and constituencies that their energies are easily diffused. They can be *too* responsive in too many directions at once. Public agencies have sought to overcome this endemic tendency by creating jobs whose incumbents are specially charged with responding to particular institutions and constituencies on the outside— legislators, the media, the courts, local communities, and interest groups. Jobs like these usually have the word "relations" in their titles, as in "Director of Legislative Relations," or "Office of Community Relations," or "Chief of Press Relations."

Public servants who hold these jobs mediate between the short-term demands of such outside groups and the longer-term strategies of the agency. This can be a subtle and difficult task. If people in such "relational" jobs lean too far in one direction and allow the outside forces to intrude too much, the agency cannot do its work. But if they lean too far in the other direction and provide too much protection for the agency, agency personnel may have difficulty discovering what their goals should be. The task of people in relational jobs, therefore, is to determine the right level and kind of responsiveness, and to help public servants on the inside maintain the right balance for themselves.

As Audrey Simmons discovers in the following case, the strategies employed by public servants in relational jobs help determine agency strategy as a whole.

Audrey Simmons and the FAA

On the outskirts of Atlantic City, New Jersey, stands a 5,000-acre Federal Aviation Administration (FAA) base. Known as NAFEC, or National Aviation Facilities Experimental Center, the base is a research center for issues relating to air traffic safety and control of the national airspace. In 1977, NAFEC employed nearly 1,500 people and was the area's largest employer. However, many employees were not local residents but technicians brought to NAFEC from other parts of the FAA. Unemployment in the area was high, particularly for minority groups. This situation, coupled with NAFEC's poor record of minority hiring, was the source of tensions between the local community and NAFEC.

Top personnel at NAFEC felt they could do little to alleviate the tensions. NAFEC already had a "temporary hire" program, in which local residents were trained for semi-skilled jobs and hired on a temporary basis; it had also instituted a cooperative education program with local colleges and universities geared to minority engineering and electronics students. NAFEC officials claimed that they hired as many local personnel as possible but that most of the jobs on the base required technical expertise which area residents lacked. Local leaders countered that NAFEC's efforts to find and train capable workers were insufficient, and that minorities were underrepresented in policymaking positions on the base.

The Trans Fair in the summer of 1977 brought matters to a head. An annual show featuring exhibits and displays dedicated to all aspects of aviation, the Trans Fair was sponsored by a private organization but held at NAFEC. The fair also provided many short-term work opportunities for local residents: setting up and taking down booths, running concessions, and performing other odd jobs. In the summer of 1977, nearly all these short-term jobs went to nonminority residents. The sponsors of the fair advertised for part-time help in a local newspaper but failed to advertise in publications widely circulated in the minority communities or to put up posters in these areas. By the time word reached the minority community that jobs were available, the jobs were gone. The angry community responded with a demonstration against the director of NAFEC, ridiculing NAFEC's claims of promoting affirmative action.

The man who bore the brunt of the community's anger was George Smith, the director of NAFEC. Smith was undecided as to what he could do to improve the situation. The base did employ an acting civil rights chief, Bill Jones, but Smith was uncomfortable with both Jones' philosophy and operating style. Jones saw his role as that of a community activist and had in the past encouraged the community to challenge NAFEC's actions. Following the outrage over the Trans Fair incident, Jones publicly blamed

This case was prepared by Beth DeHamel under the supervision of Stephanie Gould for use at the John F. Kennedy School of Government, Harvard University. Some names in the case have been altered. Funds for the development of this case and supporting documents were provided by the Office of Personnel Management and the Departments of Commerce, Defense, Health and Human Services, Housing and Urban Development, and Labor through OPM contract 61-80. This material may be reproduced by or for the US government pursuant to the copyright license under DAR clause 7-104.9(a).

Copyright © 1981 by the President and Fellows of Harvard College.

sponsors of the fair for their intentional disregard of minority unemployment—charges that made Smith's position even more difficult.

Jones had originally been deputy chief of civil rights, and was moved into the chief's position on an acting basis after the head of the office—a white man who had alienated both the community and NAFEC employees—was fired. In accordance with standard civil service procedure, the position of chief, civil rights staff was announced as a vacancy. The applicants included Bill Jones and at least three female Equal Employment Opportunity (EEO) specialists. All were interviewed by Smith. Conscious of the symbolic as well as substantive implications of his choice of a new civil rights chief, Smith hoped to find a minority woman for the position. Smith chose Audrey Simmons, then the EEO coordinator at FAA headquarters. Before coming to the FAA, Simmons had been active in community work, helping ease racial tension over housing issues.

Simmons arrived at NAFEC in September 1977, and was warmly welcomed by Director Smith. Bill Jones, however, had different feelings according to Simmons,

> As a result of my selection, which put me in a superior position to the man who had been acting chief, I had a number of problems on my hands. This man was not exactly cooperative when I started. . . . He was a very "macho" and chauvinistic male—it blew his mind to work for a woman.

Simmons' arrival as chief of civil rights caught Jones by surprise. Furious at the director, Simmons, and officials in Washington for what he felt was an underhanded attack on him and his work, Jones filed a complaint of discrimination using the agency's EEO complaints procedures. As Simmons recalls:

> He stated it this way: He believed that the director selected me for the position because a woman couldn't be effective in a job like this and [he thought] the director was trying to denigrate the civil rights program. . . . He [Jones] wanted this job more than anything in life, and he could not believe the director, knowing that he wanted the job that bad, would go and select some *woman*. FAA had never had a woman civil rights chief before.

In her first few months at NAFEC, Simmons found Jones both uncooperative and obstructive.

The difficulties were both internal and external: Jones circumventing Simmons to go to the director with issues and complaints; a tug-of-war over support staff; and other minor incidents within NAFEC. And in the minority community, where Jones was seen as one who knew how to challenge the system and get things done, his dislike of Simmons made it difficult for her to find acceptance.

Simmons dedicated her first few months to learning about the hiring and minority issues firsthand, by talking to everyone she could—telephone operators, guards, secretaries, high-level officials on the base and community leaders. She also tried to relieve the tensions between herself and Jones—by having lunch with him, by setting aside time for discussions and attempting to display interest in and awareness of the grass roots and political issues—but without much success.

By January Simmons had concluded that the poor minority employment record of the base was the result of a combination of insufficient efforts by NAFEC to reach into the minority community and the lack of technical expertise among community members. The first of these problems could be solved but the second was more deepseated. But Simmons felt that the atmosphere of NAFEC was ripe for constructive change.

> He [Smith] wanted to go out of his way to do whatever he could. It was just difficult for him to decide the right things to do. He was an air traffic man, a pilot, a technical man—not used to dealing with grass roots people. He would make brash promises to appease the community, and then not be able to come through. But he would keep trying to help—he would go into the community, make speeches at the black church, meet with anyone who wanted to see him—he really tried hard. I don't think I could have worked for him if his heart weren't in the right place.

Hoping first to demonstrate that NAFEC had a real interest in the problems of the community, Simmons set out to give local residents a participatory role in what was going on, "so people would have a sense of, yes, that's *our* government out there and not some huge monster." She worked with members of the local NAACP, the school board, the Hispanic leadership and other community groups, as well as personnel within NAFEC who were also active in the community, to gather information and plan appropriate actions for NAFEC.

By February Simmons felt ready to lead NA-FEC into a visible activity that would involve the community and give Director Smith a chance to say, "Look, I'm reaching out to do whatever I can." Since February was black history month, a committee of NAFEC employees that Simmons had organized recommended holding an awards ceremony at the end of the month to honor national and local leaders who had advanced minority rights. (Similar awards ceremonies were common throughout government, particularly in Washington, to reward individuals who supported EEO activities.) The idea soon grew into a major event—FAA officials from Washington would be invited, national minority figures would be honored with awards, and NAFEC's gates would be opened to all the local residents who wanted to attend.

Although the top NAFEC leadership were still stinging from the Trans Fair fiasco and were not eager to precipitate another disturbance, they had confidence in Simmons and gave her a virtually free hand in organizing the ceremony. The committee worked through the month to select recipients of the awards and plan the ceremony. In addition to national figures from the minority community—such as NAACP representatives—the committee members invited local officials, including the mayor and the commissioner of public works, as well as several FAA officials, including the deputy administrator, the FAA director of civil rights, and the director of the engineering and development division.

The committee also made what proved to be a controversial decision: they agreed that Director Smith should receive an award for his efforts to promote affirmative action at NAFEC. Since the 1977 Trans Fair, Smith had been actively involved in affirmative action issues—establishing contact with the local NAACP, listening to both internal and community complaints, and trying to ensure the promotion of minorities to policymaking positions. According to Simmons, the outcry over the Trans Fair hiring was a rude awakening to Smith: "He had never thought much about this before, and then a terrible thing happened. . . . I think it suddenly dawned on him that he could be viewed as a bigot and a racist. So he started doing all these extraordinary things."

The idea of presenting Smith an award was the subject of some debate within the committee, but they eventually agreed that it was an appropriate action. While a few members expressed apprehension about the community reaction, the majority felt that it would be a positive sign for the director to be rec-

ognized by his own people for his support of equal employment opportunity.

Throughout the planning period, Jones occasionally joined Simmons and the committee but was often out of the office, presumably working in the community. According to Simmons, "Since the relationship between the man [Jones] and the people of the community was continuing, I had no reason to doubt that he was, well, he certainly wasn't going to be speaking highly of me and my ability to do my job." Of her relationship with the community at that time, she said candidly,

> I guess, to admit the truth, that I was scared of the community. I decided when I have more confidence and all the support I can get from my place of work, then I would feel more secure about dealing with the public. . . . I would talk to anyone, and if they invited me to a meeting I would attend. But I didn't actively seek them out yet, because what did I have to offer? Could I say to them, hey, look, I've got jobs for everybody? No.

Preparations for the ceremony appeared to be running smoothly until a few days before the event, when word was leaked that Director Smith would receive an award. (Though the ceremony itself was well-publicized, the award recipients were not announced in advance.) Said Simmons, "We think word got out through [Jones]. He wanted to say to the community, 'See what she did? She came and made arrangements for him to get an award, when you know how he's treated you in the past.'"

The day before the awards ceremony, five community leaders arrived, unannounced, at Simmons' office. Representing the NAACP, the school board, and other community and minority groups, they demanded that Simmons withhold Smith's award and call off the entire ceremony. If she refused, they threatened to mobilize thousands of minorities from the city to disrupt the ceremony.

Simmons was stunned.

> I remember one woman, whom I had the utmost respect for, said I was "black bourgeoisie," and I didn't know what it was like to be black and poor. . . . But what could I say, "Oh, that's not true, I did come from the ghetto?" I couldn't—she wouldn't believe it; she had to know me to believe it.

Feeling her anger rising, Simmons asked them to have a seat in her office and excused herself.

I couldn't deal with it right then, so I left. I went downstairs and just stood in the hallway. . . . I thought they really could disrupt the ceremony.

And I was angry because I didn't think they had a right to tell me how to run things, and. . . . because I was doing everything I could do to make the situation right and to try to help them, and they didn't seem to understand. I was angry because things were going on behind my back that I didn't have a hand in.

With these thoughts running through her mind, Simmons went back upstairs to her office, unsure of what to do next.

Imagine you are Audrey Simmons. What do you do now?

One possibility is to accede to the demands of the community leaders and agree to withhold Smith's award and cancel the ceremony. The advantages of this option are obvious. You gain some time to deal with the underlying resentments that have been festering in the community, to which you have not devoted sufficient attention. You avoid a potentially embarrassing demonstration, in full view of high-ranking agency officials. You also avoid giving community leaders another divisive issue around which to mobilize members of the community against your agency. Finally, the entire purpose of the ceremony is to improve community relations; if it is likely to have the opposite effect, there's really no point in going forward with it.

One problem with this option is that you must first gain the acquiescence of George Smith, the agency head. Cancelling his award and the ceremony at this point would represent an admission that you have failed to improve relations between the agency and the community. Smith, as you are aware, believes he has done everything possible to meet the demands of the community for more jobs. He will be upset at what he will perceive as an ungrateful and uncooperative response from the community; he will conclude that you are not doing your job.

Another option: Negotiate with the community leaders. Seek to gain their cooperation in going through with the award and the ceremony. But what are you going to offer them? They cannot leave your office empty-handed. Their positions of leadership are founded upon their ability to deliver what their constituents want—jobs. Before they will agree to the ceremony and Smith's award, they must first be satisfied that you will deliver. And yet, you cannot give such an assurance, because Smith is unwilling (or feels himself unable) to come through with additional jobs or resources to train for such jobs.

A third possibility: Go ahead with the event even in the face of community opposition. Call their bluff. Maybe they will not be able to mobilize the community after all; their failure to do so will jeopardize their leadership positions in the community and make it more difficult for them to threaten you with similar mobilizations in the future. And even if they do demonstrate, they will learn that you don't back down easily—that you're willing to take some heat. Having learned this, they will give you more credit in future negotiations.

But this option accomplishes little. It makes a mockery of the ceremony, displays the agency's poor community relations to everyone assembled—including the press and officials from headquarters in Washington—and only increases the stakes for the next showdown (which will surely take place).

My students usually dislike all of the options. They would prefer to stall for time—maybe agree to delay the ceremony for a few weeks. In the interim, they would try to improve relations with the community by actively working in the community. They recommend that Simmons try to convince community leaders that she is really on *their* side. She should gain the trust of Bill Jones (who apparently already has convinced the community that he is working for them rather than for the agency) and get Jones to help her. She should strategize with community leaders, and with Jones, about how best to push Smith and the agency toward more jobs and training opportunities.

What's wrong with this approach? Simply this: Were you to become an advocate for the community, you would no longer be doing your job. You are not authorized to be the community's advocate. Your job is "community relations." As defined by Smith (and by the agency), this means improving relations between the agency and the community, so that the agency can get on with its primary mission, which is to undertake research on air traffic safety and control of the nation's airspace.

Smith and the agency overall want to be responsive to civil rights and the reasonable needs of the community, and part of your job is to communicate those needs. But having communicated them, your job is then to keep the lid on—to keep the community from interfering. You have *not* been hired as a "change agent" to alter the way the agency does its work or conceives of its mission. If you adopt this role, you won't last long in your job.

You are caught in the middle. Your job is to act as a "heat shield," protecting the agency from the community, but (to extend the metaphor) heat shields have a tendency to melt when the heat is turned up. Community leaders will not trust you if they perceive you as nothing more than a shield; nor will they negotiate with you. On the contrary, they will seek ways to circumvent you. You will spend more and more of your time trying to deflect their anger from Smith and other key agency personnel, a job that will be emotionally and physically exhausting. You cannot last.

And yet, if you provide no shield, you will not last either. Too much "heat" will get through. Smith and other agency officials will conclude that you are ineffectual.

The underlying problem here (and it is common to many such jobs) is that neither Smith *nor* the community is aware of the constraints and possibilities facing the other side. Perhaps there are many things that the agency could do to provide more jobs and more training opportunities without expending many resources; perhaps there are many steps the community could take to help achieve this result. But only up to a point:

The community also needs to understand the realistic limit to how far the agency can go, and the diminishing gains to be had from committing additional political resources to trying to push the agency beyond this limit.

By shielding the agency from the community (and vice versa), you prevent such mutual learning from taking place. But were you to expose Smith and other agency officials directly to the hostile demands of community leaders, it is unlikely that any learning would take place either. Mutual learning rarely occurs under conditions of too little or too much heat. Learning requires just enough heat to capture attention, but not so much as to engender defensiveness.

Thus your challenge is to conduct just the right amount of heat to engender mutual learning. You must devise means of exposing Smith and other agency officials to the demands of the community, sufficiently to fix their attention but not so much that they recoil from the challenge of responding to those demands. Similarly, you must expose the community leaders to the practical constraints operating upon the agency, sufficiently to enlist their cooperation in working within those constraints but not so much that they feel compelled to lash out at them.

Several possibilities come to mind. At the start, you might invite one or two of the more moderate leaders to meet informally with Smith. You might take a few agency officials into the community to inspect a training facility and provide advice on how to improve it. And so on. The point is that you must continue to create settings likely to conduct the right amount of heat in both directions.

The underlying principle is applicable to many of the cases we have explored so far in this book, not limited to formal relational jobs. Henderson could have been something of a heat shield for Phil Heymann's Criminal Division had Heymann allowed him to be cast in that role; but Heymann devised a more creative way of "conducting" the heat. As a result, congressional overseers and prosecutors both learned about their relative competences. Miles Mahoney did act as a kind of heat shield, standing between Governor Sargent and community groups intent on resisting the developers. Very little learning occurred on either side of the divide, however, and Miles ultimately "melted." Consider the other cases we have examined and ask yourself whether, and to what extent, the protagonist prevented mutual learning from taking place. Was Robert Hermann a heat shield between civil libertarians and hawks on national security? If so, why *didn't* he melt? Was Paul Boudreau a heat shield between the advocates for the mentally retarded and the majority who wanted mentally retarded people out of sight at minimal cost? What could he have done to avoid melting? Was Harold Brown a heat shield for Jimmy Carter? How could he have creatively conducted the heat?

chapter 8

Searching for a Strategy

Assume now that the public agency in which you are employed has established a reasonably porous boundary with outside constituents, sufficient to grasp what is demanded of it and sustain a broad mandate to take action, but also sufficient to give the agency enough discretion to develop and execute an overall strategy.

We turn now to the strategy itself. What exactly does it mean for a public agency in a democratic society to have a strategy? Several things. First, a strategy implies having priorities—focusing organizational resources on certain goals and activities. Second, a strategy suggests a long-term view of the agency's mission—of where the agency should be heading over the next three, five, seven, and ten years—and how shorter-term priorities fit within long-term goals. And third, a strategy requires some plan for how to achieve long-term goals in the interim.

None of these aspects of strategy is unique to public-sector organizations. But there are other aspects of strategy more directly related to the complex system of accountability by which public agencies are authorized to take action. Having a public-sector strategy requires a careful assessment of public priorities—not only present priorities but also priorities as they are likely to emerge over the longer term. Unlike private-sector organizations, which can predict on the basis of movements in prices and markets, public-sector agencies must rely on more subtle cues, such as a gradual shifting of public opinion, changes in the political climate, slowly emerging issues. We will be examining these aspects of strategy in the next few cases.

The first strategic step—and one of the most important, although often overlooked—is the recruitment of an agency head. The search for department secretaries, commissioners, bureau directors, and other high-level appointees is done badly when elected officials fail to see the connection between strategy and search. Under these circumstances they may turn the recruitment effort over to staffers or "headhunters" who have no special strategic competence or understanding. Or they may turn to trusted friends and associates, who may have a good understanding of the elected official's aims and inclinations but little capacity or experience to find talented people able to translate those vague inclinations into organizational strategy.

Consider the case of the Massachusetts Department of Corrections and the task confronting Peter Goldmark and his assistant, Jim Eisenberg.

Massachusetts Department of Correction

THE DEPARTMENT OF CORRECTION[1]

The Department of Correction (DOC) was established in 1919 as 1 of 15 state departments that reported to the Governor. It was, in 1972, a department of about 1,800 employees, encompassing a commissioner's office with a central staff, five major state correctional institutions, and an increasing number of small facilities. In the fiscal year 1973, its budget was about $28.5 million. The Parole Board was within the Department of Correction but not subject to its jurisdiction. The Department of Youth Services was a distinct, separately administered entity. Jails and Houses of Correction were county institutions under county management and control but with some state supervision.[2]

The commissioner, the DOC's chief executive, was a gubernatorial appointee for a term coterminous with the Governor's own term, not subject to confirmation by the Commonwealth's Executive Council. Statutory qualifications for the post required "at least five years of adult correctional administrative experience and . . . an established record of high character and qualities of leadership." The statutory salary in 1972 was $26,838.

Under the commissioner and reporting directly to him were, in 1971, three deputy commissioners. (See Appendix A.) The central staff personnel were largely career employees of the department, often having advanced through the ranks from the position of correction officer.

The central office received no standard written reports on the operation of the MCI's, although ex-

---

[1] Material in this and in the next two sections, unless otherwise noted, derived in part from Edwin Powers, *The Basic Structure of the Administration of Justice in Massachusetts* (6th ed., Boston, 1973). Derivations from this source are hereafter denoted "Powers."

[2] State institutions were termed "Massachusetts Correctional Institutions." *Jails* were primarily used for the detention of persons

awaiting trial but are also used to confine minor offenders for short sentences or to hold material witnesses. *Houses of correction* received prisoners committed by the courts for modest terms longer than those served in a jail; most jail sentences were for one month or less, whereas sentences to the houses of correction averaged from six months to a year.

This case was prepared by Alan Konefsky, Richard Peers, and Donald Simon under the supervision of Professor Philip B. Heymann for use at the John F. Kennedy School of Government, Harvard University, and at the Harvard Law School. The preparation was facilitated by preliminary research done by Sander Levin and Andrew Strenio at the Kennedy School.

Copyright © 1977 by the President and Fellows of Harvard College.

penditures were monitored. Communication between the central office and the institutions was maintained by telephone calls and by visits by central management, both routine and exceptional.

THE MASSACHUSETTS CORRECTIONAL INSTITUTIONS (MCI's)

In January, 1972, all institutionalized offenders under the jurisdiction of the DOC were assigned to one of eight state facilities, designated under the 1955 state correctional statute as a "Massachusetts Correctional Institution," followed by its geographical location. (Thus, for example, the maximum security prison would be referred to as "MCI Walpole.") Each of the eight institutions, at Bridgewater, Norfolk, Walpole, Concord, Framingham, Plymouth, Warwick, and Monroe[3] has its individual characteristics, in terms of kind of inmate population, types of facilities, degree of security, personnel organization, and management structure.

The chief administrator of an MCI was called a superintendent. Under him were lieutenants responsible for custodial care, prison industries, and fiscal management and plant maintenance. (See Appendix B.) The custodial organization rested upon a quasi-military chain of command. Correctional officers (the guards) were divided into three shifts, each supervised by an assistant deputy superintendent. Beneath them in the hierarchy were supervisors of major divisions of the MCI. Senior correction officers served below the supervisors, directing teams of guards, most of whom were assigned to cell blocks. The steward served as the business manager of the prison and oversaw the maintenance staff and kitchen, which used inmate labor. Social workers and psychological counselors were under their own organizational structure.[4]

THE CORRECTION OFFICERS

The 1,150 permanent custodial personnel of the institutions, those that kept inmates securely behind the walls, were termed correction officers. They were required to pass a written Civil Service test and meet certain physical and strength requirements. In January 1972, there were no particular educational re-

quirements for the job. Besides being protected by the Civil Service system, correction officers were represented by separate locals of the American Federation of State, County, and Municipal Employees (AFSCME, AFL-CIO). Representatives of the locals met monthly in the Penal Committee of Council 41 (AFSCME). Howard V. Doyle was council president. In 1971, however, correction officers at MCI's Bridgewater and Norfolk were increasingly discontented with their affiliation with AFSCME, and in 1972 would withdraw to form independent unions, claiming 600 members.

Traditionally termed "guards," the custodial personnel in the MCI's were, since the 1950s, officially denominated "correction officers" to denote the importance of rehabilitation as a goal of the penal institutions. The Rules and Regulations for employees at the MCI's, for example, directed the correctional officers to be "both counselor and disciplinarian." In their dealings with prisoners, they were to be "friendly not familiar, sympathetic not obstinate, vigilant not unduly suspicious, strict not unjust." The correction officers were admonished only to use that "amount of physical force necessary to accomplish the desired result."

The transformation of guards into correctional officers, however, was more rhetorical than real. The primary job of the custodial staff of an institution remained to keep prisoners confined behind the walls, to segregate inmates from society and thus to render them harmless for a time to those outside. Secondarily, such a limitation upon personal freedom was to serve to deter others from committing crimes. The custodial staff's primary role had nothing to do with "treatment" designed to rehabilitate the offender; that was the basic task of the prison's social workers and psychiatric counselors. The essential function of correctional officers, despite the change of name, remained to guard.

This organizational imperative was reflected in the guards' attitudes and behavior. The rhetoric of rehabilitation would at most stimulate marginal shifts in modes of interaction between guards and inmates. Correction officers received some training through an eight-week basic course for new officers and occasional two-week refresher courses. However, perceptions of correction officers and techniques of managing prisoners were still largely the product of the socialization process at the institution. That process inculcated a custodial mentality and approach.

In the Massachusetts correctional system, the uniqueness of each institution was reflected in differing characteristics of the job of correction officer

---

[3]The above institutions are listed in decreasing size of prison population; the last three are forestry camps.

[4]Derived from "Department of Correction."

among the several MCI's. Each institution demanded that guards play a different role, have a different attitude. Moreover, the organization and procedures varied from facility to facility. Institutions' rules, regulations, and processes were very often not even in writing, let alone in codified form. Instead, long-term staffers were mental repositories of the complex administrative processes, both official and unofficial. Such a system defied systematic review and increased the difficulty of achieving managerial control. The future Commissioner of Corrections would later describe the managerial nightmare of the MCI's:

> So, the thing is in this system, every prison is an island unto itself. And every superintendent is sort of like a dictator of that island.
>
> And in some institutions he doesn't run it. The deputy superintendent runs it, you see, and he knows everybody. He runs it out of the top of his head. I couldn't find a piece of paper, a rule or regulation, a guideline in *any* of these prisons. All of it is in the top of somebody's head.

The problem of managerial control over and within the MCI's was exacerbated by a lack of control over the personnel system. Limited by statute in its right to bargain for wage increases[5] the guards' union had turned instead to working conditions, and over the years had extracted from its employer, the Commonwealth, the contractual right to administer by the seniority system virtually all appointments, assignments, and vacation and shift selections. Thus, prison administrators were severely limited in their ability to manage the custodial staff through the application of incentives.

PRISON CHANGES AND UNREST[6]

During the late 1960s, shifts in prison social structure and prison attitudes reflected the political and social changes in the larger society. Younger inmates had been exposed to the civil rights movement, the decade's ghetto riots, the antiwar movement, and developing racial and ethnic pride and politicization. Armed with a new self-image and a new militancy,

prisoners began organizing to protect their rights and interests. The New York State Special Commission on Attica, viewing this development, described it:

> Along with the demand for respect as a human being came a new demand in the 1960s. Many inmates came to believe that they were "political prisoners," even though they had been convicted of crimes having no political motive or significance. They claimed that responsibility for their actions belonged not to them—but to a society which had failed to provide adequate housing, equal educational opportunities, and equal opportunity to compete in American life. Believing themselves to be the victims, not the aggressors, they claimed that the public should concentrate its efforts on rehabilitation of society and not of them.

This increasing militancy affected traditional inmate social organization and attitudes. First, the new political approach contradicted the maxim, "Do your *own* time," to which "right guys" subscribed and which the correctional staff itself admonished prisoners to follow. Second, the militant politicized prisoner tended to assume the role of "gorilla," the aggressive inmate who uses violence. Third, such a prisoner would tend to refuse to cooperate with correctional staff in the traditional network of unofficial contacts and relationships. Taken together, the trends demonstrated a shift in power away from "right guys" and the "thief" subculture toward the "gorillas" and a general erosion of the traditional system of social control. . . .

FURTHER UNREST IN MASSACHUSETTS PRISONS[7]

In 1971, the person attempting to cope with the job of commissioner in Massachusetts was John L. Fitzpatrick. Fitzpatrick was a career employee of the department, having worked his way up from the position of social worker. He had assumed his post in April 1970. Along with his immediate superior, Peter C. Goldmark, Secretary of the Executive Office of Human Services, he had tried to respond to calls for reform and inmate requests by introducing some ad-

---

[5]In 1972, the annual starting salary for a correction officer was $9,630, increasing in six annual increments to $12,002. This compared to $6,349 and $8,034, respectively, in 1968.

[6]This section is in part derived from Cressey, "Adult Felons. . ." and from "Department of Correction."

[7]This section is in part based on *Hearings on Corrections, "Part V; Prisons, Prison Reform, and Prisoners' Rights: Massachusetts "Before Subcommittee No. 3 of the House Committee on the Judiciary* 92nd Congress, 1st Session, ser. 15, 355–369 (1972). Description of events in Walpole is in part based on Peter Remick, *In Constant Fear* (New York, 1975), hereafter referred to as "Remick."

ministrative changes. At Walpole, for example, inmates were given more liberty to visit parts of the prison other than their own cellblock, and were no longer locked into cells during the guards' meal hours.

Such palliatives were insufficient, however. Unrest at MCIs Walpole, Norfolk, and Concord increased, and by the summer of 1971 was getting growing press coverage. Outsiders, among them correction reform and ex-offender groups, some legislators, and some professional correction officials, were speaking out on the need for change. With the uprising at the New York State Correctional Facility at Attica and its bloody suppression between September 9 and 13, both the ferment within the walls and public consciousness without increased. In the days after Attica, a number of peaceful demonstrations by large groups of inmates were carried out at Norfolk and Walpole. Commissioner Fitzpatrick encouraged the creation of inmate grievance committees, and prisoners responded with lists of requests for changes. At Norfolk, for example, requests included better food and medical attention and education programs, an end to mail censorship, a training program for guards, some black and Puerto Rican guards, abolition of the death penalty, repeal of the two-thirds law, and amnesty for the demonstrators. At Walpole, prisoners punctuated their protest with work strikes.[8] The inmates gained wide publicity in the media; a day-long meeting on September 29 in the Walpole prison auditorium among prisoners, administrators, public figures, and reporters received extensive coverage in the press and on television.

The prison protests had an effect. Mail censorship was ended immediately. The superintendent of Norfolk acceded to a number of other requests. More significantly, Governor Francis Sargent promised to introduce a prison reform bill and appointed a citizens' committee on corrections to study the Massachusetts system. The group, headed by Judge Harold Elam of the Boston Municipal Court, was to deliver its report at the end of November.

After a several-day lapse, the Walpole inmates resumed their work strike on October 5; the response of the prison administration was a lockup. [9] This second work stoppage was organized by inmates who

had emerged as spokesmen in recent weeks; Robert H. Moore, Walpole's superintendent, characterized them as "a small, hard-core group of agitators." The lockup, designed to ensure control of a potentially disruptive situation, only increased solidarity among the inmates. Negotiations between the grievance committee and the prison administration ended in a compromise: the lockup was ended on October 12, and the prisoners returned to work.

The superintendents bore the primary responsibility for handling the disturbances in their institutions, but Commissioner Fitzpatrick was also exceedingly active during these days. On October 6, while at Walpole awaiting a report from the Elam Committee of a meeting it was having with the prisoners' committee, Fitzpatrick collapsed from acute fatigue and was hospitalized. Deputy Commissioner Joseph J. Higgins assumed temporary active direction of the department.

At the beginning of November, some inmates at Walpole set fire to the metal shop and foundry, causing $30,000 worth of damage. According to guard leaders, the prisoners who set the fire were controlled by the inmate committee. According to outside observers from the Massachusetts Council on Crime and Correction (MCCC), a liberal prison reform group, inmates at Walpole and Norfolk felt discontent at the delayed implementation of promised concessions. Guards at Walpole picked up reports that trouble was brewing in Walpole. On November 5, Walpole prisoners staged another work strike, and Superintendent Moore answered with both a lockup and a shakedown, a systematic cell search for contraband. Guards found knives made from scrap metal, lengths of pipe stolen from prison workshops. pieces of chain, containers of gasoline, and a homemade pipe-bomb. Several weeks later, in response to other tips received, the prison administration conducted a second lockup and shakedown. The lockups had the additional effect of disrupting negotiations between the inmate committee and the administration. (See Appendix B.)

---

[8] Since inmates performed essential service and maintenance tasks, such as work in the kitchen and laundry, work strikes could be quite disruptive.

[9] A "lockup" is a standard control technique. It may refer either to isolation-type cells, used to confine individual prisoners for disciplinary reasons or to the "general lockup," in which an entire section of the prison or the entire inmate population is confined to its own cells around the clock. When individuals are placed in

the special isolation cells, they are deprived of numerous privileges and cannot take part in normal prison routine. In Massachusetts, inmates could be confined in an isolation unit for no longer than 15 days for any one offense.

The "general lockup" is a control technique which has been used more frequently in recent years than it was in the past, in part because formerly many prisons carried a lockup style as the normal daily routine. In a general lockup, all prisoners are confined to their own cells, and the regular prison routine is considerably curtailed. Daily activities may be reduced and many activities are cancelled. There may be armed guards monitoring in the dining rooms and there may be reduced shower privileges.

Disturbances at Norfolk would be quashed in a different way. On November 7, some 75 state police, together with guards, arrested 36 prisoners. Sixteen inmates were transferred to Walpole or Concord; others were placed in isolation. The DOC initially refused to announce changes, but the MCCC obtained details and released the arrested men's names: 10 were members of inmate negotiating committees, 4 of them committee chairmen. The Boston newspapers picked up the story, and charges and counter-charges among guards, correction administrators, the MCCC, and other actors were to fly in the following days.

The MCCC asserted that the Norfolk arrests had been forced on an unwilling Fitzpatrick by guards' union representatives, who otherwise had threatened to stage extensive sick calls. The Commissioner denied that allegation, calling the arrested prisoners threats to the peace and security of the institution, but ordering an investigation of the arrests anyway. Secretary Goldmark supported the Commissioner's action. One independent-minded Norfolk guard, George Moore, confirmed the MCC's assertion in discussions with reporters. The Norfolk guards union president, James A. Magnan, announced that the transfers were necessary to prevent "all hell from breaking loose."

Senator Jack Backman of Brookline, Chairman of the Senate Committee on Social Welfare, requested a copy of the charges against the arrested men, attacked the DOC's regulations as being "inconsistent, outdated, unavailable and unknown to the prisoners, the correction officers, and the public." The Senator requested that Commissioner Fitzpatrick hold a public hearing on the rules and procedures of the DOC. Norfolk Superintendent Ristiano was to admit several weeks later that the arrests had been requested by the guards' union, and that most men probably should not have been transferred.

In the midst of the turmoil, Fitzpatrick was advised by his doctor to resign his post for reasons of health. On November 9, Governor Sargent and Secretary Goldmark held a press conference to announce Fitzpatrick's resignation, effective December 4. The troubled state of corrections in Massachusetts, everywhere apparent, was reaffirmed on the following day, for a bill revising the two-thirds parole law died when the two legislative houses were unable to reach a compromise. As the difficulties in the prison system continued, the heat on Governor Sargent increased. On November 23, six state representatives requested the Governor to ask for the help of the American Arbitration Association in resolving the dispute at Walpole and Norfolk. Other communications to Sargent called for return of the transferred Norfolk men.

On December 3, the Elam Committee's report to the Governor, *Corrections 71; A Citizen's Report*, 44 pages in length, was released. The Committee found considerable legitimacy in the inmates' general call for reform. It concluded:

That punishment remains as the state's primary response to a convicted criminal is a critical flaw in the correctional system. . . . the fact for inmates is that there are essentially no incentives and few opportunities for growing as a person—gaining a skill, acquiring more education, actively working for the opportunity to return as a constructive citizen. . . . There is an urgent need for policies, programs, and attitudes within the Department of Correction to adapt to the clear fact that today inmates are people not just under custody but with needs to which the system must respond. . . . The demands for change have infused the prisons as they have pervaded our society, and just as they cannot be repressed with brutality on the streets, neither can they be subdued with transfer and punitive isolation inside the prison.

That these voices have not been raised before is not important. They are raised now and they carry a hopeful message if we listen before turning off. One message is that inmates want to be approached with the dignity and respect that society will demand from them once they are released. The committee feels that if inmates are made to feel like animals, they will act like animals; if they are respected as people, they will give respect to others. This is the beginning of corrections.

By not listening, however, we may force an escalation of behavior that results in tragedy. Changes are necessary so that in Massachusetts, prison disorder is not necessary to communicate a message as basic as "I am a man." . . . though security remains a responsibility of the Department of Correction, decisions about corrections should reflect inmate participation. This includes decisions about educational programs, vocational training, visiting, recreation, food, and medical care.

The needs are urgent and a perseverant public must demand change so that criminals will no longer return to society as hardened criminals but as constructive citizens.

The report made recommendations for improving key aspects of inmate life, and directed the Governor's attention to the improved training and recruitment of correctional staff. It suggested areas in which administrative action could improve the internal operation of the MCI's and the department's administrative procedures, and areas where legislation was required. Recommendations included minority recruitment of correction staff, abolition of the departmental segregation unit at Bridgewater, repeal of the two-thirds law, and more work and education release.

On December 4, Fitzpatrick's resignation took effect. Two days later, Governor Sargent announced to a group of citizens who had come to his office that he would personally visit the state's correctional facilities. Together with an assistant and Secretary Goldmark, the Governor spoke to the group of 20 for an hour and a half about the prison situation. Elma Lewis, director of the National Center of Afro-American Artists, was to say later, "We feel he made a commitment."

THE SARGENT ADMINISTRATION

In 1969, with legislative approval, Sargent had reorganized state government by establishing 10 cabinet level superagencies headed by a secretary. The duties of the secretary were to coordinate and plan the operations of the departments and agencies within his or her domain, thus relieving the Governor of the considerable task of keeping in direct touch with the operation of over 100 departments and agencies. Human Services, one of the largest and most sprawling of the new agencies, coordinated the affairs of the Departments of Public Health, Mental Health, Youth Services, Public Welfare, Corrections and a score of other agencies. In the summer of 1971, Sargent hired Peter Goldmark to head the mammoth operation.

Goldmark already had a reputation as a bureaucratic maverick when he came to Massachusetts at age 30. He was known as a man who liked action, who moved quickly and directly to accomplish his goals, and who was willing to suspend the rules of bureaucratic courtesy in order to realize his ends. A nine-year veteran of governmental service, Goldmark had begun his career in the federal Office of Economic Opportunity in the early sixties. He moved on to New York City to become deputy director of the Bureau of the Budget, and then was appointed chief of staff by Mayor John Lindsay. Young, forceful, idealistic, and broadly intelligent, Goldmark was a

bold choice for the unwieldy secretariat position, especially because, as one of his aides later said, "He had not once in his life a single moment of bureaucratic experience as a line manager. He had never been responsible for making something work. He's always been the brilliant outside guy."

On assuming his new office, Goldmark used his statutory budget review authority as a means of putting himself in a position of real influence; Goldmark was not to fill a powerless post. Instead, he asserted the right to have a voice in policy and even individual management decisions in the constituent departments of human services. His commissioners generally acquiesced, although Commissioner Jerome Miller of the Department of Youth Services avoided much loss of power to the new executive secretary. Goldmark did establish his authority in the DOC; he began issuing public statements and consulting with Commissioner Fitzpatrick on specific decisions. During the prison crisis in the fall, Goldmark, without any expertise in the correctional field, was answering Fitzpatrick's requests for advice on how to end a lockup at Walpole, and was reviewing decisions on transfers of prisoners from one facility to another. The executive secretary had Jim Isenberg, age 26, as his aide on crisis situations in the prisons. The new layer of bureaucracy that the executive offices represented thus posed major problems of jurisdiction and authority.

Another ambiguity in jurisdiction and lines of authority caused by the new executive offices was the relationship between the governor's staff and the executive secretarial structure, a difficulty never fully resolved during the Sargent administration. Junior staffers working under Flannery or Kramer on the Governor's staff assumed policy jurisdiction over certain state agencies, as young Steven Teichner did over Corrections. Yet, as secretary, Goldmark had formal authority over Corrections and assigned members of his own bureaucratic staff, such as aide Jim Isenberg, to keep watch on the department.

Sargent's personal philosophy of governing was to act as an arbiter of policy disputes brought him by his staff. Though he had developed a coherent political perspective, he had no set agenda of policies and programs he wanted to implement. Rather, he preferred to go with the flow, to allow issues to surface themselves, to manage the crisis when it arose. Then, when the critical juncture in policy choice surfaced, Sargent would allow his staff to present him with the issues, information, alternatives and arguments, from which he would select a direction consistent with the political terrain and his own beliefs.

Most of all, Sargent believed in a hands-off relationship between the governor's office and the line agencies. His role, as he saw it, was to define the broad policies of the Commonwealth and then let the department heads find a way to implement them. Sargent believed very strongly that his office and his staff could not run the agencies. Rather, his approach was to find the best person he could to head a department, to give him some policy direction, and then to back him to the hilt.

When Sargent took office, he did so with a "basic assumption" that change was needed in many areas of government. His broad tendency toward reform became particularly focused in the area of human services, especially corrections. Sargent felt that the state prison system was just not working, that it was a system which failed in its goals—incapacitation of dangerous individuals, rehabilitation of wrongdoers, and deterrence of crime—while being costly in both lives and dollars. As the turmoil under Fitzpatrick unfolded during the first years of the Sargent administration, both the governor and his staff increasingly realized the entire prison system was a political and moral embarrassment badly in need of reform. The governor's liberal instincts impelled him toward a policy of change in corrections despite the risks involved.

The Attica uprising in New York and the protests and disturbances in the Massachusetts prisons in the fall of 1971 emphasized the urgency of correctional reform. Staffers for Sargent and Goldmark considered the usual housekeeping reforms for the existing big institutions, such as limiting mail censorship, allowing media in the prisons, and getting representation of prisoners in institutional policy decisions. It was thought that the two-thirds law should be repealed, that the commissioner should be given more latitude in developing new programs and policy. They felt that correction reform in Massachusetts should include some new program, and the idea of halfway houses, a popular one, was suggested.

Jim Isenberg, a staffer in his twenties newly brought in by Goldmark because he knew something about corrections, helped clarify for Goldmark the central idea of community corrections—that there were many people in prisons who did not have to be there, that whatever supervision or treatment they needed could be provided in settings within the community.

Goldmark considered the time propitious for correctional reform.

Was it a good time to try the reform? Yes, because no matter what happened you were going to get into trouble. And no matter what you do

(. . . if you tighten up control, ease up, if you go to community corrections, no matter *what* you do), it was going to be awful, it was going to be trouble; because the system was so rotten, and everybody's expectations were so conflicting and so hot. So when whatever you do was going to be trouble, that's when you try and do something serious in government.

The idea that many people who were going to prisons should not, and the policy of community corrections as a program to carry out that conception, dovetailed with a broader approach toward the human services area that Sargent was developing, that of deinstitutionalization: moving people out of big caretaking institutions generally, in the mental health area, in care for the elderly, and in juvenile corrections, as well as now in adult corrections.

With continual unrest in the Massachusetts prisons, by late 1971 Sargent was so concerned that he made a series of extraordinary unpublicized visits to each of the state's major penal institutions. There, with only a few of his closest staff members present, he talked to staff personnel, guards, and inmates, trying to develop a feel for the problems in the prisons, and what steps needed to be taken. The Governor also held a series of meetings with prison reform groups and directed Goldmark to have his department prepare a prison reform bill.

The final product included measures that would permit reform of the traditional institutions, including improvements in custodial personnel, as well as the tools which would allow a corrections commissioner to build a community-based correctional system.

On December 20, 1971, Sargent revealed a six-point program for prison reform. In introducing his recommendations he told an audience in Waltham:

We have developed over the years a sense of security by building large walls around our prisons. We have said we are safe as long as inmates remain behind the walls. But this is a fantasy. The walls may be a symbol, but they do not protect. Ninety per cent of our inmates behind these walls will someday be released.

Sargent's six-point program to be presented to the Legislature included:

1. A statewide system of halfway houses, to be run in conjunction with a work release program that would permit inmates to work at nearby jobs during the day.

2. Establishment of a nonprofit prison industry corporation that would provide inmates with on-the-job training in useful trades and also pay them minimum wages.

3. Repeal of the state's two-thirds law regulating parole eligibility.

4. Improved training for correctional officers.

5. Increased recruitment of blacks and Hispanics into the DOC.

6. Establishment of staff-inmate councils in the prisons.[11]

THE SEARCH

Fitzpatrick's resignation in late 1971 presented Sargent and Goldmark with the opportunity to lay the critical cornerstone of a new reform program: the appointment of a corrections commissioner to implement it. Once a policy of reform, including community corrections, had been decided upon, the clear need was for a commissioner who could define and effect the considerable changes that entailed. Reardon said of the time,

> We had decided on the policy that we were going to go forward with, and the question became not just finding a commissioner of corrections, but finding one who was compatible with the philosophy that we were espousing. . . . There was no question that we were going on a liberalization effort. . . . This was a decision that was made by Sargent and worked out by the staff.

Sargent felt strongly, from the beginning, that this new commissioner would have to come from outside the Massachusetts Department of Correction, and probably out of state. He felt that no one from within the Massachusetts system, no one who had grown up and been trained within that system, would have the freedom and capability to alter the program fundamentally. The search for an outsider began.

Goldmark assigned his aide, Jim Isenberg, to search for a replacement for Fitzpatrick. The system of "check-outs" adopted for the job-search was something formerly not used in Massachusetts government; it was a method introduced by Goldmark, who demanded more thorough procedures than most administrators on a "check-out." Isenberg began talking to corrections and law enforcement officials

throughout the country, collecting names, checking possible candidates, and then touring the country to interview the stronger prospects. Sargent's and Goldmark's staffers concerned with the search discovered that the corrections area was one with a relative scarcity of talent. Reardon recalled, "There was not a reservoir of well-trained, good, bright, enlightened people who were chomping at the bit to be commissioner of corrections, here or anywhere else." Isenberge compiled a list of 20 individuals who were to be considered serious candidates for the job. From that group, Goldmark, Isenberg and Teichner narrowed the list down to three finalists,[12] each with distinctive attributes and each with something different to offer:

(1) Jim Short was a retired army lieutenant colonel. In his early 50s, Short was an imposing figure, 6-1/2 feet tall, almost 300 pounds in weight. He seemed forceful, accustomed to command and to military administration. Short was the superintendent of a small suburban prison in a major Northeast metropolitan area. He was reported to consume alcoholic beverages avidly. It was thought that he would be able to develop personal contacts and a good working relationship with members of the state legislature. Short had had little experience in dealing with black prisoners, and virtually none in handling major prison crises such as riots. It seemed that he would be fairly progressive and would be willing to take the risks a reform policy would entail.

(2) John Boone, in his late 40s, had been in the federal corrections system for 20 years. He had started as a guard at a federal prison in his home state in the South, had worked his way up through the ranks, and was currently superintendent of one of five prisons in the District of Columbia system. Boone had held posts involving classification and parole and community relations. He had also instituted a program of community corrections at his present assignment. Boone, however, appeared weak in administrative experience. Boone was black; in Massachusetts there were few blacks in the correctional administration at any level, although many inmates were black.

Boone's philosophy of correction was different from the conventional liberal approach as well as from the traditional theory. The traditional perspectives demanded strict custodial methods, including, if necessary, moderate physical coercion to control the prisoners. The standard progressive philosophy moved away from this, and used instead a system of

---

[11] Points 4, 5, and 6 could be implemented without legislation.

[12] Names of unsuccessful candidates have been changed and certain identifying characteristics have been modified in this case study.

rewards and punishment, the giving and withholding of privileges, in order both to control inmates and to rehabilitate them.

Boone was against this philosophy of "behavior modification"; he felt it broke down personal integrity. Boone's philosophy had at its core the emphasis on individual worth and the development of personal responsibility. His theory was to give prisoners the maximum opportunity to control their own lives, both within the correctional institutions and without, through the minimum form and amount of institutional controls, custody, and supervision appropriate for each person, based on his or her personal characteristics. Boone's philosophy of personal responsibility meant giving inmates as much participation in policy and management and as much freedom as possible within the institutions, and getting as many prisoners as possible out of the traditional custodial setting.

(3) Fred Rankin, in his late 40s, was a solid administrator in the field of corrections. He had a great deal of experience, gained in California, in a department in which professionals with academic credentials like Rankin could work their way up in the system. Rankin was currently a superintendent. He received good marks in administration, being described by one observer as "a manager's manager." In a state correctional department which was one of the most control-minded in the nation, Rankin had a reputation as being "too liberal," and was considered a progressive thinker. In California, he was in charge of an institution with an innovative approach. Rankin subscribed to the behavior modification school of penology. He was the only one of the three finalists with academic background in management: he was a product of the public policy program of Stanford University. Goldmark and Sargent were a bit uneasy with Rankin's more easy-going California style, and wondered how he would relate to the constituencies of the Massachusetts corrections commissioner, internal and external, and in particular how he would deal with the Massachusetts bureaucratic style. Unlike the other two candidates, Rankin did not project a particularly dynamic personality, but rather seemed mild mannered.

Each of the three finalists was invited to Massachusetts to meet with Goldmark. Each spent hours talking with the executive secretary and had opportunities to visit departmental facilities. The names of the three candidates were submitted to Sargent, and, in late November 1971, the governor met separately with each finalist for about 30 minutes. The choice, ultimately, lay with the governor, who would have to decide which man could best head the volatile, potentially highly visible, Department of Correction in a time of unrest and change.

APPENDIX A.
Department of Correction Organization

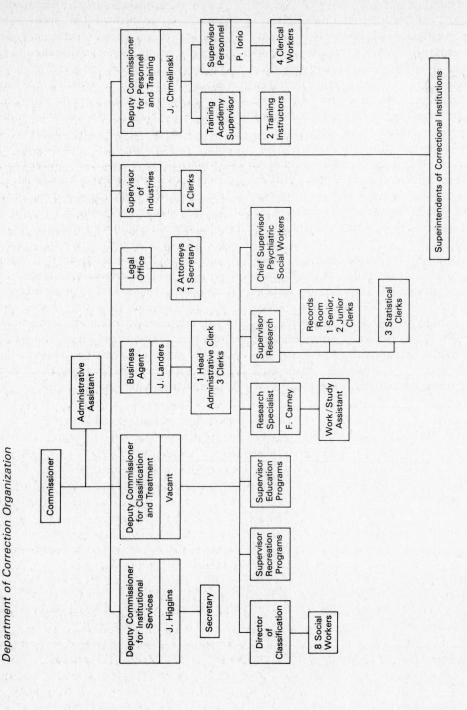

Source: Department of Correction

APPENDIX B. THE BALLAD OF WALPOLE
(Fall, 1971)

Attica happened—and then—
600 voices cried—"REFORM"
Then bent their backs in idleness.
"REFORM!!" they called, "Or we won't work!"
And beyond those walls a tiny echo said—
    "reform"

"There's many things that we don't like!"
"REFORM!!!"
A humane act so long denied.
"REFORM"
"reform," the echo whispered back.

A meeting with the press—"DENIED!"
But then they changed their minds,
And every inmate had his chance to—
Gripe—Complain—and cry.

"REFORM!" they shouted far and wide,
    "REFORM!"
"It's time we joined the other states!"
"REFORM!" and give these men a break—
"REFORM!" and help them rehabilitate.

So T.V. passed the word and papers took a stand—
The men went back to work,
And waited for that helping hand.
But all the while, deep down inside, they cried,
"REFORM!"

The governor had a Bill it seemed
To ease the situation—
It passed the Senate like a dream,
But in the House, died of deflation.

"REFORM" the call "REFORM" the echo
    answered back.
"We need this Bill for show of faith
To make our lives worth living."
But all they heard was this from hacks "Forget
    that crap reform!"

So wondering if this were true—they tested—
"REFORM! they called—the echo was the clue—
And it came back much softer. "reform."
What were they do to?? Just set a fire or two !!
"REFORM"

A week went by with nothing said,
So they quit work again, "REFORM!"
And this brought wrath from Warden Moore—
    "Amen!"
He locked them in their cells again.

And then a search of cells and grounds—
Some knives and pipes were found, and then—
I've heard it sworn—They found a .25 with loaded
    clip,
That they themselves had planted. . . .

So now the call "Reform" is dampened by locked
    cells—
No echo answers back. . . .
Not much has changed—No Bills have passed—
Who knows now what will happen???

Then they tore the prison down and forgot about
    "Reform."

by an Inmate
Box 43, Norfolk, Mass.

    Imagine that you are Jim Eisenberg and you have just been assigned by your boss, Peter Goldmark, the job of searching for a new Commissioner of Corrections. This is an important task. Goldmark does not directly supervise the Department of Corrections; the new commissioner will have a great deal of discretion to fashion a strategy. How do you begin?

    The first thing you have to decide is what you're looking for: What are the criteria that a new commissioner should meet? You could try to come up with some out of your head, but a safer bet would be to sit down with Peter, and perhaps even try to get some of the Governor's time, to solicit their views. You will soon discover (as do my students when they try to role-play this exercise) that neither Peter Goldmark nor the Governor nor, for that matter, anyone else around them has a very clear idea what is required.

Part of the problem is that the department's objectives are unclear. "Deinstitutionalization" is favored, but this vague notion could mean smaller, securer institutions; or it could stand for more leaves and furloughs; or perhaps it could mean more halfway houses and community-treatment facilities or more generous use of probation and parole. No one has thought it through or weighed the implications of any specific strategy. What about the public's safety? The support of the guards' union? Absent a strategy, it is difficult to divine criteria determining who should implement the strategy.

But even if the strategy could be defined, it would be difficult to describe ideal qualities in the abstract. Neither Goldmark nor the Governor is especially competent at determining what sorts of characteristics are required for implementing a particular kind of strategy. Neither has any detailed experience in corrections; neither is an expert in behavioral psychology.

A third problem: There are people other than Peter Goldmark and the Governor who have an interest in the selection of the next Commissioner of Corrections and possess information and perspectives that could be relevant to the selection. Unless they are involved in some way, their interests and perspectives might be overlooked, with the result that the next commissioner would start the job handicapped by disgruntled constituents, or by certain critical weaknesses and inexperience. One such group comprises leaders of the guards' union; other possible participants include the heads of public-interest organizations devoted to public safety or to prisoners' rights, parole and probation officers, police and prosecutors, mental health professionals, and key legislators.

What all this means is that you have to design a process for developing the criteria to guide your search. And the process must be ongoing, since the criteria will become clear only as the search itself begins yielding new information about precisely who has accomplished what around the nation. Thus the two processes—the development of criteria to guide the search and the actual search—necessarily involve one another.

Thus your search is not only for a *person* but also, and simultaneously, for a *strategy*. One way to begin: Comb the nation (do a search of news clippings, consult with correctional officials and academics in the field, talk with political leaders from around the country) looking for examples of strategies—broadly falling within the rubric of "deinstitutionalization"—which seem to have been successful, according to criteria that Goldmark, the Governor, and other interested parties would accept. These strategies need not be limited to corrections; other custodial institutions might be the object of similar reforms (as we discovered in Pendleton School). The point of the exercise is to find analogies to what it is that you and the others want to accomplish in Massachusetts. Discovery of such analogies enables you to better define your objectives and thus the relevant criteria for finding a commissioner. The discovery also puts you in touch with people who were involved in the successes, some of whom may have good ideas about where you might look to find a new commissioner who fits the emerging criteria. One or two of them might be candidates themselves.

Finally, assume that you are ready to focus on some specific candidates. At this stage I ask my students to play the role of Jim Eisenberg, seeking information about a potential candidate from someone who knows the candidate or has worked with him. My students usually ask the respondent to apprise the candidate's strengths and weaknesses. The problems with this approach soon become obvious. First, Jim cannot be sure of the respondent's sincerity (she may be trying to put the best possible light on the candidate because she wants him to get the job, or the worst possible light because she wants him to be rejected). Second, Jim cannot be sure of the accuracy of the respondent's memory (she may be confusing the candidate with someone else, or she may be drawing false inferences on the basis of very little information). Third, and most important, Jim cannot be sure that the respondent shares Jim's own sense of what constitutes a strength or a weakness (she may assume that a tendency to invoke sharp discipline is a strong point, and this assumption may color every aspect of her evaluation).

One way around these impediments is to avoid evaluative questions altogether and ask the respondent instead to provide specific examples of what the candidate did under certain difficult circumstances. (Was there ever a prison riot? What did he do? Did the state legislature ever uncover a scandal at one of the institutions? What did he do in response?) And you might ask, for background: How do you know the candidate? What was his typical day like? Historical narratives like these can give you insight into the person you are considering. They also can help you (and your search committee) further clarify the description of the kind of person you are seeking.

Assume now that the search has yielded several possible candidates, among them Jim Short, John Boone, and Fred Rankin (a short summary of each is provided in the case). By this time the criteria (and strategy) are far better clarified than at the start of the process. Perhaps each of the finalists should be interviewed by Goldmark and, if possible, by the Governor. Who should be selected, and why?

At this point my students get into heated argument about the relative merits of the three candidates, according to what the Department of Corrections and the Sargent Administration seem to need. How important is it that a candidate have a strong commitment to "deinstitutionalization"? How important is it that the candidate is black? How relevant is a prison record of administrative experience? Most often, a majority of my students select Boone for the job.

In fact, the search process for the new Commissioner of Corrections failed to clarify the criteria for selection or to define the broad strategy for the department. Good management skills, in particular, were hardly considered. The candidate finally selected was indeed John Boone. In the months after Boone became Commissioner, conditions in Massachusetts prisons deteriorated, guards went on strike, and prisoners rioted. Boone was unable to stem the deterioration. The public demanded that something drastic be done, and Boone was fired shortly thereafter.

chapter 9

Implementing a Strategy

We saw in the last case that a search for the new head of an agency is also a search for a strategy—a mandate to achieve certain goals over the long term, combined with an understanding of what will be required to get there. Ideally, the search process defines long-term goals more clearly and identifies some of the likely obstacles and possibilities along the way. Such clarification helps the new agency head understand what is expected; it thus strengthens and focuses the mandate for action.

But as we have seen in many of the preceding cases, mandates are never unambiguous. The broad political environment that authorizes public servants to take action is in continuous tumult; there is rarely a unanimity of opinion among legislators, judges, chief executives, high-level appointed officials, journalists, and the leaders of important interest groups about what should be done. And even where sufficient agreement is reached to provide something of a mandate, opinions have a way of shifting. A mandate to accomplish one thing at one point in time may become a mandate to accomplish quite a different thing at a later point.

The search process can help create a consensus, at least for a time, but the new agency head must nevertheless carefully diagnose the strategic situation. How strong is the mandate to achieve certain long-term goals? Where does the mandate come from? If the vision is shared primarily by a small number of people clustered around the Governor, the President, or the agency head's immediate superior, then the mandate may not be strong enough to shift the agency in a new direction. Are there alternative visions of what the agency should be doing and where it should be heading? Where do these visions arise from, within the complex authorizing environment, and how much force and potential momentum is behind them?

The new agency head must also consider the resources within the agency, which need to be aligned with any new mandate. Are the agency's personnel willing and capable of performing the new tasks? Are the agency's traditions and culture consistent with the new mandate? And what about the standard operating procedures, the systems of initiating and reviewing actions, the methods and standards for rewarding good performance, the means of recruiting new staff, and the systems for analyzing and evaluating policy proposals? Are these management systems conducive to achieving the new mandate, or must they be altered as well?

Finally, the new agency head must decide upon particular, short-term activities and goals that begin to move the agency toward the new mandate. What exactly should the agency seek to accomplish over the new month or year? What are its specific *products* to be?

These three dimensions of the strategic challenge can be summarized in this way: The new agency head must seek to *align* internal resources and short-term objectives with the new mandate, at the same time broadening and deepening the mandate so that it can be sustained over time.

Recall Pendleton School. There, as we saw, the school's internal resources (its personnel, culture, and operating systems) were well aligned with its day-to-day products (cheap custodial care of the mentally retarded), and both were entirely consistent with its unofficial political mandate (to keep mentally retarded adults off the streets, provide a source of local employment, and spend as little of the taxpayer's money as possible). Such a perfect alignment created extraordinary stability, notwithstanding periodic intrusions by the press (in the form of shocking stories about conditions at the school) and by a few reform-minded citizens. Under these circumstances, the first challenge facing anyone who wished to change the system was to destabilize it—to shift the mandate, shake up the internal resources, and thus create the possibility for an improvement in day-to-day operations. But destabilizing the system would have constituted only the first step. To achieve lasting reform, it would have been necessary to create a new stable system, in which internal resources, external mandate, and day-to-day operations were all realigned.

As the following case shows, before 1968 the Federal Trade Commission was a stable system, and like the Pendleton School, reformers were convinced that this stable system was accomplishing the wrong things. The mandate began to change, and a new chairman was appointed. Consider his strategic challenge.

A Failing Agency:
The Federal Trade Commission

INTRODUCTION

It was October of 1969 and the Federal Trade Commission—Pennsylvania Avenue's Little Old Lady—was scrambling for its life. Never the crucible for frenzied action or high morale, the agency had nevertheless managed to hang on over the years. It was 55 years old, had friends in Congress and the advantages of bureaucratic inertia. It had held on to its budget but, more importantly, it had held onto its mandate: "to prevent the free enterprise system from being stifled or fettered by monopoly or corrupted by unfair or deceptive trade practices." In the face of the burgeoning consumer movement, it continued methodically to concentrate a goodly portion of its resources on insuring that sweaters labeled 90 percent wool really didn't contain 89.9 percent. The joke went around that three museums sat side by side on Pennsylvania Avenue—the National Archives, the National Gallery and the Federal Trade Commission.

And then in January of 1969 the bubble burst. Ralph Nader and an energetic crew of spirited law students took on the FTC and, after a summer of probing their way through a mostly hostile commission, published "The Consumer and the Federal Trade Commission." The 185-page Nader report was a searing indictment of the Commission, painting it as inadequate, incompetent, lazy, lethargic, and confused:

> Like an aged courtesan ravaged by the pox, the FTC paints heavily the face it presents to the public. Because the failures go deep the paint has to be laid on thick—thick as a mask. Keeping the mask painted is perhaps the one activity the Commission dedicates itself to with energy. Its working materials are public relations, secrecy and collusion.

Nine months later, an ABA commission issued its own report on the FTC. Their language was more subdued but their message was no less disturbing than Nader's. Either the FTC undertake wholesale reform or "there will be no substantial purpose to be served by its continued existence."

Reeling from these charges, the Commission awaited the next blow. It came from President Nixon in October of 1969. He asked a California attorney, Caspar W. Weinberger, to become chairman of the FTC, handing him the broad mandate to begin immediately the "reactivation and revitalization" of the Commission. The old FTC, a "political dumping ground" as one Commissioner called it, had come face-to-face with the potent force of this consumer movement.

THE EARLY YEARS OF THE FTC

On December 21, 1913, in Woodrow Wilson's first State of the Union Message, the seeds of the FTC were sown. Wilson called for new antitrust legislation and Congress provided Wilson with two, not one, pieces of legislation. The first was the Federal Trade Commission Act, passed September 26, 1914. Its heart lay in a simple ten-word statement: "Unfair methods of competition in commerce are hereby declared unlawful." The Commission was created to make that policy work, to give it precise contours and develop the enforcement mechanisms that would make the policy live. Two-and-a-half weeks later, President Wilson signed the Clayton Act, a piece of legislation which, among other safeguards against unfair business practices, forbids mergers or acquisitions that substantially curtail competition. Taken together, these two pieces of legislation apparently provided the FTC a broad power to design a more healthy relationship between the American people and American business. However, it had never turned out quite that way.

From the very beginning the FTC was plagued by the political force of patronage. To avoid this, the

This case was prepared by Randy I. Bellows under the supervision of Professor Philip B. Heymann for use at the John Fitzgerald Kennedy School of Government, Harvard University.

Copyright © 1976 by the President and Fellows of Harvard College.

original FTC Act declared that no more than three of the Commission's five members could be from the same party. Yet in the 1920s, Republican administrations made the FTC a convenient dumping ground for political patronage.

President Roosevelt tried to change things but met with little success. According to the Nader Report:

> President Roosevelt, recognizing the FTC's potential, tried to reform its personnel and use it to spearhead his New Deal program. However, his attempt to remove the worst of the Commissioners was rebuffed in 1935 by the Supreme Court in the case of *U.S.* v. *Humphrey's Executor*, on the grounds that a Commissioner's position was quasi-judicial. Roosevelt gave up on the FTC and used it to his political advantage by granting it as a political dukedom to Senator Kenneth McKellar of Tennessee. The dukedom was managed for McKellar and "Boss" Crump's Memphis political machine by another Tennesseean, Commissioner Edwin C. Davis, from 1933 to 1949. Throughout this period, positions were openly given because of personal connections and political patronage, with Southern Democrats receiving the lion's share.

> The Republican years from 1952 to 1960 were lean years for Tennesseeans at the FTC, but they managed to survive, and, with a Democratic administration and Mr. (Paul Rand) Dixon's appointment, things were back to normal. Most of the top staff now at the Commission either came during the period of the "Tennessee gang" or are clubhouse friends. As one disgruntled observer stated to a Wall Street Journal reporter in 1963, "The atmosphere of the agency was like a southern county courthouse, and it is again." From what we saw, nothing has changed since.

For example, when Paul Rand Dixon was appointed chairman of the Commission by President Kennedy, staff Republicans in high positions were given a choice of resigning or becoming trial lawyers at the bottom level of the organization. Of the nearly 500 attorneys on the staff of the Commission in 1969, only some 40 were Republicans.

As could be expected from the political milieu in which it drew personnel, staff quality suffered. The Hoover Commission, which undertook a study of the FTC in 1949, found the agency full of much "deadwood" and said:

> In the past, the Commission has applied a policy of promotion from within. That policy has enabled the Commission to obtain some men of real competence, but in other cases, limited ability, plus sheer longevity, has won positions of importance. . . . Future appointments and promotions should discount mere seniority and instead should emphasize ability and experience.

Even more important to the agency's lethargic history were confusion and ambivalence as to its purpose. The law itself was simple and direct: the agency should eliminate unfair methods of competition. What was unclear was who was it most important to protect against whom: American industry against cheaper foreign competitors; small business against big business; or consumers against deceptive sellers? In addition to its original charter, the agency was given several other responsibilities. In 1936, the Robinson-Patman Act was passed to protect small retailers against the buying power of large chain stores (which could then sell more cheaply to consumers). Accepting the premise that chain stores and big manufacturers could obtain goods far cheaper than the smaller independents, Congressman Wright Patman co-authored the Act, "to protect the independent merchant, the public whom he serves, and the manufacturer from whom he buys, from exploitation by his chain competitor." Two years later, the Wheeler-Lea Amendment to the FTC Act broadened the Commission's mandate far beyond the elimination of "unfair methods of competition." The Amendment read, "Unfair or deceptive acts or practices in commerce are also illegal." The FTC explained in *Your Federal Trade Commission*:

> This amendment benefited the buying public. The FTC could now proceed, not only in matters that adversely affected competition, but also in situations where it could be shown that consumers were being deceived or treated unfairly.

In addition to these broad statements of policy, the FTC was given through the years a variety of other responsibilities: protection of the public against false advertising in the sale of food, drugs, devices and cosmetics; protection of the consumer in credit transactions; insuring the proper labeling of fur, wool and other textiles; prohibiting the sale of dangerous flammable fabrics; and regulating the packaging and labeling of certain products.

To implement these responsibilities, the Commission was empowered to issue cease and desist orders after formal adjudicatory proceedings prohibiting the respondent from again engaging in the practices the Commission found illegal. The order became final, and subject to penalties for violation, only at the conclusion of a course of judicial review that could go from the Court of Appeals to the Supreme Court.

In deciding whom it was most important to protect, the Commission often came down squarely on the side of American industry. The times in which the FTC acted provide an answer why. Almost immediately after the Commission's creation, the United States became involved in the First World War and witnessed the emergence of Japan as a textile and synthetic manufacturer of major proportion. This posed a real threat to the American textile industry which responded by persuading powerful Congressmen to insure that the FTC's first interest was protecting American industry against foreign competition. As the nation entered the Great Depression, the motivation changed but the results were the same. Now, industry needed to be protected in order to insure jobs. Attacking industry was attacking jobs. Few voices argued for regulation that could harm or interfere with the laissez-faire capitalism that had ruled the Twenties. After World War II, the FTC concentrated more on protecting small business against big business—but protecting business was still its purpose. As to the consumer, it was believed, protecting industry would protect him too. The choice was doubtless made easier by a process of decision that relied heavily on complaints as a source of information. Competitors were more forceful, credible, and frequent complainants.

Whatever its goals, the FTC plainly wasn't doing a very good job of pursuing them. In 1949 the Hoover Commission scored the agency for its tendency to get involved in protracted litigation or other proceedings in trivial matters.

> As the years have progressed, the Commission has become immersed in a multitude of petty problems. . . . The Commission has largely become a passive judicial agency, waiting for cases to come upon the docket, under routinized procedures, without active responsibilities for achieving statutory objectives.

> In the selection of cases for its formal dockets, the Commission has long been guilty of prosecuting trivial and technical offenses and of failing to confine these dockets to cases of public importance.

Not much had changed by 1969 when the ABA Commission wrote:

> Since its establishment in 1914, a succession of independent scholars and groups have sounded much the same themes in their criticisms of the FTC, including the absence of effective planning and failure to establish workable priorities, the consequent tendency to become involved in too many trivial cases, the delay and unnecessary secrecy in FTC operations, and the uneven quality of staff. . . . Virtually all critics of FTC performance have emphasized its continuing failure to establish and follow clear priorities of administrative action. Gerard Henderson, an early critic of the FTC, noted that the agency too often became involved in trivial matters, and attributed this deficiency to a lack of orderly planning.

But who was complaining? Surely not industry, much of which felt that any governmental regulation was too much and that the FTC already interfered entirely too much. If the FTC was prosecuting trivial cases, if it took 16 years to get the liver out of Carter's Little Liver Pills, who was complaining? With no potent lobbying force behind them, commissions critiquing the FTC came and went, but there was no one to fight for their recommendations.

In the Sixties, though, there was a difference. Some indication of the change was the increase in the circulation of Consumer Reports which tripled in the five years after 1963 and then doubled again in the next 5 years. By 1973 it reached over two million purchasers with a median income of $16,000 (an estimated six million total readers). When the consumer movement began to coalesce, it was quickly realized that the Wheeler-Lea Amendment, outlawing deceptive trade practices, could bring substantial protection to consumer transactions. The Federal Trade Commission thus became the natural, even the inevitable, target of the consumer movement. Its mandate included protecting the consumer against deceptive practices. Even had the FTC been doing a magnificent job in this area, it could hardly have avoided the scrutiny and criticism of the consumer movement. But the FTC was not doing a magnificent job. In fact, "The Little Old Lady on Pennsylvania Avenue" was so decrepit by the late Sixties that when Ralph Nader brought together seven young activists for an investigation, it was a "sitting duck." They were Nader's Raiders and it was the FTC study that gave them their name.

NADER, THE ABA AND THE FTC

Nader's Raiders. It was a curious group Nader had put together to make his first detailed foray into an administrative agency. They included the great-grandson of one President (William Howard Taft IV) and the future son-in-law of another (Edward F. Cox). Despite these establishment credentials, Chairman Paul Rand Dixon did not welcome them. Wrote Charles McCarry, in his book *Citizen Nader*:

[The Raiders] were, Nader believes, the first citizens many of the bureaucrats had ever seen in their offices. Accustomed to deal with the representatives of industry and trade associations, or with the agents of consumer organizations, they were understandably confused by a group of persistent youths who demanded to know the most intimate details of the Commission's work.

The Raiders' technique, in brief, was to demand access to the Commission's files and budget and to request interviews with leading officials. There was great reluctance on the part of Chairman Dixon to accede to either request. The Raiders, in the end, secured a good deal of data by threatening to sue under the Freedom of Information Act, and by less conventional means. After commencing on June 17 with their interviews with upper officials of the Commission, the Raiders were foreclosed from further interrogation by Dixon's ruling that they had "had ample opportunity to complete their interviews with our personnel, and . . . after August 23 they would no longer have unlimited access to staff members." The Raiders regarded this action, coming after more than two months of interviewing, as "an illegal lockout."

In their report the Raiders speak of "a tacit yet institutionalized fear—radiating outwards from the Chairman's office," which hampered their search for facts. They interviewed some officials of the Commission in secret, and a good deal of the book was derived from the information developed in these clandestine meetings.

The Nader Report was released on January 2, 1969. It created a sensation. "It made headlines all over the country," recalls Robert Fellmeth, one of the authors of "The Consumer and the Federal Trade Commission." Said Fellmeth, "I thought, are these people crazy? We're just a bunch of students. It was Nader's press agentry and the fact that we just said it."

What they said constituted a blanket indictment of just about everything in and about the Commission: its personnel, its politics, its purposes and its penchant to live on in obscurity. As McCarry pointed out, it was not "a scholarly work or even an assay into journalism; it is, as it was intended to be, an activist's tract," replete with "unattributed quotations and assertions that are not always supported in their context by facts." Given this caveat, the report still describes a Commission with monumental troubles. At the top of the list was its personnel.

The authors wrote:

. . . it is highly appropriate to mention that alcoholism, spectacular lassitude, and office absenteeism, incompetence by the most modest standards, and a lack of commitment to the regulatory mission are rampant. . . . They are well known to the Chairman, who somehow has found that they add to the congenial environment and unquestioned loyalties that surround his office.

That was just the opening shot. Said the authors, much of the criticism for the agency's poor personnel track record could be traced to Chairman Dixon himself. Instead of recognizing the nonpolitical nature of the regulatory agency, Dixon inculcated it with politics. The Raiders wrote:

When Mr. Dixon became Chairman in 1960 (a Kennedy Democratic appointment), it seems that the "best men" were all Democrats. Any Republican in a high position was offered the choice of becoming a trial lawyer at the bottom of the organization chart or resigning.

As a result, fourteen highly experienced career men left the Commission almost immediately.

Only one Republican holds a position of any prominence in the operating bureaus of the FTC: Charles Moore, who recently succeeded Sam Williams as chief of the Bureau of Field Operations. Mr. Moore is a Republican, but in his case there is an extenuating factor—he comes from Johnson City, Tennessee. There are advantages for the ambitions at the FTC in being born in Tennessee or, for that matter, in any small town in the South.

Dixon was prejudiced against "Ivy League lawyers" and saw to it that they didn't infiltrate the FTC, said the Raiders.

As a result, graduates of prestigious law schools such as Harvard and Pennsylvania, which have very capable antitrust departments, have a poor chance of joining the FTC, compared with graduates of law schools like Kentucky and Tennessee. Eleven Harvard graduates from the classes of '67 and '68 applied to the FTC, and only four were offered appointments. From the University of Pennsylvania, only three of nine applicants were given offers and from New York University only three of thirty-four applicants made it. However, from the University of Kentucky it was nine out of eleven and from Tennessee six out of sixteen.

Said the Raiders, it was possible that these law students from Southern schools were more qualified than the Northern graduates but that the facts did not bear out this conclusion. They cited higher LSAT scores in the "national" law schools, tougher admission policies and the fact that twice as many Northerners were applying for FTC jobs as Southerners (though twice as many Southerners were hired).[1]

Beyond all this, the Raiders said, Dixon's hiring and personnel policies were overtly political. The Hatch Act of 1964 prohibits the soliciting of political funds by government employees. The Civil Service Commission forbids party discrimination in hiring.

Yet in the case of the present regime at the FTC, the Hatch Act and the Civil Service Law are treated as mere rhetoric. Most attorneys at the FTC are labeled as either Democrat or Republican, and their party affiliation has a definite bearing on the positions they are offered. . . .

Besides permitting his staff to violate the spirit and the letter of the Civil Service Law in promotion and hiring, Chairman Dixon himself has violated the Hatch Act. Highly reliable sources at the FTC revealed that until recently Mr. Dixon was notorious for dunning the agency's personnel as far down as the GS-14 level for political contributions.

His methods would make any chairman

of an alumni fund-raising committee jealous. Members of the staff have testified to receiving solicitation cards from the Democratic National Committee with a code number in the corner which everyone involved knew would indicate to Chairman Dixon who gave and who did not.

The study went on to report that, although Dixon has had to abandon this method because of a threat of action by the Justice Department, he still asks subordinates to buy $100-a-plate tickets to Democratic fund-raising dinners.

In general, the Raiders wrote, Dixon was not interested in top talent. They quoted Dixon as saying to *Advertising Age* in 1961: "Given a choice between a really bright man, and one who is merely good, take the good man. He'll stay longer."

Within four years, though, said the Raiders, 80 percent of the new lawyers who come to the FTC leave anyway. Many have simply given up trying to get something meaningful done. Young lawyers write memoranda recommending complaints that are reviewed at so many levels that "months of inaction, petty changes, and misallocated attorney-hours" occur frequently. Often, two attorneys are both assigned to the same investigation, yet neither told of the other's presence. And "if an assiduous worker completes his assigned duties early and requests additional work, he is not given another investigation but is assigned to write a research paper on the Robinson-Patman Act."

Finally, the Raiders accused "friends on Capitol Hill" of unduly controlling the make-up of the agency. Staff members of the agency told the Raiders that an attorney needed a political sponsor to really get ahead. The Report cited the example of Tennessee Congressman Joe Evins. Evins was Chairman of the House Appropriations subcommittee which approves the FTC budget. The Raiders wrote:

One staff member of the FTC stated the rule: "Ambitious staff attorneys at the FTC who are from Tennessee have to know Joe Evins." For example, when a political friend, Judge Casto C. Geer, wanted to work near his home town in Tennessee, the FTC obligingly set up an office in Oak Ridge, although it does not have any offices in, for instance, Detroit or Philadelphia. Although the FTC never announced the opening of its new office, Representative Evins did make an announcement which, together with a picture of Judge Geer, appeared on the front page of *The Chattanooga Times*.

---

[1] To this, Dixon replied: "The Nader group infers strongly that the hiring practices of the Commission discriminate against "prestigious" law schools. Indirectly, I read in this charge that if a graduating student did not attend one of these schools he is adjudged a second-class lawyer coming from a mediocre school. What arrogance!"

Sometimes, however, congressional influence had more dangerous effects:

Such was the case of the flammable baby blankets. In the 1950s Representative Albert Thomas of Texas was Chairman of the House Subcommittee on Appropriations for Independent Agencies, the post now held by Joe Evins. Representative Thomas, on behalf of Texas cotton interests, influenced the Commission to rule that baby blankets were not covered by the Flammable Fabrics Law. Baby blankets, the Commission said, do not qualify as "clothing."

The Response.   At the Commission itself, the reaction to the Nader Report was mixed. Said Commissioner Philip Elman, "there has . . . certainly been some awareness even among hostile elements here that the report was largely accurate, in emphasis if not always in details. . . . It was remarkable that they got as much information as they did. Of course, it was much worse in some ways than they said."

Commissioner Dixon was less generous: "How any group could profess or claim to have made an empirical study of the activities of the (FTC) and make no mention of at least a single accomplishment is beyond me." Among the accomplishments Dixon defends was the effort by the FTC to force cigarette companies to put a health hazard warning onto cigarette packs. The FTC moved quickly on this, immediately following the Surgeon General's report, and was dogged on its persistence. Only a federal statute, pre-empting the issue by requiring a warning, finally stopped the Commission. The Raiders cite the case but label it atypical.

More to the point was Dixon's philosophical difference with the Raiders about the role of the agency. He told *Newsweek* in 1967, well before the Nader study,

We're not a civil rights agency, and we can't be policemen for the whole economy. Caveat emptor is dead and buried . . . so much so that there's a danger of going overboard in the other direction. We're trying to find the middle ground.

Dixon attacked not only the report but the reporters:

The study resulted in a hysterical, antibusiness diatribe and a scurrilous, untruthful attack on the career personnel of the Commission and an arrogant demand for my resignation. This report emanates from a group with a self-granted license to criticize a respected government agency by the use of a type of invective and a "smear technique" that newspapermen inform me is unusual even for Washington.

The history of the FTC had never been marked by entirely smooth sailing. But the Nader Report was a disruption of tidal wave proportions. It not only pointed out a path of inquiry for interested Congressmen; it also put the Nixon administration on the alert that the FTC had become a symbol of insensitivity to consumer concerns. Nixon sensed that the report was no mere aberration but a sign of the emerging consumer movement. He decided to direct a further, perhaps less biased, study. He turned to the American Bar Association and asked it to undertake its own study of the FTC. In his letter to the president of the ABA, Nixon wrote:

As you may be aware, this administration is conducting an extensive review of the Federal Government's activities in the field of consumer protection. Consumer protection has become a matter of public concern, in part it appears, because existing agencies charged with the protection of consumer interests may have failed to discharge their obligations satisfactorily.

The ABA Report.   In September of that same tumultuous year for the FTC, the ABA Commission headed by a Philadelphia Republican lawyer, Miles Kirkpatrick, delivered its report. It had little of Nader's often inflammatory rhetoric, but that made its unequivocal conclusion all the more startling:

The case for change is plain. What is required is that the changes be made, and in depth. Further temporizing is indefensible. Notwithstanding the great potential of the FTC in the field of antitrust and consumer protection, if change does not occur, there will be no substantial purpose to be served by its continued existence; the essential work to be done must then be carried on by other governmental institutions.

The ABA Commission first scored the FTC for its virtually paralyzing lack of planning. Staff attorneys did not know when to bring formal complaints or when to proceed to seek voluntary compliance. An Office of Program Review existed, but no statements of long-range objectives or priorities ever emerged from it. And, finally, once a matter was initiated there was no mechanism to keep track of it within the agency. The result: *ad hoc* decision-making run wild.

Just as serious as the failure to plan was the simple failure to get things done. Since the early Sixties, the ABA Commission found, the FTC had been doing less and less in more and more areas. Less investigations opened, less investigations closed, less formal complaints issued, less voluntary compliance and less cease and desist orders given.

The ABA Commission found the de-emphasis on formal enforcement harmful:

> For an agency employing over 400 lawyers, and charged with responsibility for enforcement of statutes in important and developing areas of law, to initiate a grand total of 23 contested cases in a year is disturbing. With such an obvious disinclination by the FTC to proceed formally, we fear that the business community may cease to take seriously the guides, rules, and other administrative pronouncements by the FTC, and also may cease to take seriously the statutes the FTC is empowered to enforce.

Furthermore, the ABA reported, when the FTC did decide to spend its money—formally or informally—the allocation was misplaced. In 1959, the Commission had been spending 16.9 percent of its total budget on enforcement related to Section 7 of the Clayton Act and 9.3 percent in enforcement work in the Bureau of Textiles and Furs. Ten years later, "during a period when the United States, according to the FTC's own Bureau of Economics, was undergoing the greatest surge of merger activity in its history," the situation had largely reversed itself. In 1969, the Commission spent 11 percent of its budget on textiles and furs but only 9 percent on antitrust activity under Section 7 of the Clayton Act. In the area of deceptive practices, the ABA report continued, the FTC still devoted little time and less money to combatting ghetto frauds and other forms of localized marketing deception. As to the FTC's complaints that it did not have the money to monitor mass media advertising and police voluntary compliance, the ABA said the FTC could have made the effort to divert resources from other programs, but did not.

In general, the ABA found the Commission's entire effort in the consumer protection area lacking:

> There is a general conviction that marketing frauds against consumers are widespread in this country and constitute a problem of major national concern. The feeling is not that business practices have changed significantly but rather that the public is increasingly unwilling to tolerate exploitation. . . .
>
> Our study has led us to the conclusion that the FTC's efforts to investigate the basis in fact for this public outcry and to find ways of coping with whatever underlying problems exist have been inadequate. It is true that the FTC's resources may not match the scope of the problem, and we do not fault the FTC for failing to still all the complaints of consumer fraud. . . . However, the FTC has fallen far short of what it could have done. It has failed to instill a sense of mission either in its own personnel or in the states and municipalities which are so badly in need of the information and expertise which should be at the FTC's disposal. Its efforts have been piecemeal, and have lacked the study and planning which are essential to identify the most pressing problems faced by consumers, and to create a unified approach toward their solution. Often the agency has seemed more concerned with protecting competitors of an enterprise practicing deception rather than consumers.

In the FTC's other major areas of responsibility, Antitrust Activity, the ABA Commission gave the FTC a mixed report:

> If the measure of the quality of FTC performance in the antitrust area is whether the agency has broken new ground and made new law by resort to its unique administrative resources, it seems clear that the record is one of missed opportunity. However, the FTC did lead the way in implementation and interpretation of Section 7 of the Clayton Act. Moreover, that program has been carried out not simply by the institution of formal proceedings, but by the publication of economic reports and the promulgation of guides, *i.e.*, by use of the full panoply of administrative resources available to the FTC.

But even where the FTC tried to make a favorable showing, it was undercut by its own staggering backlogs and delays. Wrote the ABA Commission:

> Problems of delay have vexed the FTC ever since it was established, and some of the most notorious examples of protracted administrative proceedings have occurred in that agency. . . .
>
> In the investigative stages of restraint of

trade and deceptive practice matters, it appears that despite a substantial reduction in the number of investigations, problems of delay are at least as serious now as they were in 1961. It is particularly disturbing that the most serious delay problems arise in the deceptive practice area, in which complex legal questions are seldom raised and consumers may continue to be defrauded pending completion of the FTC's investigation. . . .

In combination, the delays in investigation and litigation continue to produce decisions based on stale and unreliable evidence and to undermine effective enforcement of the statutes committed to the FTC's jurisdiction.

Finally, there was the matter of staff quality, the question on which the Nader report had focused. The ABA Commission wrote a bit more politely, but they expressed just as much dissatisfaction with the Commission's personnel, from the top on down. They found the Commission membership riddled with dissension that confused and disrupted the staff.

In that connection, we note that recent differences of view among Commissioners have reached unusual levels. This dissension, relating not only to enforcement philosophy but also to questions to how the agency ought to be run, has become a matter of public record. . . .

We do not mean to suggest that it is inappropriate for Commissioners of an independent regulatory agency to express publicly their deeply held views. . . . But there does come a point at which bitter public statements reflecting disunity among Commissioners begin to affect the performance of any agency. There are indications at present that members of the staff of the FTC, trapped between radically different philosophies of enforcement among Commissioners, are perplexed as to how to perform their duties, and increasingly demoralized by the bitter exchanges among the Commissioners.

Problems with the FTC did not stop at the highest level though, according to the ABA report. Like Nader, the ABA Commission members raised the problem created by "pressure from Congressmen to hire or promote particular individuals." But the problem of staff quality was not solely Congress' fault. Even with recent FTC efforts at more aggressive recruitment, the ABA still found that recruitment techniques were not adequate. Much of the

problem had to do with the attitude of the senior staff members hiring new attorneys.

We were informed by the bureau chief in charge of recruitment of field office attorneys that this latter policy [of not permitting field office attorneys to engage in trial work] is based on the assumption that young lawyers are not competent to engage in both trial and investigative work—a view of the capacity of young lawyers that we doubt is shared by the Department of Justice or by many private employers in the United States. The same senior staff member also told us he preferred to hire older men—because they tended to be loyal and remain with the FTC. He also reported that he gave less weight to law school grades than to other factors. If there is a formula better designated to avoid hiring bright and energetic young men, we have not heard of it.

The ABA concluded that "unless it attracts new personnel of high quality," the FTC would not be able to implement its present programs, let alone anything new. There was, said the ABA, just too many instances of incompetence in the agency—particularly at senior levels.

The ABA Commission Report was not entirely critical. It credited the agency with improving its operation in several respects. It cited efforts to improve the FTC's rules of practice and procedure, experimenting with new administrative techniques, such as trade regulation rules, and developing new doctrines of merger. Also, said the ABA, opinion writing had been placed "on a more responsible basis." On the whole, though, the ABA found the commission a real disappointment:

its performance when measured against a reasonable standard of acceptable government operation has been disappointing. When actual performance is measured against the potential, which the FTC continues to possess, the agency's performance must be regarded as a failure on many counts.

The ABA provided the President with a host of recommendations for upgrading the agency. In the consumer protection area, it recommended that the Commission undertake a major pilot project in 8 or 10 urban areas, focusing on the prevention and study of retail marketing abuse, particularly in ghetto areas. In the antitrust area, it called for long-term planning, renewed recruitment efforts to hire a quality staff, and a reorganization of the Bureau of Economics. As to process, it asked that the FTC pass rules governing *ex parte* communications.

The ABA also recommended that Congress give the Commission broader preliminary injunction powers. The study had recognized that one of the major problems with the FTC was the often futile use of cease and desist orders, coupled with excruciating delays. As a result, a deceptive advertiser could run his ads year after year while his lawyers battled it out with the FTC through various administrative proceedings. If a cease and desist order was finally given, it only told the advertiser that he couldn't run the ad in the future. No punishment was given for past conduct. The ABA recommended the use of preliminary injunction to halt deceptive and other unfair trade practices during the course of FTC proceedings. In addition, the ABA recommended that the highest priority be put on cleaning up the backlog of pending cases and reinvigorating the Office of Program Review. Finally, it called for better supervision of matters already within the FTC and more effective delegation of authority to the FTC staff.

A More Radical Proposal. In a separate dissenting opinion, one member of the ABA Commission, Richard A. Posner, had his own recommendation: kill the agency off completely and give its functions to various other branches of government. Posner had done what the other members of the ABA Commission would not do: the unthinkable act of considering the fundamental validity of having an FTC at all.

Posner, who had earlier worked as a staff assistant to Commissioner Elman, attacked the basic assumption that an administrative agency was the suitable forum for dealing with consumer problems. Wouldn't it be better, he asked, to let the courts fashion remedies and "if the courts hesitate or stumble in adapting common law principles to novel circumstances" let the legislature come in with its own solutions? Admittedly, most consumers did not have enough at stake to bring a case to court. But they could aggregate claims and, more importantly, the competitors of deceptive sellers would have a tremendous incentive to sue. Add some stricter criminal penalties, Posner said, and you'd have a judiciary with real muscle to protect the consumer.

Posner was quick to admit that there were those situations where a competitor would not have an incentive to sue another competitor—where the fraud was industry-wide. In those cases, he said, competitors would still have the market incentive to make their product safer, or better, or portray it more honestly. Furthermore, by requiring competitors to go into court to protest other manufacturers' sins, you would be imposing a higher entrance fee than allowing competitors to simply complain to the FTC. This would eliminate harassing tactics.

Not only was the FTC ineffective, Posner said, but in many cases it caused positive harm. He particularly focused on instances of slight or questionable fraud where the FTC imposed requirements on manufacturers to provide extra information on every product label (*e.g.*, requiring watchbands to bear the country of origin). The result, he argued, was that a cheap product could no longer be sold as cheaply. In many other cases, he added, the FTC embroiled itself in contests about deception that established no really important principles for consumer protection. Analyzing a series of fraud cases from 1963, Posner concluded:

In fiscal year 1963, one is forced to conclude, the FTC bought precious little consumer protection for the more than $5 million that it expended in the area of fraudulent and unfair marketing practices, and the many millions more that it forced the private sector to expend in litigation and compliance. Besides wasting a good deal of money in tilting at windmills, the Commission inflicted additional social costs of unknown magnitude by impeding the free marketing of cheap substitute products, including foreign products of all kinds, fiber substitutes for animal furs, costume jewelry, and inexpensive scents; by proscribing truthful designations; by harassing discount sellers; and by obstructing a fair market test for products of debatable efficacy.

Finally, Posner challenged the proposition that fraud was rampant in the slums, calling widespread ghetto fraud a proposition often based on "unverified and often incredible assertions" by dissatisfied consumers. Even if the accusations were true, he said, "given the state of our knowledge, it is premature to unleash the FTC on the problems of poor consumers. Study should precede action." He added that a campaign of compelling greater disclosure by slum merchants could have just the opposite effect of that intended. Information is not free, he pointed out, and the result might well be higher prices, "a curious way to fight poverty."

In concluding, Posner challenged the basic assumption under which the FTC operated: that an administrative agency was competent to deal with the problems entrusted to the Commission. He criticized his colleagues for their "resolute air of optimism," for their belief that "better leadership and better staff, with greater appropriations, with a renewed sense of dedication'' could save the agency. Their mistake, he said, is in their concentration on ''management efficiency,'' in their belief that if you made an agency more efficient it would be more effective.

But management efficiency won't solve an agency's isolation from Presidential interest and control, said Posner. It won't solve the dependence of the agency on the beneficence of Congress. It won't solve the lack of personal incentive that would motivate the agency staff to move aggressively into the consumer protection field. In fact, agency members and staff who want to keep their jobs and their appropriations have a tremendous incentive to do just the opposite—to encourage conciliation with organized economic interests and influential Congressmen.

The result was that the FTC took the side of already organized economic pressure groups (establishment firms), rather than that of new entrants or silent consumers. They concentrated on trivial fraud cases and, in the antitrust area, not on the most monopolistic industries but the most competitive ones (for example, food, textiles, and retail and wholesale distribution).

The answer, said Posner, was the judicial system. Over the past 50 years, when the FTC stayed ''adrift in its backwater,'' the court system made enormous strides. The crucial fact, said Posner, ''is that the updating of the judicial process appears to be proceeding more rapidly than the reform of the administrative process.'' Finally, more prestige was housed in the court system. A court appointment was often not a steppingstone but a terminal destination. He wondered what would happen if you made administrative appointments lifelong.

Posner admitted that the time to abandon the FTC had still not quite been reached, ''not on the basis of the kind of evidence that I have been able to assemble for the purposes of this statement.'' Instead, he called for the freezing of the Commission's appropriation at the present level and withholding from it any new responsibilities. This would force the agency to justify its ''dubious'' existence. ''If no justification were forthcoming,'' he concluded, ''the freeze would be maintained and the forces of inflation and economic growth would gradually effect a practical repeal of the regulatory scheme.''

NIXON ACTS

President Nixon chose to go with the ABA Commission's majority plan for reorganization and reform. He asked Congress for technical changes in the FTC Act to broaden its applicability to areas ''affecting'' interstate commerce, not just ''in'' interstate commerce. He asked Congress to give FTC the power to seek preliminary injunctions in cases where to wait for a cease and desist order would eliminate the effectiveness of formal action. In addition, he made proposals to eliminate the FTC backlog, asked the Bureau of the Budget to make a management study of the FTC, and ordered the FTC to start initiating field investigations rather than waiting for complaints to come to the door.

But of all Nixon's recommendations none was more important than his nominee for the chairmanship of the FTC. The ABA Commission had recognized this when it called for the appointment of a Commission Chairman:

> with executive ability, knowledge of the task Congress has entrusted to the agency, and sufficient strength and independence to resist pressures from Congress, and Executive Branch, or the business community that tend to cripple effective performance by the FTC. Because an urgent responsibility facing the new Chairman will be to unify the agency, we believe that it is important to appoint to this position someone not previously affiliated with it.

Nixon appointed Caspar W. Weinberger to the post. Weinberger is a San Franciscan born attorney who came East for his education (Bachelor's and law degree from Harvard) and went back West to make his name. At the name of his appointment he was 52, and had risen up the Californian chain from state assemblyman, to GOP bigwig, to budget advisor to Governor Ronald Reagan. In the last post, he'd earned a reputation for streamlining the Finance Division. Weinberger did not enjoy a reputation as a consumer advocate but as a tough manager and a fiscal conservative. Nixon suggested that Weinberger focus on the ABA recommendations and reported to Congress that Weinberger had assured him ''that he intends to initiate a new era of vigorous action as soon as he is confirmed by the Senate and takes office.''

WEINBERGER TAKES OVER AND IMMEDIATELY HAS A PROBLEM

Before agreeing to chair the Commission, Weinberger did a quick check to make sure he'd have enough Commissioners behind him to act. He found little to worry about on this score. Not only did Mary Gardiner Jones and Philip Elman agree to support him, but so did Paul Rand Dixon. When Dixon was chairman of the Commission, he was perennially embroiled in disputes with his fellow Commissioners. A Commission chairman ought to be in charge, he felt, and he told Weinberger not to worry about his support.

Weinberger first faced Senate confirmation hearings before the Commerce Committee. Although he had no problem being confirmed, the Senate tried to impress upon him their own view of what was wrong with the Commission. The following interchange with Utah Senator Moss illustrates well one of their primary concerns: Commissioner Elman's charges of political patronage.

> *Senator Moss.* In the reports that we have had recently on the Federal Trade Commission there has been criticism leveled at the quality of managerial and policymaking personnel of the Commission. The Commission has been accused of making its personnel choices in response to the political whims from Capitol Hill.
>
> I have heard it said that many of the severely criticized employees have boasted that no Commission Chairman would dare to fire them. How are you going to meet this dilemma?
>
> *Mr. Weinberger.* It seems to me you meet it by the basic test that you want the most competent, able people that you can possibly get in all of the positions at the Commission, and some of them have very definite duties of a specialized nature that require expertise and some of them have a very definite requirement of managerial talent but there are other requirements.
>
> It seems to me that if you use the basic test of trying to get the most able people for the particular specialty required, that this would be the best route to follow. I think it is fair to say in applying that test that I or anyone in this position would welcome the suggestions from anyone, and certainly there is no reason to suppose that Congressmen or Senators wouldn't have some very good suggestions to make, but in the final analysis the final responsibility would rest with the Commission, or in some cases with the Chairman, and under those circumstances I would want to fulfill that responsibility by trying to assure myself and the other Commissioners that we had obtained the most competent qualified person we could get and that would be the policy I would want to follow.

> *Senator Moss.* One Commissioner had leveled criticism at Congress for its toleration or even instigation of a political spoils system in the appointment and advancement at higher staff levels of the Commission. I want to assure you that you have my full support, and I am sure the full support of my fellow Senators, in eliminating any spoils system which may exist.
>
> The American consumer deserves a Commission staff with the highest degree of professionalism and dedicated to the public interest.
>
> *Mr. Weinberger.* That is my feeling, and I am very glad to hear you say it, sir.
>
> *Senator Moss.* I want you to know it is my feeling and I am sure it is the feeling of the other members of the committee. We have too serious a problem on our hands to tolerate anything that is even suspicious of being a spoils system.

The Senators considering Weinberger's confirmation were also particularly concerned with the feeling that the FTC had fallen under too much Presidential domination. Senator Hartke questioned Weinberger about this:

> *Senator Hartke.* Do you look upon this position in the Federal Trade Commission as primarily responsible to the Congress or primarily responsible to the President, or to both?
>
> *Mr. Weinberger.* I was advised by the chairman of this committee just a few moments ago that this was an arm of Congress, the Federal Trade Commission; and I intend, as I mentioned to Senator Moss, to consult frequently with the Senate Commerce Committee and with the appropriate committees of the House on matters that occur or in which it would appear there is some new direction desirable to take. . . .
>
> It is difficult for me to say at this time whether the Federal Trade Commission should be regarded as a creature of Congress or a creature of the President, or both. I have difficulty in answering that.
>
> I do feel that it was created by the Congress with the President's approval in 1914, and that this should certainly be in the background of anybody's mind administering it. The Congress has passed certain acts directing the Commission to do certain things, and the President

has signed those. And those obviously should be followed.

    Senator Hartke. Let me make it perfectly clear to you, that under the Constitution and under the law which created it, the responsibility is only to the Congress, and not to the President, in any regard whatsoever.

    Mr. Weinberger. The reporting responsibilities?

    Senator Hartke. No; the direct authority. This is not in regard to the President, but in regard to the Presidency—that this is an arm of the Congress, and it is not an arm of the administrative branch of the Government.

    It doesn't mean that you cannot take recommendations from the President, but they really, in the totality of the scene, can only have the same weight that any other individual, probably, in the Government, can render.

Hartke had good reason to emphasize the FTC's obligation to Congress rather than to the President. History had shown that the Commission was too often the agent of Presidential desires.

    Basil Mezines, a veteran of the FTC who became Weinberger's executive director, emphasized just how true this was. He used Presidents Kennedy and Johnson as examples. Kennedy, Mezines said, got off to a bad start with business due to the run-in he had over steel prices. The business community began to spread the word that Kennedy was antibusiness. Kennedy was sensitive to this kind of criticism and, according to Mezines, made sure that the newly appointed Dixon did not proceed too vigorously. When Johnson came into the Presidency, he came into it with the commitment to get along well with business. According to Mezines, Johnson called Dixon into the White House and told him not to be "stirring things up." "So," says Mezines, "Dixon went on a big kick that he loved business too" and began to process more complaints administratively rather than judicially. The other Commissioners followed suit. "Every Commissioner of the FTC was going around saying how they loved business," continued Mezines. "It was a kissing contest. . . . There was no enforcement."

    Such attitudes were not solely the province of Democratic Presidents either. According to Mezines, who came to work for the Commission in 1949, Eisenhower was no better. "Eisenhower was the last person in the world who wanted the FTC to do some-

thing. He didn't know what it was or where it was. It could've been a skin disease for all he knew." As a result, the attitude and efforts of the FTC were far from frenzied.

    But if the Senate wanted to make sure that the FTC did not take its orders from the President, who was it to take its orders from? Obviously, the Congress. And, as the Nader report and the ABA Commission study showed, there were serious problems with this too. "With political antennae, of considerable sensitivity," said the Nader report, "successive FTC chairmen have placated the Congress by servicing requests of its key committee chairmen, providing them with exclusive information for public release and attention, and cajoling the better of them through a variety of delaying techniques, admirable only for their ingenuity."

    Often the best way to placate Congress was to enforce the laws Congress was interested in enforcing. One of the best examples of this was the extraordinary attention paid to enforcement of fur labeling laws by the Commission. This might at first seem strange. But Southern Congressmen controlled the FTC appropriation and oversight committees and had strong textile industry constituencies. According to Mezines, even a strong consumer advocate like Senator Warren Magnuson, who came from a state with a big fur industry (Washington), was an influence in seeing that the FTC paid special attention to labeling laws. Coupled with the Southern block of Tennesseeans, fur labeling became a natural high priority.

    In the final analysis, Congress unquestionably had authority to direct FTC activities. As Mezines put it:

> Don't forget the FTC is a creature of Congress. . . . They are not like a department . . . which is part of the executive. Therefore, they're subject to the will of Congress. The FTC has always responded and done what Congress wanted it to do. If Congress wanted to push ghetto fraud, that's what they'd be doing.

    In effect, therefore, there was a dual criticism of the FTC: first, that it was really too close to both Congress and the President to act as a quasi-independent agency; and, second, that the mandate it was getting from Congress was not good enough for an agency of the FTC's potential. Whether anything could be done about the former criticism was highly questionable. But the latter criticism—that Congress' mandate to the FTC was wrong—not only was well taken, but was being acted upon. In 1969, Congress itself was beginning to feel the signs and pressures of the consumer movement. As Senator Abe Ribicoff said, in congratulating Nader's Raiders on their work:

> I have got a hunch that your testimony and your report have shaken up the FTC and I wouldn't be a bit surprised if some of their methods wouldn't undergo a change. I would hope so.

Ribicoff's sentiment, though widespread enough to give Weinberger important Congressional support, was far from universal. In particular, the sentiment was not at all shared by the Congressman with the strongest influence over the FTC's budget, Tennessee's Joe Evins.

Evins made this quite clear, even before Weinberger could settle into his new position following confirmation. Immediately before Weinberger's first appearance in front of his House Appropriations subcommittee, Evins asked to see him for a moment. Evins took him into a small room, which Weinberger later described as reminding him of a confessional. He handed Weinberger a slip of paper with the names of three FTC employees on it and told Weinberger to make sure they were taken care of. At the committee hearing that followed, Evins went out of his way to lambast former Commission Chairman Paul Rand Dixon. An FTC veteran in attendance perceived this as a threat of sorts to Weinberger, the message being, "I can do this to you too." Evins' committee was then in the midst of considering the FTC's budget request. Weinberger knew that displeasing Evins could cost him as much as a million dollars from a total budget of about $20 million.

Imagine that you are Caspar Weinberger, the new chairman of the Federal Trade Commission. Tennessee Congressman Joe Evins, chairman of the House Appropriations Subcommittee, has just met with you privately and given you a note, on which he has written the names of three FTC employees. He asks you to "take care" of them, presumably meaning that you should bestow upon them special favors, including, perhaps, promotions. What do you do?

In order to decide, you need to understand why your decision is potentially important to your larger strategic challenge. The Federal Trade Commission has been a stable system, much of whose authority has come from Tennessee legislators like Joe Evins. They want the agency to protect small businesses—particularly in the textile industry—from unfair foreign competition, but they don't want the FTC to do much else. Above all, they regard the agency as a source of patronage for loyal supporters. The Commission's internal resources have been aligned with this mandate: Agency personnel do very little of anything; many are drawn from Tennessee; they have had mediocre academic records; the best of them soon leave. And its day-to-day output (what there has been of it) is exactly as you might predict, given the mandate and the resources.

But the mandate is shifting. The American Bar Association's report, coupled with the Nader Report, have focused public attention on the agency's inadequacies. To state the matter another way, the relevant public with an interest in the agency has been enlarged sufficiently to create the *possibility* of a broader source of authority, imposing new and higher demands on the agency. Richard Nixon, the new President, has promised reform. Your challenge: to further broaden and deepen the mandate for reform, and to align the agency's internal resources and short-term objectives with the new mandate.

Implementation of any strategy begins with small steps. Strategies often succeed or fail in the details. That is why I often ask my students to consider *exactly* what they would do in a given situation—avoiding grand strategic formulations in favor of specifics. So what exactly do you do now that Evins has given you the note? To make matters a bit more complicated, assume that you discover that one of the three employees is incompetent, one is merely undistinguished, and the third is quite productive.

One option: Promise Evins that you'll take care of his three friends, and then give each of the three a promotion. This will put you on a good footing with Evins from the start, and keep him content. He'll trust you and be more willing to give you the benefit of the doubt when you begin making changes. The last thing you want right now is for him to see you as an opponent, intent on overhauling the entire agency. If you cross him, he will quickly organize the old political constituency against you. The emerging reform constituency may not yet be strong enough to save you. Displeasing Evins could also cost the agency $1 million of its appropriation (about 5 percent of its budget).

But consider the negative consequences of this option. Agency employees will know that Evins's friends received promotions because of Evins's request (the "old-boy network" is an enormously effective communications system). You will thus be signaling to the agency that it is to be business as usual: The old authorizing environment is still firmly in control, and you have no intention of altering the patronage system. As a result, the most competent employees (some of whom had hoped that your appointment would represent a new direction for the agency) will search for new jobs outside the agency; and the least competent will feel more secure, refraining from searching for new jobs.

You will have missed an opportunity to send a powerful signal to the contrary. Such a signal is not only a means of retaining good current employees and discouraging incompetent ones, but, even more important, it is one of the few concrete ways you have of convincing good *prospective* employees that the ground rules have changed, that they thus might find the FTC an attractive and challenging place to work. Further, it's a means of convincing the newly emerging sources of authority (the ABA, the consumer movement, the Nixon Administration, the media) that you take their concerns seriously and are prepared to act on them. This, in turn, can fortify their resolve.

My students puzzle over this. Some of them want Weinberger to hand the note back to Evins immediately, notifying him in no uncertain terms that Weinberger will no longer tolerate patronage at the FTC. But this tactic carries with it all the disadvantages of displeasing Evins without creating any of the advantages of a clear signal to everyone else. (It occurs in private, where only Evins gets the clear signal.) Some of my students want Weinberger to politely pocket the note, then return to the FTC and promote the competent employee but fire the incompetent. But this signal will be clear to Evins (you fired one of his friends) while being somewhat less clear to everyone else (after all, you promoted one of Evins's friends).

As is becoming apparent, this is a case study in *signaling*. Public servants often have few instruments at hand for directly mobilizing resources and strengthening mandates. Implementation of a new strategy thus frequently requires indirect tools—in particular, the use of small decisions to communicate larger intentions. Employees, elected officials, journalists, and others whose work affects (and is affected by) the work of public managers are continuously on the lookout for such signals, which, in turn, elicit from them either cooperation or opposition. And the patterns of cooperation or opposition so generated tend to shift the entire system this way or that. The choice of whether to use a small decision to signal large intentions thus depends upon how much cooperation, relative to opposition, is likely to be generated. And *this* result will turn on who is likely to receive the signal and what they are likely to understand by it.

Weinberger needs to send a loud signal to his emerging sources of authority and to potential resources (such as future employees). It must be loud, because these sources of authority and outside resources are still somewhat diffuse. They lie outside the old system and are thus less able to pick up subtle cues than are people who have constituted the agency's authority and resources in the past—people who are likely to be in close touch with one another and on the alert for any sign of change.

At this point, some of my students conclude that Weinberger should politely accept the note but not commit himself one way or the other to Evins. Then he should return to the agency, release the note to the press, and promptly fire all three employees (which, incidentally, is exactly what he did).

chapter 10

Sustaining a Strategy

Strategies for public agencies are not simply implemented, as architectural drawings or military plans are implemented. There is no specific point of time at which a public strategy has been put into *effect*. This is because the authorizing environment—comprising legislators, executive-branch officials, judges, journalists, interest-group leaders, and the larger public behind them—is in continuous flux. Not only do administrations come and go, but appointed officials come and go even more frequently; and, with the possible exception of incumbent legislators whose generous campaign contributors ensure a long tenure, elected offices change hands at a fairly rapid clip as well. In addition, the public's attention span is short, and its memories are even shorter. What seems an important issue today may fade by tomorrow. The media are fickle, sometimes even sensational, in their choice of story. Interest-group agendas shift as the public's attention shifts. What was once conventional wisdom becomes an outdated assumption; yesterday's fads become today's jokes.

This fluidity notwithstanding, it is still possible for a public agency to maintain a strategic direction long enough to achieve some continuity over time, thus giving the public a return for its earlier investments in personnel and new programs. With enough care and leadership (of the sort we discussed in Chapter 3), a mandate can be sustained that will allow the agency's new capacities to be fully demonstrated. And the demonstration, in turn, may gain a degree of public trust, which allows further positive momentum.

There are many cases of such virtuous circles, sometimes lasting for decades. At the federal level, several agencies are exemplars of sustained excellence and relatively consistent policy making: the State Department, the Securities and Exchange Commission, the Antitrust Division of the Justice Department. Similar examples can be found in state and local governments. These agencies are not sheltered from politics; they remain accountable to the public. But their mandates have been sufficiently clarified and supported by the authorizing environment and their internal resources and operating systems have performed sufficiently well that they have earned a measure of trust and respect. The trust and respect have, in turn, given these agencies (and their leaders) enough independence that they have been able to survive short-term fluctuations in the authorizing environment. They have surmounted momentary fads and immediate crises, fashionable solutions and cure-alls, because they have performed consistently and well.

The lesson is not that public agencies should avoid dramatic initiatives and new directions. Caspar Weinberger embarked upon a fundamental new strategy for the Federal Trade Commission; Pendleton School needed a dramatic reversal; Audrey Simmons had to bring about a major shift in the way the agency and the community perceived each other. Sometimes abrupt change is necessary. The point is that in order for such a new strategy to be sustained, the agency must in effect strike a deal with the public (and with those who mediate between the public and the agency): If it meets the new standards that the public believes are appropriate for judging its success, the public will trust that it is doing what it should be doing. So long as it *continues* to adhere to those same broad standards and seek the same long-term goals, that trust will be maintained.

Under these circumstances, problems arise only when public servants take their mandates for granted— when the strategic momentum seems so strong and secure that agency officials stop worrying about fulfilling their side of the bargain. Consider, for example, the plight of the Federal Trade Commission ten years after Caspar Weinberger first set it on a new path.

Mike Pertschuk and the Federal Trade Commission

In March 1977, President Jimmy Carter appointed Mike Pertschuk, head of the Senate Commerce Committee staff, to the position of chairman of the Federal Trade Commission. As described by one admiring adversary,

> Pertschuk was the single most influential person in this town on consumer issues for the last half of the 1970s. Every significant consumer group in this town recognized that Mike Pertschuk was the accomplished leader in the consumer field. There were always people on the House side and people down at FTC and people here and there but Pertschuk was the eminent leader in the same sense that Nader was St. George the Dragon Killer.

This "eminent leader" seemed eminently well-suited to his new mission: during the 1970s, the FTC had emerged from its rather inglorious past to become one of Washington's most aggressive bureaucracies—an army, in short, worthy of such a general.

This case examines the first year of Pertschuk's chairmanship. In particular, the case provides a brief

The case was prepared by Arthur Applbaum, Research Assistant, under the supervision of Stephanie Gould, Editor, Case Program, for use in the Senior Managers in Government Program at the John F. Kennedy School of Government, Harvard University.

Copyright © 1981 by the President and Fellows of Harvard College.

background on the FTC, surveys Pertschuk's early management initiatives, and chronicles the ensuing battles with Congress and industry. . . .

THE REPUBLICAN YEARS

After Weinberger's departure in 1970, the commission began writing on the slate which he had succeeded in wiping clean. His successors—Miles Kirkpatrick, Lewis Engman, and Calvin Collier—undertook a vigorous recruiting effort to people the FTC with bright, young attorneys. This left the agency in 1977 with a few seasoned middle managers, having some six years of experience, and a large crop of talented, green, and highly volatile line attorneys. The turnover rate was high, for the FTC couldn't compete with the salaries its rising stars could command in the private sector.

Between 1970 and 1977, FTC activities became increasingly forceful. The Bureau of Competition, for example, moved steadily from an emphasis on monopolistic conduct to monopolistic structure. Previously, the mainstay of the bureau had been penny-ante price discrimination cases under the Robinson-Patman Act. In 1967, 173 investigations of violations of the Robinson-Patman Act were initiated; by 1976, that number had been reduced to six. The bureau was gunning after larger game, aiming at the structural sources of market power. Under the novel theory of "shared monopoly," the FTC undertook mammoth actions against two oligopolies: the four largest breakfast cereal manufacturers and the eight largest petroleum refiners.

The changes in the consumer protection effort were even more radical. Prosecution under the protective Wool and Fur Product Labeling Acts virtually ceased, and the agency abruptly moved away from nickel-and-dime cases drawn from the mailbags. Deceptive national advertising became the bold new focus: the FTC took on the questionable claims of Wonderbread, Bufferin, Excedrin, and Listerine. The bureau developed two new weapons in the advertising campaign: the ad substantiation program, putting the burden of documentation squarely on the shoulders of the advertisers, and the doctrine of corrective advertising, a daring legal remedy that eventually sustained numerous court challenges.

MAGNUSON-MOSS

The passage of the Magnuson-Moss Act in 1975 substantially extended the reach of the FTC's regulatory arm. Previously, the agency's major regulatory weapon had been the cease-and-desist order, issued to particular firms after case-by-case adjudicative proceedings. Although the commission also issued something called "trade regulation rules" (industry-wide regulations that spelled out, with the force of law, how an industry should conduct business), these rules in fact surfaced very infrequently before 1975—at first because of agency sluggishness, and later because of doubts about the agency's legal mandate. In 1972, for example, a district court held that the FTC couldn't require that octane ratings be posted at all gasoline pumps, voiding one of the few TRRs then in existence.

In 1975, however, Congress settled any such doubts by adding express industry-wide rulemaking authority to the Magnuson-Moss legislation (which contained, as well, other provisions strengthening the agency's powers). Rulemaking under Magnuson-Moss required somewhat more rigorous attention to due process than do informal administrative procedures—oral hearings and some degree of cross examination, for example, were required, and a written record had to be established—but formal rules of evidence did not apply, and the commission could expedite the proceeding in various ways.

Chairman Engman eagerly set out to exercise the FTC's newfound authority. In the span of eight months, fourteen consumer protection rulemaking proceedings were initiated. Pertschuk eventually inherited seventeen pending ventures that cut a broad swath across the American market: funeral practices, used cars, credit practices, over-the-counter drugs, eyeglasses, mobile homes, hearing aids, food advertising, health spas, vocational schools, flammable plastics, appliance labeling, protein supplements, care labeling, franchises, home insulation materials, and gasoline station lotteries.

Some of these rules struck at the very core of the trade practices of certain industries. The used car rule would require that used car dealers provide a warranty, or, in a later form, inspect cars and post the results of the inspection. Many professions protected by state licensure laws or anti-competitive voluntary "ethics" were to become the subjects of investigations. The eyeglass rule would invalidate state laws that prevent the advertising of optical services and otherwise restrict the competitive sale of eyeglasses.

The FTC initially cast its net wide, proposing rules in very broad, ambitious versions. The funeral rule, for example, which in its final form was simply an itemized price disclosure rule, originally went so far as to stipulate that no profit might be made on the sale of flowers. As one observer commented, "People saw the rulemaking process as essentially a legislative process: put a bill out there, have a lot of hearings all over the country, invite feedback, massage it, work it." But the commission didn't fully anticipate the anxiety the iterative process would provoke in industry:

> The agency naively thought that you could put these proposals out there and have them looked upon in a somewhat nonthreatening fashion by the industry, and have a good legislative process, and get people working together to put together the best outcome from the public policy standpoint. In fact they were viewed as terrible threats.

The original rules struck out at industry abuses in two directions at once: eliminating the incentive to misrepresent and dictating specific practices. "To remove existing restraints on market competition *and* to specify in detail how these businesses must operate once the barriers were eliminated" may have been, according to one observer, regulatory overkill.[1] The vocational school rule, for example, proposed a grab bag of disclosure provisions, practice restrictions, and consumer remedies. A school would have to inform the student of its dropout and placement rate; would not be permitted to say certain things in recruiting students; would have to provide a "cooling off" period after signing a contract within which a student—free from any contact from the school—must reaffirm his intention to enroll to validate the contract; and would have to refund prorated tuition to dropouts. The hearing aid rule would grant the consumer the right to cancel the purchase within a month, but also would prohibit a variety of misrepresentations and require door-to-door vendors to present a card to the hard of hearing stating that they are selling a product.

Some observers thought the new rules to be not only politically provocative, but legally dubious as well. Robert Pitofsky (an FTC bureau director in the early '70s and a commissioner in the late '70s) commented that:

> Many rules and cases initiated in the mid-1970s were extremely ill-considered, and some legal work developing those projects was poor. . . . I'll give you a few examples. The proposed rule mandating that the precise language approved by the FDA for over-the-counter drug labeling be used in TV advertising—which would have

introduced into 30-second commercials such memorable words as "antiflatulent," "antiemetic," "antitussive," and "hyperosmodic" —was not based on any intelligible legal theory and was simply contrary to common sense. The attempt to bring a monopoly case against DuPont, challenging its behavior in building some new plants to produce a product by a substantially more efficient process than any of its competitors, was one of the "wrongest" cases since 1890. Both the rule and the case were thrown out unanimously by the commission after years of wasted effort; they should not have been started.

The agency also didn't anticipate the lengthiness of the process. Most of these proceedings were to require three to four years to complete, acquiring along the way a written record of up to 100,000 pages. Almost all of the rulemaking proceedings inherited by Pertschuk were still a year or eighteen months away from final promulgation, and had not yet been revised in response to public scrutiny.

ENTER MIKE PERTSCHUK[2]

At the time of his appointment to the FTC in March 1977, Pertschuk had been the chief counsel to the Senate Commerce Committee. In choosing Pertschuk, Carter was pursuing his policy of appointing liberal public interest advocates to subcabinet posts: Joan Claybrook, head of Ralph Nader's Congress Watch, became administrator of the National Highway Traffic Safety Commission; Carol Foreman, executive director of the Consumer Federation of America, was appointed assistant secretary of Agriculture for Consumers. Carter promised Pertschuk independence from White House interference, expected in turn that Pertschuk demonstrate independence from personalities on the Hill, and encouraged the new FTC chairman to pursue the interests of the consumer.

To assist him in the task of managing the FTC, Pertschuk sought to assemble a staff that would be evenly balanced between outsiders and insiders, and between proven consumer advocates and equally public-spirited but more cautious voices. Bill Baer, one of Pertschuk's advisers who served on the transition team, recalled the qualities the chairman wanted:

---

[1]Ernest Gellhorn, "The Wages of Zealotry: The FTC under Siege," *Regulation* (Jan/Feb 1980), p. 34.

[2]Mike Pertschuk generously supplied the writer with the texts of a series of addresses in progress. This case relies on many of his insights.

What he was looking for initially was people who were outstanding lawyers, with some clear evidence by their past activities that they had a sense of public interest activities, and an appreciation for consumerism. He really wanted to have a feel that these were people that knew right from wrong and had a sense of purpose and commitment. All the people he brought in had both private bar experience and public interest experience, so there wasn't the tendency to take somebody right out of Nader's Raiders and put him in a position of responsibility.

For example, Pertschuk reached inward to appoint his chief aide-de-camp, Chris White. White, who was recruited during the Republican shakeup, had risen to one of the assistant bureau director slots in Consumer Protection. To run BCP, he brought in Al Kramer, and made Tracy Westen Kramer's deputy director. Law school classmates, Kramer and Westen had extensive experience practicing a spirited brand of public interest and consumer law. For general counsel, Pertschuk appointed Mike Sohn, the paradigmatic lawyers' lawyer, whose litigation work for Nader's Center for Auto Safety Pertschuk had come to know and esteem.

In the area of antitrust, where Pertschuk felt least knowledgeable and confident, he deliberated carefully, eventually choosing a bureau director, Al Dougherty, with years of FTC experience and bureaucratic savvy. He was less concerned about making weighty appointments in the area of his greatest strength: congressional and public relations. The Office of Public Information withered under Pertschuk's rule from the political control center of the FTC to a press office. In congressional matters, Pertschuk intended to direct much of the action himself. He therefore appointed Nancy Chasen to the post of assistant general counsel for legislative affairs and congressional liaison—a woman with experience as a congressional staffer and consumer lobbyist in the House, but with no independent base on the Hill. Recalled Pertschuk:

> I had assumed that I would have little difficulty with Congress because I enjoyed good relations with key committee members, especially in the Senate, and also had the support of the President. I had asked Nancy to run the Congressional Relations office because I knew her to be an experienced and effective lobbyist. If there were troubles, I assumed that, working with Nancy, I could handle them myself. I did not put any emphasis on building the Congressional

Relations staff or integrating its work with that of the line bureaus at the commission. Since the new challenge for me was running the agency, that's where my energies and focus went.

INTERNAL POLICIES

To the management of the FTC Pertschuk brought a predilection for negotiation and consensus building born of his legislative past. Over the next few years he was to negotiate unanimous decisions among the five FTC commissioners with atypical frequency, and he extended his collegial ways to his dealings with his top managers. Early on, for example, Pertschuk initiated a series of weekend retreats for the upper level staff under the direction of an organizational psychologist.

Out of the retreats and other such interchanges evolved what Pertschuk called the "management team." Although he had initially been disposed to seek policy guidance primarily from those bureau directors principally involved in any particular issue, "at some point," he recalled,

> Sohn and the bureau directors asked for a regular meeting because they felt there was a tendency for people not to be included, so we evolved various structures of meetings to respond both to having the management team together and also the need for working directly with the bureau directors who were the key operating officers.

The team—the chairman; the bureau directors of competition, consumer protection, and economics; the general counsel; the director of the Office of Policy Planning and Evaluation (OPPE); and the executive director—met weekly, usually with Pertschuk's top aides, the assistant general counsel for legislation, and the public information officer.

Pertschuk's intent, Sohn observed, was not only to reduce personal conflicts, but to broaden the spectrum of views incorporated into decisions:

> I think, as time went on, he saw the need for more perspectives than just the enforcement perspective. He brought in others to get reactions that weren't so much the reactions of the law enforcers. The two bureaus tended to be— quite naturally, it's not a reflection on the people—a reflection of what they saw their mission to be. They tended quite naturally to want to push in the direction of more and more vig-

orous regulation. But the economists will tell you that the last ounce of regulation is probably not cost justified. The general counsel will tell you that the courts may raise an eyebrow about this if you go too far.

But the chairman's approach at all times conformed with his nonconfrontational philosophy of management, according to Bob Reich, head of the Office of Policy Planning:

> [His goal was] eliminating conflict, or reducing conflict as much as you could; creating collaboration, creating an environment where people could be very creative, reducing turfness, eliminating as much as you could ego—giving people ego gratification, not through so much their identification with different parts of the bureaucracy, but through their identification with the entire organization. And a lot of emphasis on group development.

This style of management contrasted sharply with that of Republican chairman, Lew Engman. "Engman's management philosophy," in the words of former executive director Margery Smith, "was to have very strong, very opinionated people in each major organization and have them fight. He loved it." The idea, apparently, was to promote healthy debate and self-scrutiny. The result was perpetual internal warfare. Under Engman, for example, the Office of Policy Planning and Evaluation had become the antagonist of the operating bureaus. As one former staffer recalled: "They didn't like *anything* and they criticized *everything* except for a couple of pet projects. There were some very huge battles as you can imagine. . . ." What the bureaus chiefly resented was OPPE's tendency to take its potshots at the final stages of a proceeding, faulting projects on economic or efficiency grounds after months or years of work had been invested. Reich noted that OPPE ". . . had, by Pertschuk's time, so antagonized the legal staffs that much of the legal staff would not return calls to OPPE. It was the worst example of how an evaluation unit can break down."

Pertschuk addressed this situation by removing "E" from OPPE:

> I wanted an Office of Policy Planning which could work with the bureaus and is extremely sensitive politically—with a small "p"—to coordinate, to bring task forces together to force the bureaus to think through some of their programs, but not to be in a position where they were polarized from the bureaus.

To help his office participate with the bureaus in the early stages of policy formulation, Bob Reich initiated two planning projects: policy planning sessions for the commissioners, and interoffice task forces for the staff. Said Pertschuk:

> One of the things we did was to develop the whole process of policy planning sessions, which really gave the commission an opportunity to shape initiatives very early. Every four to six weeks the commission held a policy planning review session in which the policy planning staff would put together everything that was going on in a given area, all ongoing activities, with an update—a review of the general situation, economic situation, and then a series of options for future activity. So the commission at that point would indicate, forget about this and concentrate on that, which had never really been done before.

And of the task forces, White observed:

> They tended to give the Policy Planning Office something of a steering wheel, and something of a set mandate, which would allow them to work with the organizations and to bring organizations together. And so a lot of basic information flowed back and forth.

Some similar changes were wrought in the general counsel's office, which, under the Republicans, had been used chiefly (in Chris White's words) "to ride herd over some of the more freeswinging tendencies of the bureaus":

> Pertschuk's approach was to make sure the General Counsel's Office was doing what it was supposed to be doing and that was giving opinions of the law: a likelihood of successful merits, how well the case had been put together, and resisting the temptation to add in an additional view of the policy.

As well as encouraging cooperation among the previously combative bureaus, Pertschuk encouraged all his managers to give free rein to their creative spirits and, as Reich put it, "to let every flower bloom." He placed a premium on innovative ideas that would probe the outer limits of FTC's mandate to eliminate "unfair and deceptive" practices. As White put it, "There was a lot of talk about getting out there and go, go, go, and back up the troops, throw the football."

The emphasis on vigorous consumer advocacy

often promoted a combative stance towards the objects of rulemaking. As Reich recalled,

> Some staffs got very adversarial: funerals is a good example, or used cars or vocational schools. The staff really perceived—perhaps rightfully—venality on the part of businesses affected. There were *highly* adversarial relations between the FTC staff and industry trade associations and lawyers.

It remained a topic of debate within the FTC whether—in fulfilling the commandment to be intellectually fruitful and multiply regulations—the FTC's legal cadres proceeded as an orderly phalanx or as an unleashed mob. One view was that, not only were the staff attorneys under fairly tight supervision, but that in many proceedings they were engaged in pruning the provocative first attempts of former administrations. Kramer certainly felt that he had the troops under control. So Pertschuk to some extent may have reaped a harvest the Republicans had sown. Others pointed out, however, that there was an incubation stage in Pertschuk's time in which FTC rulemaking activities were pretty much invisible to top management. As Reich explained it:

> what happened was that rulemakings were commenced in 1975, 1976. Once they went back to the staff, there was no institutional means for monitoring these rulemakings. They did not get back to senior staff until they were already at the presiding officer and hearing stage—in other words, not until the staff had already compiled its record and made its case, and that was often two or three or sometimes four years after the initial commencement of the proceeding. So when the rulemakings bubbled up again to senior staff and to the commission, [they were] very, very broad, in some cases quite radical—perhaps rightfully—ideas that had not yet been narrowed and focused. The narrowing and focusing did not happen until the political pressure was brought to bear on the agency.

Robert Pitofsky took yet a third view: that the troops were under control, and under orders to inflict heavy damage.

> It's true that many rules took on a scope and direction during rulemaking well beyond what the commission originally authorized, but I rarely had the feeling that the senior staff was unaware of that process. Most of the rules that ran aground—used cars, hearing aids, over-the-

counter drug advertising, and presumptive illegality of some conglomerate mergers—seem to have had the support of the bureau directors until the commission began to balk. Two exceptions were funerals and food advertising.

EXTERNAL POLICIES

Very early on Pertschuk voiced his intention of keeping top FTC officials at arm's length from the business community and the Washington bar. At his confirmation hearings he stated that

> It is . . . my intention to keep to an absolute minimum social contact with those who had an economic stake in commission activities. In some cases, this will mean curtailing social relationships which I value, but cynicism and public skepticism of the integrity of government is at a fever pitch, and I believe that it is essential for government servants to scrupulously avoid even the appearance of collusive relationships.

In accord with these sentiments, Pertschuk declined the invitation to serve as a member of the governing council of the American Bar Association antitrust section, a position traditionally filled by the FTC chairman and the Assistant Attorney General for Antitrust.

> I refused on the grounds that the Bar was a private trade association whose self-regulatory activities were as subject to FTC scrutiny as the anti-competitive excess of optometrists or dentists. . . . I wouldn't serve on the Board of Governors of the American Medical Association, so why should I with the Bar?

He planned to speak less frequently than customary before industry groups, and to reduce the number of meetings held with business representatives. For example, Jeffrey Joseph, chief lobbyist for the US Chamber of Commerce, who waited two years for an audience with Pertschuk commented:

> Pertschuk took the position that business had enough people in Washington to take care of their interests, no one looked out for the consumer, and he wasn't going to meet with business. He didn't need to talk to business. He set the stage. All we could do in business is say, look, if you won't talk to us, we'll find some other way of getting your attention.

The *ex parte* rule, prohibiting the use of off-the-record communications between litigants and commissioners in reaching a decision, was to be interpreted broadly and enforced seriously. Dick Leighton, counsel for the Grocery Manufacturers of America, recalled the changes brought about by Pertschuk:

> Up until Mike came in, the commission as a whole used to meet regularly with different industries, sit down, have lunch or something, and discuss what was going on. The Grocery Manufacturers of America was one of them. Once a month we would meet, have lunch, and kick things around. That was perceived as bad when Mike came in. They closed the door and became largely dependent upon information generated by their staff. They controlled all information and the *ex parte* rule prevented people from going directly to the commission and saying, hey, there's something wrong here.

Pertschuk also issued, at the urging of the operating bureau directors, but over the objections of others on the management team, a meetings policy limiting contact between the respondents' counsel and top management. Lawyers would be granted meetings with the bureau directors only if they had first tried to resolve the matter with lower-level staff. The "meetings policy" was intended to address such concerns as those voiced by Senator Fritz Hollings (D-S.C.) at Pertschuk's confirmation hearing:

> if you don't have a Washington lawyer who can see the commissioner off the record, or know how to talk to the staff, and everything else, you can't represent anybody before the commission. That disturbs me no end.

Pertschuk was also concerned with ensuring due process, maintaining the morale of lower-level staff, and precluding even the suggestion of collusion:

> For years I had heard tales, deeply resented by the staff of the commission, of cases laboriously developed by rank and file commission lawyers only to be compromised, as one of the barons of the FTC bar, drawing upon a carefully woven fabric of personal and professional relationships, gained access to senior commission officials and commissioners as members of the club and obtained not only an audience but a "sweetheart deal."

Finally, meetings were often seen as a waste of time. One top manager observed that:

> Often meetings don't tell you anything more than you can tell from the paper. I think there was concern about managing your time schedules. The bureau directors are sitting there with 300 attorneys apiece.

But there were some dissenting voices within the FTC. Chris White, then assistant to the chairman, recalls his position:

> It was idiotic, and I'll tell you that because I've told everybody. I've been in a zillion of those meetings. Half of my career, you know, was in the Bureau office. And I never went to one in which the enforcement goals of the Bureau weren't advanced. I never went to one in which one of two things happened: your credibility in the facts was shaken and you went back and decided whether or not something had to be modified; or the representatives of the company that wanted to settle the cases hanged themselves. That was much the preferred option, to let them come in. They would test out their arguments and nothing they had would shake us a bit.

Public Statements. Pertschuk made no speeches, with the exception of congressional testimony, for the first six months of his administration. "And I did that—which was a good idea generally—because I needed to learn the job. But also to maintain some quiet."

He shattered the quiet in November, appearing to be following through on his oft-repeated promise of turning the FTC into "the largest public interest law firm in the U.S." Speaking before the Action for Children's Television conference, he presented his legal and philosophical thinking about an issue that was to become his major policy initiative: children's advertising.

> Commercials do not disclose their nature—that is, the economic interest of the advertiser in convincing the viewer. To the small child it is as if a trusted friend urged the consumption of a particular product, not for personal gain, but solely out of concern for the child. . . .
>
> If there is one salient public policy which rises commandingly from centuries of common and statutory law, it is that the commercial ex-

ploitation of children is repugnant to a civilized society. . . .

Moreover, children have become the target market for products that promise immediate satisfaction. With food, this often means instant pleasure—and the danger of long-term malnutrition. . . . They cannot protect themselves against adults who exploit their presentmindedness. . . .

It may be that only a ban on the advertising of these products on programs directed towards the young child can help remedy their inherent defect. . . .

Pertschuk explains why he spoke out so forcefully:

I had come as the candidate of the consumer groups. And I had to do something early to establish my good faith with them, because they are easily dissatisfied, and I felt it was important to maintain their trust. And that was sort of the strategy but also I wanted it. I basically felt close to them and I felt an identity with them. And so it was important to me not to be dismissed as just another coöpted bureaucrat. . . .

Later that month, the chairman presented before the New England Antitrust conference some similarly strong views on antitrust policy:

I have become increasingly convinced that current antitrust policies lack clarity and conviction. . . . The antitrust enforcement agencies have often been lacking in historical perspective and imagination. Tending to think only like litigators or to restrict themselves to a narrow allocative efficiency approach to economics, they have failed to provide leadership in their most important and fundamental area of responsibility: taking the broad view and attempting through enforcement initiatives and the power of information to bring the structure and behavior of major industries and indeed, of the economy itself more in line with the nation's democratic, political and social ideals.

According to Pertschuk, "the antitrust speech was not part of a strategy. It was basically worked on by Albert Foer [Assistant Director of Competition for Special Projects] and Al Dougherty, and it was the first effort to try and articulate my evolving philosophy. So it was basically a fairly straight-forward statement."

The bureau chiefs contributed their own public statements to the image of a new activism at the FTC. Al Kramer, for example, put forth the position that scrutiny of advertising should be based on the total "sensory experience" created by the ad message, not just the words involved. "The media have left the written word behind in a cloud of dust and have created a new environment of multiple sensory experiences of which the written word is a minor part." And Al Dougherty pressed forward some ambitious antitrust theories developed under the Republicans: no-fault monopoly—the notion that structural concentration should be prevented regardless of observable effects on the competition, and shared monopoly—that oligopolistic industries share market power, and therefore should be broken up.

Pertschuk's positions were no secrets—his stand on children's advertising was well known, and a dictation tape containing parts of his emerging competition philosophy was leaked over the summer. But the stridency of his words and the boldness of his ideas shocked nonetheless. Al Kramer recalled the effects on industry: "The rhetoric was just another thing that made it easy to focus on Mike as the overzealous leader. We could have done more to shop polish over our image, and not to add to the tarnish." Another management team member said that "Certain of his comments on the children's advertising rulemaking were taken as personally attacking businessmen who advertised to children."

Policy Initiatives: Kidvid. In keeping with the sentiments voiced above, Pertschuk quickly set his staff to work on a bold rulemaking initiative to regulate television advertising directed at children. Legally, he saw children's television, or "Kidvid," as an area ripe for FTC intervention on two counts: as a point in theory, he read the ancient Anglo-American legal tradition insulating children from commercial exploitation as marching orders, and as a point of fact, he cared about the influence of advertising on children. In announcing his intentions to pursue Kidvid rulemaking at a congressional hearing in April, Pertschuk said, "As a citizen and as a parent, I am deeply concerned about the economic, social, and psychological effects the TV advertising has upon our children and upon their families." The principal culprits, and therefore targets, were advertisements for sugar cereals and junk food, which posed a dental and possibly a nutritional hazard to children.

Pertschuk was motivated as well by a variety of strategic considerations. Although the FTC was working on a gaggle of rulemaking proposals begun under Engman and Collier, Pertschuk felt that he had to make his own mark to reassure his consumerist constituency.

> When I discovered there were very few other things left that were really coming up in the agency, that is, there were very few new initiatives that were going to bubble up at least until new people had taken over and developed their own, then it became even more important to get the children's proceeding on the line and out, because that was a visible, strong position. . . . And so children's TV became the principal vehicle to demonstrate that we were serious.

According to Bob Reich, Pertschuk thought he had found in Kidvid a potent symbol that would probe the frontiers of deception and unfairness and broach the question of protecting the vulnerable.

> I think he thought that this was a terrific bootstrap issue. Pertschuk is a great, clever politician, in the sense that he understands the symbolic role of politics. He understands that you need symbolic issues that have certain ingredients—public drama—that can easily be communicated to the public, that draw almost a gut reaction from people. And that secondly can be translated into legislation, or particular proposals. And third, and perhaps most importantly, that open up other issues, which are kind of key foot-in-the-door issues. Nader's Corvair was a perfect kind of issue, because *Unsafe at Any Speed* had all of those aspects to it. Pertschuk thought that children's advertising was that kind of issue. Nader disagreed. He thought it was a terrible issue, because it would not galvanize people.

Pertschuk later remembered Nader's warning: "If you take on the advertisers you'll end up with so many regulators—with their bones bleached—in the desert."

The children's advertising rulemaking seemed to have the support of Pertschuk's congressional backers. Previous FTC chairmen had been chided (probably under Pertschuk's urging) for not pursuing the issue. At the confirmation hearing, Senator Warren Magnuson endorsed a venture into Kidvid:

> Now, we've all been interested here in children's advertising; it's a difficult, complex subject. . . . Now I would hope that you would

take a good, long look when you talk about advertising [with the FCC]. I hate to narrow this down, but the abuses seem to be in children's advertising, advertising directed to children.

Senator Hollings, who chaired both the appropriations subcommittee and the communications subcommittee (and who later forcefully opposed Kidvid rulemaking) encouraged the proceeding at the outset. Bill Baer reported that the senator told Pertschuk privately during the April appropriations hearing process: "Look, I want you to do something. I am going to put the money in the committee report directing you guys to take a look at the problem of children's advertising."

One congressional staffer hypothesized that Pertschuk chose Kidvid because he was familiar with the terrain: "My theory is, Mike's last major thing that he actually staffed himself was the hearings in the early '70s on children's television. So when Mike went to the FTC he wanted to do something that he knew something about, and that was Kidvid."

THE VIEW FROM THE HILL

At the time Mike Pertschuk took over the FTC, the Congress he had worked with for over a dozen years was undergoing a transmutation. The congressional reforms of the early '70s and the emergence of the "mediagenic" candidate with weak party allegiance was diffusing the once formidable power of committee chairmen, diluting the authority of legislative leadership, and increasing the likelihood of bills getting rewritten on the floor. The reforms also gave rise to a new brand of special interest politics. Said one industry observer:

> Everybody has a subcommittee, everybody has a voice—democracy with a small "d" to the point of absurdity, to the point of disarray. Special interest politics resulted from that. Everybody had a forum to call a hearing, to initiate an investigation, to initiate an amendment effort. When you had six or ten members who really had the ultimate power in the House, which they did in the old days, then special interests had to compete with each other for the favor of that member or chairman. In these days when you have a plethora of subcommittees, and a guy is trying to make a name for himself in the newspaper, then he looks for a special interest to champion.

The changes on the Hill were political as well as structural. The celebrated conservative shift so apparent by 1980 had begun to take its toll on congressional liberals as early as 1976. With no economic relief in sight, the voices crying out for government regulation began changing into (or being replaced by) voices demanding regulatory reform. These conservative sentiments were augmented by the post-Watergate mistrust of the "imperial presidency" and its bureaucratic baronies.

The FTC's two oversight committees—the Senate Commerce Committee and the House Interstate and Foreign Commerce Committee—remained left of center amid these shifting currents. Chairman Warren Magnuson (D-Wash.) in the upper chamber and Harley Staggers (D-W.V.) in the lower were counted among the more liberal members of the new Congress, and—regardless of the waning interest in consumer issues among their brethren—their committees continued proposing legislation to strengthen the consumer's hand. But by 1977, even these committees were beginning to show the effects of the times.

A number of prominent liberals had vanished from the ranks of the Senate Commerce Consumer Subcommittee. Its chairman, Frank Moss (D-Utah), was defeated in 1976, as were members Vance Hartke (D-Ind.) and John Tunney (D-Cal.). John Hart, the subcommittee's vice chairman, died that December, and John Pastore (D-R.I.) retired. Although clearly sympathetic to consumer causes, the new Consumer chairman, Wendell Ford (D-Ky.), as an advocate remained unproven. Finally, Magnuson himself was to give up the Commerce chair late in 1977 to head the Appropriations Committee. The highly touted staff painstakingly built by Pertschuk also had begun to disperse. Some, like Pertschuk, entered the administration. Others, sensing the upcoming retrenchment, moved on.

In the House Bob Eckhardt (D-Tex.) assumed the chairmanship of the Commerce Consumer Protection Subcommittee. Eckhardt, author of the Toxic Substances Control Act, was a staunch consumerist; he received in 1976 a 100 percent rating by the Consumer Federation of America, and 0 percent from the National Associated Businessmen. But the full House clearly lagged behind the gentleman from Texas in consumerist zeal.

These changes in Congress in part reflected changes in the world outside—in particular, the world of industry lobbies. When Magnuson-Moss was signed into law in January 1975, business interests had barely whimpered. The affected industries

assumed that the rulemaking process would take years, and they trusted that, under a Republican administration, they wouldn't be hurt too deeply. And, as Jeffrey Joseph, chief lobbyist for the US Chamber of Commerce, remembered:

> Magnuson-Moss was done with a business community mostly unaware. We started getting calls from major businesses around the country saying, we just heard that this bill passed, what is it? Although it had been going through discussion in the Congress for four or five years. Business didn't even want to try to fight against something with a consumerist handle on it. They weren't that sophisticated. They weren't well organized. I think a lot of people were concerned about their image.

Inflation and economic stagnation, however, were taking their toll on the popularity of consumerism, and by the end of the year, a bill to establish a separate Consumer Protection Agency—legislation that had surfaced in Congress every year since 1970[3]—could barely squeak through the House (although it had passed the House with a three hundred vote margin five years earlier). To hear Joseph tell it, "It was suddenly legitimate. You didn't have to feel ashamed as a member of Congress to vote against something Ralph Nader wanted."

Members of Congress with waning consumerist sympathies found themselves courted by a business community that had rewritten the rules of industrial lobbying. The formation in 1972 of the Business Roundtable, a periodic meeting of the top chief executive officers in the country, sparked an awareness of the possibilities of cooperation among firms. As David Dunn, a lobbyist with the Patton, Boggs and Blow firm commented:

> [Individual companies had] learned not to try to fight by themselves. They learned to find people who were similarly situated and form *ad hoc* committees with these people and have a concerted, organized effort across the board of a number of industries who were similarly situated to fight the thing together. If you put ten different companies or ten different trade associations in one room you're bound to have a

---

[3]For years, no more than a handful of legislators had dared vote against creating a consumer agency. Legislation had passed both chambers overwhelmingly and repeatedly, but never in the same years.

plant in a lot more congressional districts and a lot more states than if you're just one person.

Dick Leighton, whose law firm Leighton, Conklin, and Lemov handled over three-quarters of the trade rule regulations, says industry became more willing to exercise the legislative option:

> Most people who have been around Washington long enough realize that if you just limit yourself to taking clients' problems to court you've severely limited yourself. If the client has a problem, and it's FTC-oriented, either you get the FTC to take action to solve the problem, or if they're attempting to enforce something against you, you're not limited to procedures at the FTC. Hopefully, you could go to the Hill or go to court or go to public opinion to preempt the FTC.

Also, the legalization of corporate political action committees (PACs), allowing corporations to make direct contributions to political candidates, changed the complexion of relations between industry and Congress somewhat. Said Leighton:

> Contributing through PACs means that you get on a first name basis with people, to talk over your problems. Some would say, you influence them. I don't know if that's the case. I know definitely that it is not always the case. But at least it opens the door so you can talk to someone. It makes it easier to come in and say, "Here's my point of view."

Finally, the industry lobbyists of the new order studied and learned well the tactics developed and plied so resourcefully by the public interest lobbies in years past: grassroots organizing. As Dunn commented:

> They learned the lesson of the public interest groups—to motivate the average constituent. The most powerful lobbying tool there is are the people that vote to elect or reelect a congressman or senator. Writing letters. Speaking on your behalf. That is the most powerful tool. Period. Bar none.

By the time industry and the Carter White House joined battle in 1977 over the latest (and last) attempt to create a consumer agency, the ways business pursued its interests had been transformed. Dick Leighton remembered:

> For the first time in history, you had "the coalition": National Association of Manufacturers, Grocery Manufacturers of America, the US Chamber of Commerce, National Federation of Independent Business, all together, and thousands of people underneath them, in a highly structured, organized way, taking positions, moving, dividing up the Hill, and lobbying. Tremendous power was brought to bear.

Small, middle, and big business closed ranks to defeat the proposal: the National Federation of Independent Businesses (NFIB), representing one-half million small businessmen; the Chamber, with its 2,700 state and local branches, 1,300 trade associations, and 90,000 merchants and manufacturers; the National Association of Manufacturers (NAM), speaking for 13,000 industrial companies; and through the Roundtable, 200 of the country's corporate giants. Business representatives claimed that they simply rode the changing mood of the country. A General Motors representative told reporters: "It's an overstatement to say that business turned Congress around. I see it more as Congress becoming more aware each year that the bill cannot stand on its own merits, and turning itself around." (But in one congressional office, for example, while mail was running heavily against the consumer agency, a poll taken in the same district showed that 61 percent of the voters wanted it. A nationwide Harris poll showed Americans 52 percent to 34 percent in favor of a consumer agency.)

By Pertschuk's first summer in office, the Consumer Protection Agency was in serious trouble. Encouraged by its advances, the coalition of business interests unleashed its newfound skills on another pending piece of consumer legislation: the FTC Improvements Act.

THE FTC IMPROVEMENTS ACT

In May 1977, the House and Senate Commerce Committees began to consider HR 3816, the FTC Improvements Act, which also contained a three-year authorization amendment. The bill, which would broaden significantly the powers of the FTC beyond those granted by Magnuson-Moss, had two particularly controversial provisions:

- Class action suits, permitting groups and individuals to seek redress for violations of the FTC rulings in the courts;

- Equitable relief, authorizing the FTC to petition the courts to place in receivership companies that face FTC penalties and that are likely to dissipate their assets.

Pertschuk had in fact had a hand in drafting the legislation and, while he was still on the Hill, had tagged the authorization onto the bill, reasoning that authorizations are rarely voted down. The subcommittee hearings on the legislation were indeed warm and uneventful, with both committees reporting similar bills that were overwhelmingly favorable to the FTC.

The balmy climate of the subcommittee in May, however, proved a poor predictor of conditions in the full House in October. On October 3, HR 3816 finally reached the House floor and was promptly dismembered: both the class action and equitable relief provisions were stricken by 2–1 margins. Ten days later, the House was considering an even more severe rebuke to the agency, in the form of a legislative veto amendment offered by Jim Broyhill (R-N.C.). This particular amendment called for what was known as the one House veto: if one House voted its disapproval over any FTC rulemaking, and the other at least acquiesced, the rulemaking would be void. (Legislative vetoes over the actions of other executive and independent agencies had been offered in many forms over the years, but never before had a blanket provision been applied to such a wide range of an agency's activities.)

The opposition to the class action and equitable relief provisions seemed to have been stimulated by the coalition of business lobbies discussed above; but even some components of industry appeared to regard the veto extreme. The Chamber of Commerce, which was to embrace the effort later on, had gone on record a few months earlier against the veto in general:

We have felt this can be manipulated and we would be falling into a snake pit if we take issues to Congress rather than rely on the experts at the agencies. . . . Continued uncertainty is sometimes worse than a bad decision.

And another lobbyist for a prominent Washington firm commented:

I personally prefer the Congress to improve their abilities at writing legislation to start with and when a change needs to be made you make a change. You don't let the agency trot down the rosy path doing what it thinks is right and then call them up short and destroy their credibility in the public eye. And put them constantly on the defensive from then on out. They spend hundreds of man-years trying to put a regulation together, and then at the last minute, you cut their legs off? I don't think that's the way to do it.

The primary force behind the veto drive was neither industry, nor Broyhill, the bill's sponsor: rather, it was Elliot Levitas (D-Ga.). The successor to Georgian Andrew Young in the House of Representatives, Levitas personified the new congressional trends: unfettered by the old order, right of center, and a proponent of bureaucratic accountability. Levitas had irked the leadership and threatened committee chairmen in the past by persistently proposing amendments to bills that would grant Congress veto power over administrative regulations. Bob Eckhardt, floor manager of the FTC Improvements Act, was "totally, unalterably opposed to a legislative veto on constitutional grounds and on policy grounds," said Peter Kinzler, a senior member of his staff; and the House leadership, although silent, clearly wasn't pleased with Levitas.

Largely thanks to the efforts of Levitas, the legislative veto amendment eventually carried by a vote of 272–139, and HR 3816, by now hardly an "improvements" bill, was approved by a similar margin. The conferees, led by Harley Staggers and Eckhardt, barely avoided House instructions not to compromise on the veto provisions. Levitas settled for permission to participate in the conference negotiations. Faced with the House actions, Wendell Ford (D-Ky.) dropped the class action provision from the Senate version of the authorization improvements bill, after which the Senate package perfunctorily passed 90–0, without any mention of the legislative veto.

While all this was transpiring in Congress, the FTC itself was scarcely visible on its own behalf, although in an October 6 speech to the National Press Club—one of his earliest public statements—Pertschuk did take a slam at industry's opposition to the class action provision:

It's interesting to see what business says when consumers ask not for more government but for the right to defend themselves. As you know, pending before Congress are the FTC Amendments of 1977, a measure that would give consumers their own private right of action in the marketplace. . . . And the reaction of the business lobby to all this? A lobbying effort by the business protection interests full of the typical gambits. There are mass mailings of form letters to all congressmen. The Fortune 500 lobbyists including GM, Montgomery Ward, Sears, Penneys and Firestone, join with the Chamber of Commerce and the Business Roundtable, descend upon the Hill, misrepresenting the intent, substance and impact of this straightforward and important consumer protection measure.

But no one at the FTC evidenced any concern for the potentially much more serious legislative veto issue. Nancy Chasen, Pertschuk's choice for assistant general counsel for legislative affairs, didn't come to the commission until December. She explained:

I've forgotten when my predecessor left, but it almost doesn't matter, because he didn't have Mike's confidence. Whether he was there or not, it's almost incidental. Mike really had nobody running that staff until December. . . . There was no sense in the FTC, in December of '77, that anything was wrong on the Hill.

FIRST CONFERENCE: FEBRUARY

The conference committee on HR 3816 met in February. House conferees conceded to the Senate on all major points without much misgiving—the House majority at the conference were all part of the Commerce Committee majority. Eckhardt fairly presented Levitas' case, but the senators would have no part of the legislative veto affair, considering the procedure an unconstitutional usurpation of executive prerogative by an uppity lower chamber. "The veto had fallen off several major conference reports in other areas in the previous Congress," said Kinzler. "So we weren't quite aware of the strength of the [House sentiment for] legislative veto." David Dunn concurred:

Bills get amended on the floor all the time. You go into conference and you clean it up. And then when it comes out of conference people say, well, you know, it's a conference, they agree on it, we have to give a little and take a little and they accept the conference report. Very rarely do you have a conference report rejected.

In consequence, Eckhardt's staff anticipated no problems in selling the product of the conference to the full House (in spite of the fact that, earlier that month, the House had finally rejected the annual

proposal for a Consumer Protection Agency. As Kinzler recalled: "We thought that we could finesse the veto as long as there was no class action, and that we actually had the freedom to put the equitable relief section back in."

According to Kinzler, the Chamber of Commerce had agreed to a modified version of the equitable relief provision:

I cut a deal with the Chamber for a pared-back equitable relief section, and they withdrew their opposition. So the conference report on the FTC authorization filed on February 22, 1978 retained an equitable relief provision, and paid only lip service to "congressional review."

The Senate routinely approved the report by a voice vote the day it was filed. In the House, Eckhardt anticipated no formidable opposition; according to Kinzler: "The Republicans, Broyhill didn't expect to beat us, we didn't expect to be beaten, we didn't send out 'Dear Colleagues' and stuff, we didn't expect more than 100 to 150 votes against us."

Nancy Chasen, still settling in to her new position at the FTC, was reassured that she needn't become involved.

I got to the FTC in December. I never went up to the Hill myself until February, because it was a rudderless office. So I sat there trying to get myself together. I checked in several times a week with the people who were working in the substance of the authorization bill. And they said, oh, everything's fine, everything is terrific, the bill is coming along, Eckhardt's subcommittee is doing this or that, and everything is terrific, don't worry.

Chasen finally made her first visit to the Hill on February 28, the day of the HR 3816 debate:

I went because I looked around my office to see if anybody had gone up there, and I saw everybody's coats and thought, this is ridiculous, nobody is going to be up there. I better get up there in case something is wrong.

Indeed, something was. The conference report precipitated vituperative attacks on what one member characterized as "one of the most dangerous agencies in Government":

As I travel across my district in Oklahoma, the cry most commonly heard is for Congress to bridle the bureaucracy. Our most effective control would be to have review and veto over the rules and regulations which are imposed daily upon the people of this representative democracy by a bunch of faceless, nameless bureaucrats. And of all the agencies which are running amok, the Federal Trade Commission is the absolute worst example.

Levitas had, apparently, been very busy. Chasen commented:

He is the most tenacious person I have ever in my life come across. . . . If he wants a legislative veto, it's in this committee, it's in this general bill, there are a couple of special bills. Every place you turn there is Levitas. He does not miss an opportunity and it is very hard to do that because there is so much going on on the Hill that you have to have either very good staff or very good antennae. . . . He got down on the floor and you never saw him standing by himself in the corner like a liberal consumerist. Levitas was always talking to somebody. He always had his arm around some other guy's back.

Peter Kinzler echoed Chasen's admiration: "It was only Elliot working the floors like crazy," says Kinzler. "Elliot is a lone ranger. He works people like crazy and he works them well." In fact, however, Levitas appeared to have had some substantial help. The NAM, NFIB, and GMA had used the list of names garnered in their fight against the establishment of a Consumer Protection Agency to stimulate opposition to the conference report.

Whatever the cause, the House was up in arms. While his colleagues were castigating the FTC, Levitas himself refrained, confining himself to arguments for a structural solution to the problem of unelected agencies wielding broad, quasi-legislative powers.

This House overwhelmingly . . . adopted a provision which allows the elected Members of Congress—those people who suffer the inconvenience to seek election by the people—to have some say-so about the rules and regulations established by the FTC, to say that when the FTC legislates—and this is just what they do with their rules and regulations—that someone elected by somebody at some point has an opportunity to say whether it is good or bad legislative policy. . . . Taking this provision out, which the House put in overwhelmingly, takes

away not only from the Congress but also from the American people this opportunity of government by consent of the governed.

Other congressmen lambasted the equitable relief section, claiming that overzealous FTC attorneys might use the threat of receivership to force the signing of consent orders by innocent small businesses:

Regardless of how the FTC goes about getting a receiver appointed over a business, that business is irreparably harmed. That is what we are talking about. We are giving the power to libel and slander a small business to the FTC—that is exactly what happens. Their reputation is irreparably harmed, and their ability to carry on business is curtailed. . . .

This is from the majority on the conference: "Nevertheless, the possibility exists that some few overzealous staff people may be tempted to suggest equitable relief as a negotiating device, even when they know it would not be proper." That is what the conferees admit, an overzealous staff, a few overzealous staff people. Are there a "few overzealous people" in the FTC? I am surprised at that, because there are millions of them, millions of them.

The tone of the debate, according to Chasen, was more bellicose than the words themselves.

It was just unbelievable. What you don't see in the Congressional Record is that the Republicans were stamping their feet and yelling and cheering. It was really a circus . . . the intensity of the emotion of the people who opposed the agency and the personalized kind of attack that it was—there was really an irrational strain about the debate.

The House rejected the conference report on the FTC authorization and amendments bill by a vote of 146 to 255. Mused Kinzler: "109 votes is an extraordinary margin for a bill that you planned to win and the other side thinks he's going to lose. When we had the hell beaten out of us, it came as a surprise to everybody, including Broyhill." Kinzler went on to observe that, "We came back from the first conference underestimating the power of the drive, the institutional drive, desire of the House to have a legislative veto." David Dunn, a prominent Washington lobbyist, however, saw in the loss a direct rebuke of the FTC:

They underestimated the problems that they were causing the congressmen back home. They just underestimated the number of complaints that congressmen were getting back home from their funeral directors, from the used car dealers, and their optometrists and their doctors and dentists and everybody else. The FTC was getting into everybody's business and the FTC became the symbol of big government in the living rooms, in the backyards of all the towns of America.

COMMUNICATION PROBLEMS AT THE FTC

If Dunn's observation quoted above was, indeed, the message, it was still not getting through to the FTC. Chasen described the aftermath of the rout:

[I called] Mike from the Hill after the debate, and I said, I think you have real problems here. I then wrote a memo saying things are not good, and I circulated it to members of the commission and the management team: The February 28 debate on the FTC Improvements Act conference report defeated by a vote of 146–255 is attached. Much of the debate focuses on the absence of a legislative veto provision. I urge each of you to read the debate thoroughly, as it indicates quite clearly the tone of congressional disaffection for much of what the FTC is doing.

The memo was pulled back because it was too inflammatory. Somebody in Mike's office read the floor debate and concluded that it wasn't that bad. The stamping of the feet and the hooting and the howling doesn't come through when you read the floor debate. It's one of those things where you really had to be there. So I agreed that it could be called back because it would cause problems—that the more conservative members of the commission would stamp up and down if they read my memo, it was giving them ammunition, and it's just asking for trouble. A somewhat milder memo was put on top.

So that was the state of things on March 1, 1978. There was no real acknowledgement that anything was wrong, or appreciation for just how bad that floor debate had been.

Part of the reason why Nancy Chasen's premonitions were widely discounted by the management team, according to Pertschuk, was her style:

Although Nancy was an experienced and effective lobbyist, she served up raw her anxieties over the deterioration of our congressional position, and that made me less likely to focus on them. She had begun early to communicate her anxiety over the state of our congressional affairs, but I wasn't prepared to deal with her concerns. Much of a manager's day, as you know, consists of a series of crises, both real and imagined, that demand attention. Others had learned that I absorbed bad news best if it was modulated.

Kinzler added: "Nancy's very excitable, and she was seeing through the eyes of the consumer movement." And part of the problem might have been her lack of recognition within the FTC. As Pertschuk reflected:

Nancy had to land running, in a sense, without any specific background in the work of the agency. She was an outsider. She was a woman. She obviously needed to build up a grounding in the work of the agency and the confidence of the management team. I should have made sure that she got help and support in that effort and I didn't.

Chasen concurred:

It's very hard to have that kind of responsibility and be out in left field. I was not a person who had emerged from the bowels of the FTC, as Bob Reich did, for example. He knew everything that was going on at the FTC. I was a Hill person. The only credibility an outsider has being pulled in is the mantle of the chairman, the mantle of somebody else's power. And I didn't have that. Well, I couldn't pull the agency together.

But the problem also seems to have stemmed from Pertschuk's own reluctance to allow a dissonant reality to disturb his world. As Chasen explained:

Mike's feelings in all of this were very human kinds of things. He just didn't want to have this problem! It's a professional failing. I think he made a mistake. And mine is a professional failing, because I didn't check up on him.

I would come back to the FTC, and I'd say, Mike, Congressman whoever really doesn't like you. And he'd say, I don't know him. And I'd say, it doesn't matter. He thinks he knows *you*. I think you better go see him. So there's a period of a few months where Mike is having a hard time dealing with the fact that people don't like him. People know who he is, and they don't like him. . . .

Part of the problem was that Mike lacked a feeling for the raucously democratic nature of the House, assuming that it more closely resembled the "civilized" personality of the Senate. That misperception added to the impression that I was exaggerating the intensity of House feelings.

Pertschuk admitted that he was not inclined to listen:

Again, it may very well be that I didn't hear the predictions of how serious things were because I discounted them. Instead, turning upon the bearer of bad tidings, I came increasingly to believe that Nancy tended to see crises as larger than the reality and therefore that her alarms were exaggerated. We all tended to dismiss her alarms as exaggerated but she turns out to have been right.

KIDVID RULEMAKING

While Congress was lambasting the FTC on February 28, a second proceeding was taking place only a short walk down Pennsylvania Avenue from the Hill: Mike Pertschuk presented the commission with the staff's rulemaking proposals on children's advertising. The chairman had kept promising his consumerist constituency a speedy gestation period—at one point staking his salary against a self-imposed deadline at the annual meeting of the Consumer Federation of America. For months, staffers in the Bureau of Consumer Protection labored over a variety of remedies, including a flat ban on any advertising directed towards children below the age of eight. Pertschuk could not muster three votes on the commission to recommend that extreme a solution, so the initial notice of proposed rulemaking issued in April by the commissioners was actually a set of alternatives to be considered: limiting the number of ads for sugared products directed at children, controlling advertising techniques, requiring the disclosure of nutritional information, banning advertising for sugar-coated products, and banning all children's advertising.

A dismayed and outraged assemblage of business interests—broadcasters, advertisers, cereal manufacturers, grocery manufacturers and sugar concerns—saw $600,000,000 worth of children's advertising revenues threatened by the FTC action. The

subtleties of the document offered no solace. Says Pertschuk:

Though I myself and other members of the commission made it plain that a majority of the commission was firmly opposed to any form of ban on children's advertising, that news never caught up with the initial proposal.

The initial proposal, which listed a ban as one possible alternative, perplexed industry. As David Dunn recalled:

How can we oppose it when we don't know what it is that they're proposing? If you're a defendant in a criminal case and people tell you, well, we think you may have committed a robbery, you may have committed a kidnapping, and you may have committed murder. We're going to try you for all three. We don't know which we're going to select. How do you defend yourself? Well, you figure you're going to defend yourself against murder. That's what industry did. They figured the ban was the worst.

From the perspective of an industrial representative, the FTC had struck a hard-nosed and contentious posture. Dick Leighton, attorney for the GMA, recalled the commission's first steps:

To announce the proposal of Kidvid they had set up quite a media event, leaking the stuff to the press but not to the affected industries.

After the commission voted on the proposal they had a champagne party. It was kind of hokey. When you're talking about affecting billions of dollars of interest and you've already ticked off hundreds if not thousands of people who were waiting for an adversarial proceeding, and you hold a champagne party before the thing is even done, you say, my god, is this wired, or what?

The conduct of the Kidvid proceeding exacerbated already strained relations with Washington's attorneys. Recalled Leighton:

They would do small things on a continual basis that got you personally mad. They had some surprise new procedures that were tried for the first time in this proceeding, including one that had to do with the introduction of evidence, which Mike Sohn said was virtually identical to an FDA regulation. I practice a lot in the Food and Drug area, and I didn't know this FDA regulation, so I had an associate here call the person listed in the federal register to ask for a cite. He calls up and says "I represent the GMA, could you give me a cite on that regulation?" He says "Do you have a law library?" "Yes." "Then look it up." CLICK. That is typical of what we were faced with early on. They thought they had us. It was very unprofessional, and it's usually not the way lawyers work among each other. We all understand we have our own problems with our own clients. Now it only took one call like that for me to say, okay, I'm going to get that rascal. He's not going to do that to us. It's that type of attitude which took us the next step. People had a personal commitment. Each one of us had three or four of those attempts to embarrass the client, attempts to embarrass you.

Leighton's sense of pique seems to have been widely shared within the Washington bar, which by this point had pretty much closed ranks against the FTC.

When it lost the Washington bar, the FTC lost a valuable messenger, informant and mediator. As Reich ruefully recalled: "The Washington bar had been the main ambassadors of the FTC to the business community. It was through the Washington bar that the business community was reassured by the FTC." Baer regretted the lost intelligence attorneys had provided:

> By being a little more formal in the meeting policy, by keeping a little more distance, I think we probably denied ourselves an important source of critical information. By having Washington counsel in, by going out on the cocktail circuit a little bit and talking to people, those are the ways in which you pick things up.

Attorneys also played the role of negotiators, according to Baer, forestalling efforts by businessmen to circumvent regulatory channels:

> They translate, both ways, to and from. They are trying to make a deal. Where you have industry whose tendencies are to fight all the way, and an agency that is prosecuting to the end, the Washington lawyers say, "Wait a minute, let's talk it through," and that sort of stuff. By alienating that group and by cutting off access we made it harder for them to buffer and gave them fewer incentives to buffer.

Leighton more or less concurred with this view. He observed that, if the FTC had not taken such an adversarial stance,

> we could have gotten some of the more enlightened companies to say, let's go in and bargain a little bit, and get half a loaf. But they got everyone 100 percent against them, willing to commit war chests and time, the personal time of Chief Executive Officers, saying, we cannot allow this to happen. They basically accused well-know businessmen of deliberately trying to foreshorten the lives of kids.

Other observers commented that, with such high stakes, confrontation was inevitable, provocative staffers or not: "When you presented so fundamental a challenge to the broadcasters, they had no choice but to defend themselves in Congress. You awoke the sleeping giant."

Once awakened, the giant was a formidable one. What it lacked in grass roots support was compensated for by money and sophistication. Tommy Boggs of the Patton, Boggs and Blow firm attracted a consortium of 32 principals to fight the Kidvid rule. The *Washington Star* reported a war chest of $16,000,000 (the total budget of the FTC in 1978 was only $64,000,000). Recalled Pertschuk:

> One of the business lobbyists told me that, because of the ban proposal, the first amendment implications, it was easy for the children's lobbyists to raise money from other groups like General Motors and Bristol-Meyers, because they saw this as an attack on all advertising.

David Dunn described the coalition and its organization:

> The companies were basically a broad-range of advertising agencies, advertising associations, food companies, and the networks—the people who gain revenues from advertising of food products. Those were the economic interests we brought to bear against the Kidvid proposals.
>
> There were three basic groups. There was a litigation group which was headed up by a sister law firm of ours. Then there was the regulatory and *ad hoc* committee. Those were the people who put together the comments and addressed the regulatory proceeding itself, with regulatory representatives from each company or each trade association. And then there was the legislative, of which we were. I guess we

were what you might call the secretariat of the principal—we were the planning mode. And ours was a much smaller group. What we tried to do was to put together the best lobbyists in Washington, the most experienced from the sugar industry, the broadcasting industry, from the cereal industry, from the top industry, from the food and chocolate industries. We amount to about eight people.

One path the Kidvid opponents chose was to file suit to disqualify Pertschuk from ruling, in his capacity as quasi-judicial commissioner, in the children's television proceeding, claiming that he had prejudged the outcome. But the main vehicle for their campaign against the rulemaking was the up-coming appropriations legislation. The authorization bill, in limbo between conferences, was now un-amendable.

So we decided to do the one thing that we could do. Amend the appropriation bill. You can't legislate on an appropriation bill. It's against the rules of the House to require an agency to take an affirmative action as a condition to the appropriation. However, you can write into the appropriation certain guidance language which does not require them to do anything. It just states that this is law.

Boggs and Co. wanted to state that the FTC is prohibited from pursuing the children's advertising rulemaking.

THE NATIONAL NANNY

On March 1, 1978, the morning after the House vote and the commission meeting, the *Washington Post* ran an editorial, entitled "The National Nanny," that changed the contours of the Kidvid debate:

The FTC as National Nanny

The Federal Trade Commission has now agreed to consider imposing major restrictions on television advertisements aimed at young children. The primary goal of the proposal is to reduce the amount of sugar children eat. Few people, least of all thoughtful parents, will disapprove of that goal. But the means the FTC are considering are something else. It is a preposterous intervention that would turn the agency into a great national nanny.

The proposal has three parts (or "op-

tions," as the staff naturally describes them). A complete ban on advertising on programs aimed at children under eight years of age; a ban on all ads on programs aimed at children under 12 for those sugar-coated products most likely to cause tooth decay; and a requirement that if ads for other heavily sugared products appear on programs aimed at children under 12, such ads be balanced by separate dental and nutritional ads.

Now, it is true that children watch many hours of television and see thousands of advertisements that cause them to demand that their parents buy certain products, mostly candy and cereals with huge amounts of sugar in them. And parents often yield to those demands, with the result that children eat more sugar than is good for them—from which the FTC's staff concluded that government must do something about the ads to protect the children.

But what are the children to be protected from? The candy and sugar-coated cereals that lead to tooth decay? Or the inability or refusal of their parents to say no? The food products will still be there, sitting on the shelves of the local supermarkets after all, no matter what happens to the commercials. So the proposal, in reality, is designed to protect children from the weaknesses of their parents—and the parents from the wailing insistence of their children. That, traditionally, is one of the roles of a governess—if you can afford one. It is not a proper role of government. The government has enough problems with television's emphasis on violence and sex and its shortages of local programming, without getting into this business, too.

The government can try to warn children (and parents) about the dangers of eating too much sugar. It has been doing so for generations and it might as well keep trying. If a case can be made, warning labels can be required and limitations on the amount of sugar added to foodstuffs can be imposed. Television situations can be encouraged—perhaps even required—to carry dental health ads during children's programs.

But a flat ban on commercials involving, as it would have to, certain judgments a government shouldn't be encouraged to make or enforce, would make parents less responsible, not more.

As Bob Reich described it:

The National Nanny symbol transformed the debate over children's advertising at a very early stage away from the question should large companies use complicated, sophisticated psychological manipulation against young children into a very different question, which is should government come between the parent and the child.

The *Post* had hitherto been a staunch supporter of the FTC, and in fact, subsequent editorials can be read as attempts to repair the damage done by coining "the National Nanny." But the paper was incensed by what it saw as careless disregard for First Amendment rights. Said Sohn, "The rulemaking involved free speech issues, to which the *Post* has always been very sensitive." (*Post* publisher Katharine Graham's position as owner of advertising media, both print and tube, may have contributed to the constitutional consternation.) The *Post's* previous position on FTC matters heightened the impact of this turnabout. Recalled Pertschuk: "As an advocate for the children's advertisers told me later about the impact, it had such political potency because 'It was their guys, not our guys.'" "National Nanny" soon grew larger than the Kidvid debate. The phrase was picked up by other business interests, who sought to portray the FTC as the gratuitous nanny not only of the nation's children, but of its businessmen as well.

APPROPRIATIONS

The House Appropriations Subcommittee on State, Commerce, the Judiciary, and related agencies began deliberations on the FTC's FY 1979 budget two weeks after the National Nanny editorial. The public hearings in the House were, in Pertschuk's judgment, "somewhat hostile." Mark Andrews (R-N.D.), who had been so taken with the editorial that he entered it into the published record of the FTC's appropriations subcommittee hearings, grilled the chairman on children's advertising:

On page 3 of your statement you are saying you are exploring what degree of commercialization of children our society wishes to tolerate, and you are going to do that with a rulemaking. Are your rulemakings so precise that they can tell what society will tolerate?

Andrews also pressed Pertschuk about his quasi-judicial status and the question of prejudgment.

Pertschuk took pains in his opening statement to stress FTC accomplishments that *reduced* regulation—striking 111 of 152 old pre-Magnuson-Moss trade rules from the rulebooks, and writing regulations in plain English—but for the most part, his testimony evidenced a fair degree of imperviousness to congressional displeasure:

Andrews: Your statements on the staff proposals on television advertising indicate you feel the commission should construe the terms "unfair" and "deceptive" in the FTC Act quite broadly, thus breaking, as I understand it, new ground in major policy areas. The recent vote on the conference report on the FTC amendments would make it clear that the Congress wants to preserve its role in setting new public policy, and the commission's role is to execute the laws passed by Congress. I wondered if that message had been clearly received by you and the commission?

Pertschuk: Well, Mr. Andrews, I spent a number of years working on the Hill, and I am not sure that messages from votes communicate quite as clear a message as you might indicate.

Pertschuk went on to explain that the authorization vote was part of the broader legislative veto issue, and not a rebuke of the FTC. When a Michigan congressman, wanting reassurance about the FTC's new antitrust policy, asked, "You do not think bigness is necessarily bad," there was a loaded silence, and suddenly Pertschuk replied, "Actually, I do." As Chasen vividly remembered:

Everybody from the FTC slid under the chairs! You see, he couldn't have given that answer in a hostile environment. He couldn't have believed, at the point that he said that, that there was real trouble there.

The painful truth did not come crashing down until shortly thereafter, when Pertschuk realized he was about to lose a subcommittee he never thought was in danger.

The appropriations hearing had been somewhat hostile, but we had not picked up any information that anything was going on. I think I was on the Hill—I can't remember why—the day before the subcommittee was supposed to meet.

And I got word—probably from Nancy—that Tommy Boggs had been around. Right up to the day the subcommittee was meeting we had no advance notice. So I called Norm Dicks, a congressman from Washington who was Magnuson's administrative assistant, and was really a staunch ally throughout. I asked, "Have you heard anything?" He started laughing and saying, "Tommy Boggs is sitting right here and he's got eight votes to suspend the children's proceeding."

Imagine that you are Michael Pertschuk. Go back to the point at which you were appointed Chairman of the Commission in the spring of 1977, and do something that Pertschuk failed to do: Undertake what might be termed a "strategic audit" of the agency. Examine the breadth and depth of the agency's authority to take action—specifically of its mandate to vigorously protect the public from consumer fraud, monopolization, and collusion. And examine the agency's internal resources as well. What do you discover?

On the positive side, the mandate continues to be quite strong. Consumer groups have grown in strength over the years. Jimmy Carter, the new President, says he is committed to protecting American consumers. The Washington, D.C. bar association's Federal Trade Commission section is also in favor of a vigorous agency (in part, because a vigorous FTC means that corporations will pay these lawyers generously to defend them, and partly because the FTC bar comprises former FTC lawyers and officials who have a genuine pride in the agency).

Internal resources are well matched to the strong mandate. Caspar Weinberger got rid of the dead wood; most of the present agency staffers are young, enthusiastic, energetic, and bright. And the agency is already considering a number of major regulations (pursuant to new authority to promulgate industry-wide rules), on which staffers have been busy at work, covering funeral practices, used cars, credit practices, eyeglasses, and gas-station lotteries, among many other things.

But you must also be cautious. If you do this audit correctly you will find that the authorizing environment is slowly shifting. You cannot take your mandate for granted. Business groups have begun organizing themselves, using many of the same tactics that consumers and environmentalists have used over the past decade. The public has grown more skeptical of regulations, and Carter himself campaigned against "big government in Washington." Moreover, congressional leadership is no longer as predictable as it once was; the seniority system has broken down in the wake of post-Watergate reforms, and it is more difficult to negotiate with Congress "wholesale" through senior committee chairman. These days, congressional deals are struck "retail" with many subcommittee chairmen. This change may give some advantage to business groups, who are better able to mount broad lobbying campaigns on many fronts than consumer groups.

This potential problem is aggravated by all the regulations currently winding their way through the agency's administrative process. Many of the rules target small businesses which lie at the heart of local economies (go into any medium-size town in America and you'll find that the president of the Rotary Club is in one of the businesses now under seige by the FTC). These are the constituents that matter most to many members of the House of Representatives.

Note also that you face a potential problem inside the agency. Many of these proposed regulations—relying upon complex fact-finding and subtle legal arguments—are being staffed by relatively inexperienced personnel. These young people may be bright and enthusiastic, but they are not seasoned. They may make mistakes. They may be excessively zealous, antagonizing the firms and industries they are dealing with. At a time when business groups are beginning to defend themselves in Congress and the courts from what they consider to be excessive regulation, an overly zealous staff can be a major liability.

All this would argue for restraint and caution. You need to make sure that staffers proceed carefully, and that the first major regulations you issue are fully justified. You should avoid publicity, opting instead for a quiet and judicious approach that underscores the seriousness and care with which the agency is exercising its new authority. To the extent possible, maintain informal, friendly relations with the business community; listen carefully for signs of discontent, and make sure that when industries or firms are disgruntled about action the agency has taken or is about to take, you are fully prepared to justify the action to the public. The agency still enjoys public trust, gleaned during the last decade. Do not squander it.

Now look at what Pertschuk did. He restructured agency relations with the authorizing environment by reducing informal contacts with business and the FTC bar and making provocative speeches about antitrust and consumer protection. He reorganized the agency by abandoning the hierarchical system already in place (involving many layers of review, managers at each level who kept careful watch over a relatively few subordinates, and subordinates at each level who had to seek permission before taking action) in favor of a far less hierarchical one (fewer layers of review, wider spans of control, and notification of superiors only after taking action). He also sought to reduce conflict among various units, eliminate competition among them for scarce resources, abandon internal checks by certain units on the work of other units, and, in general, encourage teamwork and cooperation.

What was his overall strategy? Surely not to sustain the strategy that the agency had been pursuing since Caspar Weinberger's days. Pertschuk said he wanted to make the FTC into the "largest public-interest law firm" in the nation. He envisioned it as an advocacy agency on behalf of consumers. He wanted his staff to be bold, creative, and aggressive. His decision to seek a new regulation covering advertising directed at children fit exactly into the new strategy: The new rule would, he hoped, expose the insensitivity and cupidity of American corporations and the awesome power of advertising. It thus would have much the same effect on public opinion as had Ralph Nader's exposure, years before, of the dangerous design of General Motors' Corvair. Just as Nader's revelations had sparked the consumer movement, so, Pertschuk hoped, would the FTC's revelations about children's advertising spark a new round of public concern.

But Pertschuk's strategy failed. Congress eventually eliminated the FTC's authority to promulgate a Kidvid rule. Congress also cut back on the Commission's general authority to promulgate rules, requiring that any new rule must be subject to a congressional veto. The FTC's budget was slashed. Congress almost abolished the agency altogether; indeed, the FTC was shut down for several days. Under Ronald Reagan, the FTC lost half its staff and became as moribund as it had been before Caspar Weinberger and Richard Nixon reformed it.

Why did Pertschuk's strategy fail? He failed to pay attention to the parts of the authorizing environment that would oppose it. And he overestimated his mandate from consumers, the White House, and other sources of support; he assumed that his actions would strengthen his mandate, when in fact they undermined it. For example, by barring contact with lawyers representing businesses affected by proposed agency actions, Pertschuk in effect lost the support of the FTC alumni who were now in private practice. They wanted a vigorous agency, to be sure, but they also wanted access to the agency; without access, they had no competitive advantage over any other lawyer in town.

Pertschuk's internal restructuring exacerbated the problems of staff inexperience and excessive zealotry. Without proper supervision, and given all the activities already under way, the likelihood increased that staffers would make mistakes and unnecessarily antagonize businesses affected by their actions. Absent internal checks and institutional naysaying, agency decisions were not carefully scrutinized. As a result, the agency provided ample ammunition to business lobbies seeking to prove that the FTC was irresponsible and needed reigning in.

Pertschuk's inflammatory speeches, and choice of ''Kidvid''—the proposed regulation directed at advertisers—confirmed the worst suspicions of the business community. These tactics also served to cement an emerging alliance between small-business groups (already fretting over the FTC) and big-business groups, which included advertisers, food processors, and the media. The media were particularly concerned about Kidvid, because the proposed rule might cause a loss of advertising revenues. It also represented what was perceived to be a direct assault on the First Amendment. (The *Washington Post's* accusation that the agency wanted to be a ''national nanny'' marked a sharp reversal from the media's reaction to Nader's efforts a decade before; at that time, rather than accede to GM's desire to attribute blame for traffic fatalities to bad drivers, the media placed blame on the company.)

The question remains: Why did Pertschuk fail to perceive the relative weakness of his mandate and the danger of embarking on a bolder strategy? Why didn't he focus his efforts on sustaining the mandate already in place?

My students usually offer a variety of explanations. Perhaps it was arrogance. Pertschuk had worked as a Senate staffer and thought he understood Congress; but getting and sustaining a mandate for action is far different from working directly for an elected representative. Some conclude that he was an ideologue, willing to bet the future of the agency on his own personal views of what the public needed (shades of David Goldman and Miles Mahoney). Others blame Nancy Chasen, the Assistant General Counsel for Congressional Relations, who did not adequately sound the alarm (another example of a failed "heat shield").

But I have a different theory. After all, I was there at the time. A part of the problem lay in how Pertschuk restructured the agency. By reducing agency contacts with outside lawyers and business groups and eliminating internal checks and reviews, he made it far more difficult for himself—and for anyone else within the agency—to pick up news. He bound and gagged the FTC, rendering it unable to communicate with its authorizing environment, to clarify its mandate, and thus to test its strategy against the larger shifts that were then occurring in public perceptions and political sensibilities.

A related problem was the way in which Pertschuk defined the mission of the agency from the start. An independent regulatory agency like the Federal Trade Commission (a direct lineal descendant of the Progressivist movement in America) derives public trust, and legitimacy, from its independence, neutrality, and expertise. Like Phil Heymann's prosecutors, the FTC is accountable to the public by means of the professional standard it maintains, rather than through any direct system of political oversight.

Thus, in conceiving of the FTC as an "advocacy agency," Pertschuk misconstrued the deal between the agency and the public. And by advancing that vision as an explicit statement of the agency's mission, he implicitly cut a new deal, which relied for its legitimacy on a much closer working relationship with Congress. In effect, Pertschuk suggested that the FTC would henceforth be representing one side of a large and enduring conflict. He thus annointed the public's elected representatives to act as umpires. Under these circumstances he could only expect more political scrutiny than before.

The moral of the tale: Understand *why* the public trusts that you will make decisions in the public's broad interest. Know the real sources of your authority. Create an organization capable of listening carefully to the sources of its authority. Sustaining a mandate is no less difficult than creating one; indeed, it can be more difficult if you take the public for granted.

chapter 11

Public Deliberation

If the authorizing environment is badly split, it cannot deliver a sustainable mandate. Each side of the debate—national security versus civil liberties, busing versus neighborhood schools, the right to an abortion versus the right of the fetus, energy versus the environment, gun control versus gun ownership—checkmates the other. As soon as one side gains enough political clout to subordinate the other side, the other mobilizes itself to regain the lead. Sometimes the courts become involved, but not even the Supreme Court can provide a sustainable mandate where the public continues to be sharply divided.

So far in this book we have encountered several examples of such splits and the dilemmas they pose for public servants trying to find a mandate for action. Robert Hermann, as you remember, circumvented the debate over civil liberties and national security by casting his open visa proposal in different terms; but this was a temporary solution, at best. The underlying debate would continue, and he would have to cope with it sooner or later. Stephanie McGrail faced an electorate sharply divided over the death penalty. Harold Brown discovered a deep fissure in the authorizing environment over the use of nuclear and neutron weapons, and over military strategy in general. Michael Pertschuk ignited a simmering dispute between consumer advocates and American business.

Occasionally these disputes reflect contrasting values so deeply held that there is no room for compromise, no possibility for achieving a sustainable mandate in any direction. But more often, views have become polarized because underlying facts, constraints, or possibilities for joint gains are not fully appreciated. Recall Audrey Simmons's challenge, and similar challenges faced by many public servants cast into "heat shield" jobs. Under such circumstances it may be possible to educate both sides and in so doing create a sustainable mandate after all.

Consider the challenge facing William Ruckelshaus.

Managing Environmental Risk: The Case of Asarco

On July 12, 1983, William Ruckelshaus, administrator of the Environmental Protection Agency (EPA), announced at EPA headquarters in Washington proposed standards that would regulate arsenic emissions from copper smelting and glass manufacturing plants in the US. Arsenic had increasingly been regarded as a dangerous air pollutant and as such fell with the purview of EPA. Issuing standards for pollutants was nothing new at the agency, but this announcement attracted more than usual interest: Ruckelshaus was proposing to involve the public in helping him decide just how stringent those regulations should be.

The arsenic standards were expected to have their greatest impact on Tacoma, Washington, because of its proximity to a copper smelter owned by the American Smelting and Refining Company (Asarco)—the only smelter in the nation that used ore with high arsenic content and a major source of arsenic emissions. The proposed standards applied the best available technology to reduce emissions; but even so, there would remain a residual risk factor that might, according to EPA calculations, result in roughly one additional cancer death per year among Tacoma area residents. However, imposing further requirements to eliminate that risk could drive up the plant's costs and make it uneconomical to run. The smelter employed more than 500 people, in a state that was experiencing over 11 percent unemployment. "My view," Ruckelshaus later told a *Los Angeles Times* reporter, "is that these are the kinds of tough, balancing questions that we're involved in here in this country in trying to regulate all kinds of hazardous substances. I don't like these questions either, but the societal issue is what risks are we willing to take and for what benefits?" To get answers to that question, Ruckelshaus announced EPA's in-

tention of actively soliciting the views and wishes of the people most affected by the proposed regulations: the residents who lived and worked near the Asarco smelter. "For me to sit here in Washington," Ruckelshaus told the assembled press, "and tell the people of Tacoma what is an acceptable risk would be at best arrogant and at worst inexcusable."

RUCKELSHAUS AT EPA

At the time the proposed arsenic regulations were announced, Ruckelshaus had only recently returned to the agency he had first headed in 1970, the year EPA was established. During the brief tenure of his predecessor, Anne Burford (formerly Gorsuch), EPA had become mired in scandal and controversy, and was frequently attacked for failure to enforce environmental laws and to carry out the agency's mission. The appointment of Ruckelshaus, who was highly regarded for his integrity and admired for his work as EPA's first administrator, had done much to restore credibility to the agency, but mistrust of the Reagan administration's commitment to environmental issues lingered in the public mind.

In Ruckelshaus' view, moreover, there were other troubling uncertainties facing his second EPA administration. In the 1980s, scientists were no longer assuming the existence of a threshold of safety from carcinogens: in theory, at least, adverse effects could occur from exposure to even one molecule of a carcinogenic substance. Ruckelshaus, in a June 1983 address to the National Academy of Sciences (NAS), put it this way: "[W]e must assume that life now takes place in a minefield of risks from hundreds, perhaps thousands, of substances. No more can we tell the public: You are home free with an adequate

This case was written by Esther Scott for the Program in Ethics and the Professions. It is based on an earlier unpublished case by Richard Innes. Funds for this case were provided by the American Express Fund for Curricular Development in Ethics.

Copyright © 1988 by the President and Fellows of Harvard College.

margin of safety." In this starker world, Ruckelshaus told the assembled scientists,

> We need more research on the health effects of the substances we regulate. . . . Given the necessity of acting in the face of enormous scientific uncertainties, it is more important than ever that our scientific analysis be rigorous and the quality of our data be high. We must take great pains not to mislead people regarding the risks to their health. We can help avoid confusion both by the quality of our science and the clarity of our language in exploring the hazards.

THE ASARCO SMELTER

The Asarco copper smelting plant on the edge of Tacoma was a model of the kind of wrenching choices the EPA administrator often faced in proposing regulations. Built in 1890, the Asarco smelter, whose 571-foot smokestack dominated the landscape around it, processed high arsenic content copper ore and produced commercial arsenic as a by-product from its smelter. (Arsenic is present as an impurity in certain ores, such as copper and lead, and can be produced either as a waste or as a by-product in the smelting of these ores. The arsenic was used in the manufacture of glass, herbicides, insecticides, and other products.) The Asarco plant—the only one in the nation that used high arsenic content ore—was also the only domestic producer of industrial arsenic, providing approximately one-third of the US supply of arsenic.

In recent times, the smelter had been in shaky financial condition. World prices for copper had plummeted from $1.45/lb. in 1980 to 60 cents/lb. in 1982, and US copper processors were facing intense competition from Japan. At the Asarco plant, the cost of producing copper was 82 cents/lb. The plant had for awhile been able to make a profit largely due to sales of residual metals—chiefly gold—from the copper smelting process; but as the price of gold dropped, so too did the plant's earnings and, according to Asarco officials, it had been losing money for several years.

For generations, the Asarco smelter had provided a livelihood to the families of Ruston, a small company town (population 636) that had sprung up around the big smokestack, and the surrounding area. In 1983, it employed roughly 575 workers on an annual payroll of about $23 million. (According to company estimates, it could cost the state of Washington as much as $5.5 million in unemployment benefits if the plant shut down.) The smelter also contributed to the economy of the area by spending approximately $12 million locally on supplies, indirectly supporting $13 million of auxiliary business, and paying $3 million in state and local taxes. Seventy-year-old Owen Gallagher, a former mayor of Ruston and an employee of Asarco for 43 years, spoke for many town residents when he told reporters from the *Chicago Tribune*

> I've worked in the plant all my life. So have my brothers, and so have my neighbors. We're not sick. This town was built around that plant. People came here looking for fire and smoke in the 1900s to find work. Now the government's complaining about that same smoke and trying to take our children's livelihood away.

But the fact was that Asarco had long been regarded as one of the major polluters in the Northwest, and held what one report called "the dubious distinction of being the worst arsenic polluter in the United States."[1] Commencement Bay, Tacoma's industrial harbor, had been designated a Superfund hazardous waste clean-up site partially because of accumulated arsenic both in the soil around the plant and in the bottom sand of the bay. Asarco was also one of the two major emitters of sulfur dioxide (SO_2, a by-product of burning carbon fuel) in the state of Washington.[2]

Area residents affected by this pollution made no bones about their feelings. Bill Tobin, a lawyer and resident of Vashon Island—a semi-rural, middle-income community two miles offshore from Ruston—pointed out that, because of the high smokestack and prevailing wind directions, "we are the dumping grounds for these pollutants without any benefits such as jobs or Asarco tax payments." Island residents were particularly concerned over high levels of arsenic found in urine samples of their children and in soil from local gardens. "I'm not for the loss of jobs," one homeowner told the *Tacoma News Tribune;* but he added, "Numerous people who staked their life savings on a place and a home are finding they can't enjoy the land because of the emis-

---

[1] Barnett N. Kalikow, "Environmental Risk: Power to the People," *Technology Review* 87 (October 1984): 55. As a result of studies of workers exposed to arsenic in copper smelting and arsenic manufacturing plants, a number of widely respected groups, including the National Academy of Sciences and the National Cancer Institute, concluded that inorganic arsenic was carcinogenic in humans. It has been linked to skin and lung cancer.

[2] The other was a coal power plant in western Washington.

sions of the Asarco plant.'' Vashon Island was by no means the only reluctant host to emissions from the smelter. Neighboring Tacoma received tons of air pollution from the plant, and little by way of taxes from the smelter to compensate. One member of the Tacoma city council described the effects of the smelter as ''somebody standing on the other side of the city line with a thirty-ought-six and firing it into Tacoma.''

Over the years, efforts to control pollution from the Asarco smelter came primarily from the regional level.[3] Since 1970, the Puget Sound Air Pollution Control Agency (PSAPCA), a regional air pollution authority, had issued a variety of orders aimed at reducing both SO_2 and arsenic emissions; but Asarco had either failed to comply and paid the relatively small penalties, or delayed action through litigation and variance proceedings.

However, despite the court battles and delays, PSAPCA had made some headway in getting Asarco to comply with its orders. As Asarco officials were quick to point out, the company had spent about $40 million over a ten-year period in equipment and practices designed to reduce pollution; it had also agreed to curtail operations when meteorological conditions would cause high ambient SO_2 levels. In the late 1970s, Asarco and PSAPCA negotiated a compromise agreement covering both SO_2 and arsenic emissions. For the latter, Asarco agreed to install, by 1984, secondary converter hoods, which would reduce ''fugitive'' arsenic emissions that were not funnelled up the smokestack (and were considered more dangerous because they were less likely to disperse before reaching the public).[4] According to later EPA estimates, the cost of the converters would run to roughly $3.5 million in capital outlay (Asarco put the figure at $4.5 million), along with an estimated $1.5 million per year in operating and maintenance expenses. These costs were expected to result in an estimated product price increase of 0.5 to 0.8 percent.

While these local efforts were ongoing, EPA had been, more or less, out of the picture. Under the provisions of the Clean Air Act, the federal agency was required to identify, list, and promulgate National Emission Standards for Hazardous Air Pollutants (NESHAPs) for substances believed to be detrimental to human health. EPA had listed inorganic arsenic as a hazardous air pollutant in June

1980, but had decided the following year not to issue a NESHAP for it. This decision chagrined PSAPCA officials, who felt that a ruling from EPA would give them another tool to use in their dealings with Asarco. But, as it turned out, EPA was soon forced to take a stronger hand in the matter. In late 1982, the state of New York, concerned about arsenic emissions from a Corning Glass manufacturing plant in New Jersey, took EPA to court. The US District Court subsequently ruled that the agency must publish proposed national standards by July 11, 1983, six months later. Thus was the stage set for Ruckelshaus' experiment in risk management.

TAKING IT TO THE PUBLIC

The Risk Assessment. On July 12, 1983—the same day that Ruckelshaus announced the proposed regulations on arsenic emissions[5]—Ernesta Barnes, administrator of EPA's northwest regional office, appeared before the press in Tacoma. ''We ask the public's help to consider the very difficult issues raised by arsenic air emissions,'' Barnes told the assembled reporters. ''Together we must determine 'What is an ''acceptable'' or ''reasonable'' risk to public health from arsenic emissions.''' To aid in that process, she announced public hearings in Tacoma on August 30 and 31, to be preceded by ''public workshops and other activities to inform you of the many technical issues involved.''

The hearings—wherein the public had an opportunity to present testimony—would have been held anyway, because the proposed standards for the Tacoma smelter were part of a national rulemaking process. What was different, said Ernesta Barnes, was the workshops. The ''underlying theory,'' she explained, was that the decisionmakers had a ''moral responsibility'' to provide ''adequate information'' and opportunity for discussion in advance of the hearings, ''so that when the actual public hearing was held, those that had chosen to become especially well informed would have not only their own values on which to base their testimony, but also better information about what the facts actually were.''

At the press conference, Barnes provided a

---

[3]Under the provisions of the Clean Air Act, EPA routinely delegates many of its powers to regulate and enforce to the states, which in turn can delegate their powers to regional authorities.

[4]The actual order from PSAPCA to install the hoods was not issued until 1981.

[5]The standards actually comprised three sets of regulations—for copper smelters processing high arsenic content ore, for copper smelters processing low arsenic content ore, and for glass manufacturing plants. The Asarco smelter in Ruston was the only facility in the US that fell into the first category. The risk assessment (and resulting standards) for high arsenic content copper smelters thus applied only to that one plant.

brief sketch of some of the technical issues the workshops would cover, outlining the risk assessment EPA had performed as part of the standard-setting process. EPA analysts had used a dispersion model to calculate concentrations of arsenic at over 100 locations within approximately 12 miles of the smelter, and combined those figures with "unit risk numbers"[6] derived from previous epidemiological studies of workers exposed to arsenic. The results of EPA's analyses yielded an estimate of some 310 tons of arsenic emissions spewed out each year by the Asarco smelter, and the risk of up to four related cancer deaths per year within 12 miles of the smelter.

Because EPA considered inorganic arsenic a non-threshold pollutant—i.e., even the most minute trace of it could not definitely be said to be harmless—it determined that the arsenic emissions from the Asarco smelter should be, in the language of the proposed standards, "controlled at least to the level that reflects best available technology (BAT), and to a more stringent level if, in the judgment of the administrator, it is necessary to prevent unreasonable risks." The appropriate BAT, Barnes explained at the press conference, was the converter hoods Asarco had already agreed to (and had in fact begun installing) in its negotiations with PSAPCA.[7] The hoods would, she said, reduce arsenic emissions from the smelter to 189 tons per year. "The number of related cancer cases within a twelve-mile radius of the plant," she added, "would drop from four per year to one a year."

Ruckelshaus was free to impose on his own a "more stringent level" of emission control. He could, for instance, set emissions standards that would require Asarco to use a lower arsenic content ore[8] or to convert to electric smelting. However, Asarco maintained that the added cost of shipping the low arsenic ore would force the company to close the smelter. Similarly, the expense of switching to electric smelting would amount to $150 million in capital outlays, and could also precipitate a shutdown. It was to consider such options and their im-

plications that Ruckelshaus sought public involvement. "Should we interpret the legislative intent of the Clean Air Act to mandate a total shutdown to produce zero risk to public health?" Barnes asked at the Tacoma press conference. ". . . Or is there a level of risk that is acceptable to the community and consistent with the law?"

Reaction. The workshops were not scheduled to start until mid-August, but debate on the issue began as soon as Barnes' press conference was over. Ruckelshaus' proposal to involve the public in the final decisionmaking received, not surprisingly, intense coverage in the local media, but it was widely reported in the national press as well. Many of the headlines depicted Tacomans as facing a stark choice: "Smelter workers have choice: Keep their jobs or their health" (*Chicago Tribune*); "What Cost a Life? EPA Asks Tacoma" (*Los Angeles Times*); "Tacoma Gets Choice: Cancer Risk or Lost Jobs" (*New York Times*). Most articles quoted Tacoma area citizens who stood on opposite sides of the fence on the issue, citing their fears of ill health or unemployment. "I'm concerned about getting lung cancer," one resident told the *New York Times,* while the head of the local union representing the workers at the smelter countered, "Simply dying from cancer is not different from a man losing his job and then committing suicide."

Many observers were critical of Ruckelshaus for what one area resident called "copping out." "It is up to the EPA to protect public health," said Ruth Weiner, head of the Cascade Chapter of the Sierra Club, in an interview with the *New York Times,* "not to ask the public what it is willing to sacrifice not to die from cancer." Another local citizen told a *Los Angeles Times* reporter, "EPA came in recently and found that our drinking water was contaminated and just cleaned it up, saying they'd find out why later. Now, why aren't they just cleaning this mess up instead of asking people how much cancer they would like to have?"

On the day he announced the proposed regulations, Ruckelshaus had told the press that he was not seeking a referendum from the people, only seeing if a consensus emerged from the public meetings; however, he added, in a remark that was widely quoted, "I don't know what we'll do if there is a 50-50 split." Perhaps in part because of that remark, the notion persisted among the public and some of the press that Ruckelshaus was in fact taking a vote. This idea received its harshest expression in a July 16 *New York Times* editorial, titled "Mr. Ruckelshaus as Caesar,"

[6]In its proposed regulations, EPA defined a unit risk number as its estimate of the lifetime cancer risk occurring in a hypothetical population which is exposed throughout their lifetime to a concentration of one microgram (1/28 millionths of an ounce) of a pollutant per cubic meter of air.

[7]In fact, some critics felt that EPA's (albeit involuntary) entry into the regulatory scene delayed installation of the hoods, while Asarco waited to learn what EPA would propose as best available technology.

[8]Asarco-Tacoma used ore that contained four percent arsenic; the remaining 14 smelters in the US used ores with 0.7 percent or lower arsenic content.

that compared the EPA administrator with a Roman emperor "who would ask the amphitheater crowd to signal with thumbs up or down whether a defeated gladiator should live or die." For Ruckelshaus to "impose such an impossible choice on Tacomans," the editorial stated, was "inexcusable."

Ruckelshaus responded to the editorial in a July 23 letter to the *Times* insisting that "no poll of Tacoma's citizens will be taken." The people of Tacoma were being asked for their "informed opinion," not a decision, he continued. "They know that the right to be heard is not the same thing as the right to be heeded. The final decision is mine." Ruckelshaus continued to defend his position despite the criticism. "Listen," he told the *Los Angeles Times,* "I know people don't like these kinds of decisions. Welcome to the world of regulation. People have demanded to be involved and now I have involved them and they say: 'Don't ask that question.' What's the alternative? Don't involve them? Then you're accused of doing something nefarious."

Controversy Over Numbers. Disagreements with EPA over the proposed arsenic regulations were not limited to how the agency was handling the process. Even before the official round of workshops and hearings began, EPA's risk calculations were being called into question. Just days after Ruckelshaus announced the proposed regulations, Asarco officials noted that their own figures on arsenic concentrations in the vicinity of the smelter—based on routine monitoring on the site—were significantly lower than the estimates—based on a computer model—provided by EPA; in a letter to EPA (later published in the *New York Times*), Asarco asserted that the agency had "overpredict[ed] maximum ambient concentrations of arsenic by a factor of 10." It soon turned up that EPA's model had some serious flaws—most notably the assumption that the smelter was on flat land, when in reality it was on the side of a steep hill. EPA quickly announced its intention of revising its estimates; and when they were published, the agency's new figures for overall arsenic emissions were indeed lower: 115 tons per year (instead of 310), to be lowered to 85 tons (instead of 189) with the installation of the converter hoods.[9] However, these new estimates were not available until late October— too late for the workshops but in time for the public hearings; in the meantime, there was uncertainty

about what were the right figures and whom to trust. One leaflet distributed by the union at the time of the workshops asserted that the "figures used for the computer model were from 410% to 2267% higher than the actual figures."

Other questions about EPA's calculations arose around the time the workshops were to begin. Dr. Samuel Milham, Jr., of the Washington State Department of Social and Health Services, told the *Los Angeles Times* that EPA's projections of possible lung cancers were "baloney." Milham, who had conducted studies in the Tacoma area, found elevated lung cancer rates among retired Asarco workers, but, he added, "we have been looking for extra lung cancers in the community (among those who do not work at the smelter) and we haven't found them. Nothing."

THE WORKSHOPS

Against this backdrop of well-publicized controversy, the northwest EPA office (Region 10) began conducting its workshops, aimed at acquainting residents with the details of the proposed regulations in preparation for the upcoming hearings. The first workshop was held on Vashon Island on August 10, 1983, followed soon after by two more in Tacoma itself. All three workshops (which were covered by local and national TV) were well attended, particularly the two in Tacoma, which drew environmental groups, local citizen organizations, and a large number of smelter workers, who had come at the urging of their union representative. (The importance of stacking the aisles with large numbers of supporters, one observer noted, might have stemmed from a lingering feeling that Ruckelshaus was going to make the decision by counting heads.)

The format of all three workshops was basically the same: after a formal presentation by EPA staff, the audience divided into smaller groups in order to encourage dialogue and permit more individual response to specific questions. EPA national headquarters sent two key policymakers—Robert Ajax, chief of the Standards Development Branch, and Betty Anderson, director of the Office of Health and Environmental Assessment—to assist in the process. They, along with Ernesta Barnes, rotated among the groups, answering questions. Each group had a "facilitator" (hired by EPA for the occasion), a recorder, and three EPA staff from the regional office. "Every comment [from the public] was recorded . . . and [later] typed up," says Barnes. To accompany discus-

---

[9]In announcing these lower figures on October 20, 1983, Ernesta Barnes did note that the amount of fugitive emissions released near ground level was higher than originally estimated.

sion, staff from the Region 10 office prepared and distributed a number of handouts for the workshop, including illustrations of how hooding helped control emissions, excerpts from Ruckelshaus' NAS speech, and fact sheets on arsenic controls and risk calculations.

EPA had come prepared to discuss risk assessment figures and dispersion models and present graphs and charts, yet many of the questions they encountered had little to do with verifiable "facts." "The personal nature of the complaints and questions made a striking counterpoint to the presentations of meteorological models and health effect extrapolations," wrote Gilbert Omenn, dean of the School of Public Health at the University of Washington, in a letter to Ernesta Barnes. (Omenn had been hired by EPA to observe and help evaluate the workshops.) People asked about the symptoms of arsenic poisoning, about other health effects from arsenic, about the advisability of eating produce from Vashon Island gardens. One person asked whether it would be necessary to remove a foot of dirt from her garden to make it safe (and who would pay for it); another wanted to know what effect arsenic emissions would have on animals. Ruckelshaus, who had received a personal report on the Vashon Island workshop, later recounted that, after EPA health experts finished their presentation, "A woman got up in the audience and said, 'Last week, my dog ate some spinach and dropped over dead. Did he die of arsenic?'" There were more sobering moments as well, Ruckelshaus noted, as when "another woman got up and said, 'Will my child die of cancer?'"

Nevertheless, technical matters such as the risk figures and epidemiological studies formed the basis for the majority of questions. Several inquiries focused on EPA's dispersion model and the reliability of the proposed control equipment. One resident wanted to know if any studies had been done on birth defects or miscarriages in the area; another asked whether the risk posed by emissions from the smelter was greater than the risk from ambient carbon monoxide from cars. This last question highlighted EPA's difficulties in explaining adequately the risk numbers in a relative context. Although EPA had prepared a table illustrating comparative risk, it was described as "cluttered" and needing fuller explanation. One critic commented, "How can they expect a relatively unsophisticated public to understand what these risk figures mean when the environmental establishment in this state doesn't even understand them?"

Several questions betrayed a lingering hostility toward EPA for not resolving the issue on its own.

"Seems like EPA is leaving the interpretation of the law up to the public," one resident commented. "Why has Asarco continued to obtain variances from complying with the law? What authority does EPA have to do this?" Another resident asked, "At this point in time is Asarco in violation of any clean air requirements? If so, why are they allowed to operate? Why is EPA spending taxpayers' money for this process if Asarco is not violating any laws?" "We elected people to run our government, we don't expect them to turn around and ask us to run it for them," said still another. "These issues are very complex and the public is not sophisticated enough to make these decisions. This is not to say that EPA doesn't have an obligation to inform the public, but information is one thing—defaulting its legal mandate is another."

In the end, the workshops got mixed, but generally favorable notices. "Many of the questioners were impressively well informed," Gilbert Omenn wrote. "I expect that some rethinking of elements of the *Federal Register* notice and the presentation of certain assumptions and facts will result from [the workshop]." "We also got educated," agrees Randy Smith, an EPA analyst from Region 10. "The questions raised at the workshops sent some people back to the drawing board."

CLOSING ARGUMENTS: THE HEARINGS

At the conclusion of the workshops, several groups asked EPA to postpone the formal hearings, slated for late August, to allow them more time to prepare the testimony. The agency agreed, and the hearings were rescheduled for early November. In the meantime, EPA participated in a few more workshops run by others—the city of Tacoma and the Steelworkers Union, where the comments and questions bordered on the openly hostile. ("I have seen studies which show that stress is the main source of cancer," one worker told an EPA representative. "The EPA is one main cause of stress.") By the end of the summer, all the interested parties were gearing up to present their arguments at the public hearing.

The hearings began on November 2, 1983. A panel of EPA officials (made up of representatives from the regional office, EPA headquarters, and EPA's research facility in North Carolina) presided over a three-day period, as roughly 150 people representing a variety of groups or just individual concerns offered their views on the proposed arsenic regulations. Their testimony ran the gamut from sophisticated technical arguments for more controls to anxious complaints that EPA was asking Tacoma residents to vote on a death sentence for one of their fellow citizens.[10]

PSAPCA's Testimony. Harvey Poll, chairman of PSAPCA, was first to speak at the hearings. The PSAPCA board had evaluated EPA's proposed standard, Poll told the hearing panel, and concluded that it had some serious shortcomings. The board's primary objection was that the proposal did not establish arsenic ambient air quality standards. (EPA was, however, constrained by statutory requirements, which directed the administrator to set technology-based, not ambient air, standards in issuing NESHAPS.) PSAPCA was also concerned that because the new hooding would reduce SO_2 emissions, Asarco would be able to operate the smelter more often (instead of curtailing operations during adverse meteorological conditions), thereby actually increasing the total volume of plant-wide arsenic emissions. PSAPCA wanted EPA to consider requiring Asarco to install a flue gas desulfurization system (at a cost several times higher than the $3.5 million for secondary hooding) or, more drastically, to force the company to convert to a new smelting technology at a projected cost of roughly $130-$150 million. PSAPCA had already issued a compliance order forcing the company to choose one of these options by 1987 in order to reduce SO_2 emissions (and, of necessity, arsenic emissions) by 90 percent.

Asarco's Testimony. Next to testify was Asarco, which had hired the public relations firm of Hill and Knowlton to organize and present its case at the hearings. In addition to Armand L. Labbe, an Asarco vice president and former manager of the Tacoma smelter, the company employed five expert witnesses to refute EPA's numbers and modeling assumptions and to assert that "there *now* exists an ample margin of safety" from arsenic emissions from the smelter [emphasis in original]. Most of the experts were affiliated with universities and each boasted an impressive curriculum vitae with relevant experience.

"Epidemiological studies demonstrate that arsenic emissions from the Asarco Tacoma smelter are not at levels that pose a health risk to the public living in the vicinity of the plant," Labbe flatly stated. Tom

Downs, a professor of biology at the University of Texas, disputed EPA's extrapolations of health effects: "[EPA's assumptions about exposure to arsenic] is like saying that the effects of taking five aspirin tablets a day for a lifetime are the same as the effects of taking 500 aspirin tablets every day for 1% of a lifetime."

Despite its assertion that, in the words of Asarco attorney C. John Newlands, "the Tacoma Smelter is now in compliance with Section 112 of the Federal Clean Air Act," the company stated its support for EPA's proposed arsenic standards—and at the same time outlined its opposition to ambient standards or to efforts to reduce emissions further. Asarco also detailed the projects—some of them voluntary—the firm had undertaken over the years to control SO_2 and arsenic pollution. Summing up the firm's position, Labbe reminded his listeners that a prolonged depression in the copper industry had hurt the Tacoma plant's ability to compete, and that the smelter had lost money in recent years. He concluded: "We are unable to commit additional expenditures beyond installation of BAT under present conditions."

Environmental Groups. A host of environmental groups appeared at the hearings—ranging from long-established organizations like the American Lung Association of Washington (which, according to staff member Janet Chalupnick, played a key role in coordinating a coalition of clean air groups) to more recently formed groups like Tahomans for a Healthy Environment.[11] For the most part, the environmentalists' testimony was critical of EPA—arguing that its proposed regulation did not go far enough—and supportive of PSAPCA's more comprehensive recommendations. Several environmental organizations opposed EPA's "best available technology" approach, asserting that it effectively discouraged the development of new technology to improve emissions control. "By allowing a company to only install the available technology it says is affordable, the EPA is creating a situation in which the company is still allowed to emit substantial amounts of toxic substances but may be inclined for financial reasons to resist development of improved control technologies," said Brian Baird of Tahomans for a Healthy Environment. "If BAT standards are regularly used," he continued, "It seems reasonable to anticipate that the pace of technological development of all types of pollution control will be substantially

---

[10]According to one observer, a number of witnesses at the hearing were confused about the meaning of the term "risk," assuming that the risk of one additional cancer death meant the certainty of the fatality—not the worst-case probability.

[11]Tahoma is the Indian name for Mt. Rainier.

slowed, because the market for Better Available Technologies will not only have been removed, it will have been significantly undermined.''

In its testimony, the National Audubon Society reiterated Baird's point: ''. . . If EPA finds zero emissions of a pollutant to be impossible, they should set the standards at the lowest levels possible rather than at the levels achievable through pollution control technologies easily affordable by the polluting industries. In order to protect [the public] health, standards must be used to force technological innovation in pollution control rather than to simply reinforce the status quo.'' Similarly, Nancy Ellison of the Washington Environmental Council chided EPA for proposing only the ''absolute minimum'' in regulation; nor did the council agree, she told the panel, ''that the only choices available are hood installation or smelter shutdown. This is not a jobs-versus-the-environment issue.''

The Smelter Workers. As Ellison's remark indicated, environmentalists in the area had been making an effort to reverse the longstanding pattern of labor vs. environmental interests, and to find common ground with the workers in resolving arsenic emissions problems. Further evidence of a fragile alliance between the two groups was observable in the testimony of Michael Wright, an industrial hygienist for the United Steelworkers union. ''No one has to convince our union that arsenic at high levels is risky,'' said Wright. ''We know what arsenic has done to many of our union brothers and sisters in the Tacoma Smelter and other copper smelters. It was the death of our members which provided the conclusive evidence that arsenic causes lung cancer.'' Wright went on to urge EPA to encourage the development of technology which would make the plant safer for workers and community residents by reducing pollution.[12] He supported the installation of secondary hooding and research to determine if further controls would be useful and economically feasible.

Not surprisingly, the union spoke out against requiring control equipment that was too costly, and would therefore force the plant to close. Referring to a study which he used to estimate the health risk of forcing the smelter to close, Wright claimed that the stress resulting from unemployment could cause 84 deaths in Pierce County over a six year period.

[12]The Occupational Safety and Health Administration—not EPA—was responsible for setting safety standards in the workplace itself. According to Ernesta Barnes, OSHA had already issued regulations requiring workers to wear respirators in the smelter.

''That,'' he asserted, ''is a considerably greater risk of death than what EPA predicts from arsenic after the installation of secondary hooding.''

Following Wright's testimony, individual smelter workers spoke before the panel. In what was often emotional testimony, several members of the ''25 year club''—people who had worked at the plant for more than a quarter of a century—made their case. ''I'm 88 years old and I ain't dead yet. I'm still breathing,'' said Ross Bridges. The workers reflected on the good life the smelter had made possible for them and their families. If the smelter closed, they maintained, it would leave them jobless. ''No high-tech industry moving into Tacoma is going to hire me,'' one man lamented. ''The smelter is all I've got.''

Vashon Island Residents. Residents of Vashon Island (which, except for Tacoma's North End, received the majority of emissions from Asarco) provided equally emotional testimony of the trauma they had experienced as a result of the arsenic pollution. One man came to the hearing sporting a gas mask, several were clad in hospital patient garb, and some carried young children to the podium to make their point. One woman, who claimed to have been diagnosed by her doctor as ultra-sensitive to arsenic, tearfully told the panel that she and her husband had been forced to sell their small farm for a fraction of its worth—due to depressed real estate prices on the island—and leave the area. Michael Bradley, chairman of a group named Island Residents Against Toxic Emissions (IRATE), made note of a recent cautionary statement issued by a local health agency warning against eating vegetables grown in the arsenic-laced soil on the island. ''If Asarco cannot clean up their act and prevent this kind of pollution then they should be forced to close,'' he stated angrily.

POSTMORTEMS

After three days of testimony, the hearings came to an end. Ruckelshaus was not expected to make a decision on the final standards for arsenic emissions until February or March of 1984. In the meanwhile, some assessment, at least of the process, had already begun. From an administrative point of view, the brunt of managing the tasks of informing and involving the public had fallen on Ernesta Barnes and EPA's Region 10 office. According to one source, roughly 30 people from the regional office had worked full-time for four months on the Asarco case.

Randy Smith of the Region 10 office told one reporter that the "process proved terrifically costly and time-consuming."[13]

But the regional office did feel that there had been an internal payoff for them in a greater appreciation by EPA headquarters of what it meant to be "on the front lines." The regional staff felt that because of their frequent contact with area groups, they were better able to engage the public's participation. "After a while," remarked one regional staff member, "we realized we couldn't let [headquarters staff] do the spiel [in the public workshops]. The people from headquarters were just not enough in touch with the local level. . . . They were too scientific." Another regional office commented:

> At headquarters [in Washington, DC] they thought we were a bunch of bozos out here in the region. They could not understand why we were scrambling and bending over backwards to organize the workshops and put out easily digestible information for the public. When they arrived in Tacoma, however, and found themselves face-to-face with a well-informed and often angry public, they began to appreciate our problem a little better.

The process also proved beneficial to the regional office from the standpoint of image and public trust. A number of witnesses and observers agreed with Nancy Ellison of the Washington Environmental Council, who complimented the Region 10 office for its "openness and willingness to share information during this process." The office's cooperation and outreach efforts had, she continued, "gone a long way toward restoring trust and confidence in the agency here in the region."

Even Ruckelshaus' decision to involve the public received gentler treatment at some hands. Ruth

Weiner of the Sierra Club, who had earlier criticized the EPA administrator for "copping out," stated at the conclusion of her testimony that the Clean Air Act "requires public involvement." She continued, "Moreover, in becoming involved, the public begins to appreciate the difficulty attendant on making regulatory decisions, the ease with which EPA can be made a scapegoat because the agency's blunders are so readily magnified, and the inadequacy of simply identifying 'heroes' and 'villains' in environmental protection. It may have been hard work and a headache for all of us, but the public involvement is most certainly worth it."

Ruckelshaus himself was largely in agreement with this last sentiment. Back in June, in his speech before the National Academy of Sciences, he had told his audience that, in managing risk, "we must seek new ways to involve the public in the decision-making process." He continued, "It is clear to me that in a society in which democratic principles so dominate, the perceptions of the public must be weighed." Later, as he looked back on the process he had kicked off when he announced the proposed arsenic regulations for the Asarco smelter, he found validation for these views. Ruckelshaus felt that local citizens had shown they were "capable of understanding [the problem of the smelter] in its complexities and dealing with it and coming back to us with rather sensible suggestions." In fact, he added, "the public—the non-technical, unschooled public—came back with some very good suggestions as to how they could reduce the emissions of arsenic in the plant [and still keep it open]." But, perhaps, the final proof of the success of the venture would be in the decision that—as he had often repeated—Ruckelshaus alone would make. It was still an open question as to how Asarco might respond to citizens' suggestions, and whether it would feel as sanguine as Ruckelshaus about remaining open. While he pondered his decision on the final standards, the debate on his risk management techniques continued.

[13]Kalikow, p. 61.

Imagine you are William Ruckelshaus, and you must decide upon a standard for limiting the amount of arsenic emitted into the air from facilities like the Asarco smelter. Your staff at the EPA has determined that under present conditions, without any limits on emissions, the Asarco smelter will cause four cancer deaths per year in the Tacoma region. Applying the best available technology to the source of emissions will result in one death per year. Were Asarco required to purchase lower-arsenic-content ore, the hazard could be reduced further. But such a requirement would force the company to close the plant, resulting in a loss of hundreds of jobs and jeopardizing the regional economy. So which is it to be?

The law is of no help. Congress has decreed that you must provide an ''ample margin of safety'' to area residents, but these words impose on you and the EPA all the burden of determining what is ''ample.'' You want a safe environment, but you are also aware that the Tacoma economy is depressed; the national economy is not much healthier. Unemployment is high, and a decision by you to impose strict environmental controls might push local unemployment even higher.

My students usually have difficulty deciding. The choice seems to turn on how you define your job. What is your mandate, and what is the mandate of the agency? Why have you been brought to the EPA at this point? What's the overarching *strategic* problem with which you must deal?

Your problem is the lack of a clear mandate. The authorizing environment is sharply at odds over how strictly the environment should be protected—not only in Tacoma but throughout the United States. On one side of the debate are environmentalists who demand high levels of protection. To them, there is no ''safe'' level of toxic emissions. On the other side are industrialists and workers who feel that economic growth must not be subordinated to environmental concerns, and that the nation cannot afford absolute safety.

The debate has become sharply polarized in recent years, in part because of how Anne Gorsuch, your predecessor at the EPA, approached her job. She took an extreme position in favor of the economy and the ''free market'' and against the environmentalists. She was outspoken and uncompromising. Most significantly, she framed the issues in polar terms—jobs *or* the environment—and she went on a crusade against what she believed to be the excesses of the environmentalists. She polarized the EPA itself, and she drew criticism not only from staffers and environmentalists but also from members of Congress and large segments of the public. In a sense, she used the same confrontative tactics that Michael Pertschuk had used, to much the same effect.

Gorsuch left the agency adrift, without a mandate for what it should seek to do. The public no longer trusted the EPA to act responsibly. Worse yet, the public no longer knew what it wanted from the EPA to begin with. Thus your real job is to re-create a sustainable mandate—to defuse the issue and build a new consensus for what the agency should seek to accomplish in the years ahead.

You were chosen because you are trusted by both sides. You were the first administrator of the EPA when it was founded in 1970, and you have a reputation for integrity and judiciousness. So why do you choose, as one of your first acts, to focus attention on the Asarco smelter in Tacoma? Why do you personally visit the city, and why do you devise such an elaborate series of public meetings? Most puzzling of all, why do you suggest to citizens of Tacoma that you will be influenced by their opinion in this matter? The EPA is charged with developing *national* standards, not different standards for every locale. And Congress charged *you* as EPA administrator, with the responsibility for making the decision, not a large and diffuse populace.

After a while, my students begin to make the connections: Ruckel-shaus is using Tacoma to illustrate something to the rest of the nation. He wants to focus the nation's attention on what the people of Tacoma are learning and use their learning as an example of what other Americans must also learn.

What exactly are the citizens of Tacoma learning, through all the meetings and media attention? They are learning that there is no correct answer to the question of how much environmental protection is warranted, how much safety should be purchased at the expense of jobs. The choice ultimately depends on what the public *values.*

In fact, the public meetings in Tacoma provide an occasion for workers, environmentalists, and average residents to confront one another and hear one another's arguments. The meetings help the citizens of Tacoma to understand that all of them will be both advantaged and disadvantaged by any decision that is made: A safe environment is in all their interests, but so is a buoyant economy. Thus, through the course of the meetings, the issue gradually becomes redefined. It is no longer a simple choice between environmental safety and jobs. There are other possibilities, such as seeking to diversify the regional economy to become less dependent upon industries that pollute the air, and finding new jobs for Asarco workers who might lose their present jobs if the company cannot dramatically reduce its toxic emissions. (It is interesting to note, in this regard, that, although the Asarco smelter did close, Tacoma subsequently created one of the most successful Job Training Partnership programs in the nation, finding new jobs for almost 90 percent of Asarco's employees, notwithstanding the area's high level of unemployment overall.)

In other words, Ruckelshaus sees Tacoma as a microcosm of the larger strategic problem he faces. He recognizes that by defusing the "jobs versus environment" issue there, he can teach the entire nation a lesson that will help defuse it across the country. He uses Tacoma to signal larger goals and intentions, not unlike the way Caspar Weinberger used the note from Joe Evins. Ruckelshaus thus stimulates public deliberation. He creates a setting in which people can learn from one another, like the settings that Audrey Simmons might have created in order to educate both sides of the controversy she inherited.

A few years after the Tacoma experiment I asked Ruckelshaus to assess what he tried to accomplish there. His response was interesting:

> Perhaps I underestimated how difficult it would be to get people to take responsibility, to educate themselves and one another about such a difficult issue. Probably not more than a relatively few citizens of Tacoma learned that for issues like this there is no "right" answer. . . . They would have to decide what they wanted for their community. They would have to determine their own future. But even if a handful learned this lesson, then you have a basis for others learning it. You have the beginnings of a tradition of public deliberation about hard issues. And you also have all the other people in the country who watched what happened there in Tacoma, and indirectly learned the same lesson from it.

The Tacoma experiment was part of Ruckelshaus's larger strategy. In the end, he left the EPA in far better shape than he found it. He successfully defused the ''jobs versus environment'' issue and helped restore public trust in the agency.

The Ruckelshaus case is a nice one on which to end, because it neatly summarizes and integrates many of the lessons we have been pondering about the role of the public manager in a democracy.

First, we examined the relationship between personal ideals and public ideals. When you are vested with public authority, you hold a public trust. When your ideals conflict with the ideals of those who represent the public, you may seek to persuade the public and its representatives of the correctness of your personal vision, but you have no authority to act on it without their knowledge and acquiescence. David Goldman had no authority to pursue his ideal, however much we might agree with it. Like Anne Gorsuch or Michael Pertschuk (or even Oliver North, to take a more recent example), such substitutions of personal vision for public authority ultimately erode public trust.

The situation is different with respect to elected officials, whose personal ideals are part of the reason they were elected. Directly elected representatives are expected to deliberate, not act as automatic conveyor belts for public sentiment. They are thus accountable to the public for who they *are* and what they believe. The public is able to reassess these personal qualities periodically and decide whether to substitute another person comprising another set of ideals.

Second, we examined conflicts of loyalties and ambiguities in job definitions. Public servants owe their direct superiors the benefit of the doubt in balancing the attainment of certain goals against others and developing overall priorities. Miles Mahoney did not understand that part of his job was to help the Governor with the Governor's larger agenda. There are limits, of course. Public servants owe a greater allegiance to the law and the Constitution, and when political superiors ask them to take actions clearly contrary to the law or the Constitution, public servants have a responsibility to decline the request or resign.

We then turned to an examination of leadership, under circumstances in which mandates are ambiguous. Here, public servants can help relevant publics focus their attention on problems and issues and consider alternative courses of action. The public manager can thus create a mandate through engaging the attention and involvement of those who might be affected by agency action. But there may be a temptation to manipulate: Robert Hermann created a false mandate for his proposed open visa by avoiding such engagement. William Ruckelshaus, by contrast, invited it. Unlike Hermann, Ruckelshaus understood that a mandate built on false premises is unsustainable.

Occasionally, public trust rests upon the public's confidence that its servants are applying objective criteria and applying them objectively. Under these circumstances, politics invites abuses of power. Drawing the line between appropriate political oversight and inappropriate political interference is a delicate but critical task. Phil Heymann devised a procedure for doing so. In a way, William Ruckelshaus also had to convince the public that the Environmental Protection Agency would be similarly immune to partisanship. The EPA would remain accountable to the broad standards encoded in the law, but it had to avoid taking sides in a dispute that had become politically charged. Part of Ruckelshaus's job was to render political oversight of the agency less partisan, by making the public itself less partisan.

Where agency resources, agency goals, and sources of authority are all aligned, a strategy can be sustained. But this is no guarantee that the strategy conforms with fundamental standards of fairness or decency, as they are enumerated in the Constitution and by the courts. Pendleton School had a highly stable, sustainable strategy but one that arguably disregarded the basic rights of its wards. Litigation, under these circumstances, may be a means of destabilizing such a stable system, creating possibilities for new alignments between resources, goals, and sources of authority.

The media are active participants in holding public officials accountable, as they reflect and enlarge upon public concerns. The stories that journalists write or broadcast are aspects of larger public dramas already unfolding about which the public has fears or hopes. William Ruckelshaus used the media to focus attention on his Tacoma experiment, as a means of stimulating public deliberation across the country about a controversy—jobs versus the environment—already under way. He wanted to change the "story *behind* the story"—that is, the way in which the larger story about jobs and the environment was being told by Americans to each other. By contrast, the Carter Administration regarded the neutron bomb story as a single instance of irresponsible reporting, failing to grasp the larger public concerns underlying the strong public reaction to it.

Public servants often seek to protect themselves against the public by erecting buffers in the form of "relations" personnel, whose job is to keep various segments of the public happy and supportive of what the agency is doing. But these buffers can also prevent public managers from learning what the public wants and needs. I used the metaphors of "heat shields" and "heat conductors" to convey the different ways of conceiving such relational roles. Heat shields, responsible for keeping the public at bay, may eventually "melt"—losing the confidence of their bosses and of the public—if they fail to "conduct the heat" in a manner that encourages mutual learning. Audrey Simmons was on her way to melting. William Ruckelshaus's job could also be understood in these terms. He might have acted as a heat shield for the Reagan Administration at a time when the administration was under fire for the policies of Ruckelshaus's predecessor, but had he done so, he would have accomplished little. Instead, he helped *conduct* the heat—educating different parts of the authorizing environment (as well as agency personnel and the White House) about what was really at stake and about the constraints and possibilities involved in trying to protect the environment while maintaining a healthy economy.

The search for someone like Ruckelshaus to take command of an agency or a program is in fact a search for a new strategy. We examined how the search process mirrors the challenges that will be faced by the new agency head and thus why it is important to treat the search as a vehicle for better defining long-term goals.

We then turned to the implementation of strategy—the realigning of internal resources, agency goals, and mandates. Because public managers have few direct instruments of control at their command, they must implement strategy indirectly, through carefully selected signals that serve to mobilize resources and support. Caspar Weinberger used Joe Evins's note as such a signal; William Ruckelshaus used Tacoma.

Strategy needs continuous clarification and adjustment. Authorizing environments shift. The ways in which public agencies are organized can either help or hinder the manager's ability to recognize such shifts and make necessary adjustments. When he organized the FTC as an advocacy agency, Michael Pertschuk failed to comprehend the shift and the dangers it implied. So did Ruckelshaus's predecessor at the EPA. Ruckelshaus's job was to reopen the agency and render it better able to respond.

Finally, and for all these reasons, public managers are in the business of education. They must educate their staffs, public intermediaries, and the public at large. In all their activities—clarifying ambiguous mandates; forging new mandates where the public is sharply divided; aligning internal resources; and "conducting heat" across large chasms separating different branches of government, different systems of values, or different socioeconomic groups—public managers are causing learning to take place. In a democratic form of government, such learning, and the deliberation it implies, is a prerequisite to everything else.

The challenge of public management in a democracy is to be both effective *and* responsive: to get things done and to do the things that the public wants done. The two principles are at war with one another only when public managers forget their roles as instigators and convenors of democratic deliberation. Properly understood, politics and law are not constraints on effective public action; they are sources of knowledge and wisdom about public purposes.

Further Reading

I have found the following books and articles of particular use in thinking about the role of public management in a democracy.

ALTSHULER, ALAN A., "The Study of American Public Administration," in *The Politics of the Federal Bureaucracy,* ed. Alan A. Altshuler and Norman C. Thomas. New York: Harper and Row, 1977.

BARBER, BENJAMIN, *Strong Democracy.* Berkeley: University of California Press, 1984.

BURKE, EDMUND, *Burke's Politics,* ed. Ross Hoffman and Paul Levack. New York: Knopf, 1959.

DOIG, J. W. and E.C. HARGROVE, *Leadership and Innovation.* Baltimore: Johns Hopkins Press, 1987.

FLEISHMAN, JOEL L., LANCE LEIBMAN, and MARK H. MOORE (eds.), *Public Duties: The Moral Obligations of Government Officials.* Cambridge, Mass.: Harvard University Press, 1981.

GILMORE, THOMAS NORTH, *Making a Leadership Change.* San Francisco: Jossey-Bass, 1988.

GOODIN, ROBERT E., *Manipulatory Politics.* New Haven, Conn.: Yale University Press, 1968.

HARMON, MICHAEL and RICHARD MAYER, *Organization Theory for Public Administration.* Boston: Little, Brown, 1986.

HEYMANN, PHILIP B., *The Politics of Public Management.* New Haven, Conn.: Yale University Press, 1987.

KAUFMAN, HERBERT, *Red Tape.* Washington, D.C.: Brookings, 1977.

KELMAN, STEVEN, *Making Public Policy.* New York: Basic Books, 1987.

KINGDON, JOHN, *Agendas, Alternatives, and Public Policies.* Boston: Little, Brown, 1984.

MANSBRIDGE, JANE J., *Why We Lost the ERA.* Chicago: University of Chicago Press, 1986.

LAX, DAVID and JAMES K. SEBENIUS, *The Manager as Negotiator.* New York: Free Press, 1986.

LEWIS, EUGENE, *Public Entrepreneurship.* Bloomington: Indiana University Press, 1978.

LIPPMAN, WALTER, *Public Opinion.* New York: Harcourt Brace Jovanovich, 1922.

LONG, NORTON, ''Bureaucracy and Constitutionalism,'' in Norton Long, *The Polity.* New York: Rand McNally, 1962.

MAASS, ARTHUR, *Congress and the Common Good.* New York: Basic Books, 1983.

MILL, JOHN STUART, *Considerations on Representative Government,* in *Collected Works,* ed. John M. Robson. Toronto: University of Toronto Press, 1977.

NEUSTADT, RICHARD and ERNEST MAY, *Thinking Through Time.* New York: Free Press, 1987.

PITKIN, HANNA, *The Concept of Representation.* Berkeley: University of California Press, 1967.

REICH, ROBERT B. (ed.), *The Power of Public Ideas.* Cambridge, Mass.: Ballinger Press, 1988.

STONE, DEBORAH A., *Policy Paradox and Political Reason.* Glenview, Ill.: Scott, Foresman, 1988.

THOMPSON, DENNIS F., *Political Ethics and Public Office.* Cambridge, Mass.: Harvard University Press, 1987.

WEBER, MAX, *The Theory of Social and Economic Organization,* trans. A. M. Henderson and Talcott Parsons. New York: Oxford University Press, 1947.

WEISBAND, EDWARD and THOMAS FRANCK, *Resignation in Protest.* New York: Penguin, 1976.